Chicago Labor
and the Quest for a Democratic Diplomacy,
1914–1924

Chicago Labor and the Quest for a Democratic Diplomacy, 1914–1924

ELIZABETH MCKILLEN

CORNELL UNIVERSITY PRESS

ITHACA AND LONDON

First published 1995 by Cornell University Press.

Library of Congress Cataloging-in-Publication Data

McKillen, Elizabeth, 1957–
    Chicago labor and the quest for a democratic diplomacy, 1914–1924
/ Elizabeth McKillen.
        p.   cm.
    Includes bibliographical references (p.   ) and index.
    ISBN 0-8014-2905-6
        1. Trade-unions—Illinois—Chicago—History—20th century.
    2. Labor movement—Illinois—Chicago—History—20th century.
    3. Pressure groups—Illinois—Chicago—History—20th century.
    4. Gompers, Samuel, 1850-1924.   5. United States—Foreign
relations—1913-1921.   6. United States—Foreign
relations—1921-1923.   I. Title.
HD6519.C44M38   1995
331.88'09773'1109041—dc20   94-46960

Printed in the United States of America

⊗ The paper in this book meets the minimum requirements of the
American National Standard for Information Sciences — Permanence
of Paper for Printed Library Materials, ANSI Z39.48-1984.

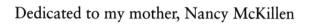

Dedicated to my mother, Nancy McKillen

Contents

Preface

THIS book originated from a desire to reconcile the insights of diplomatic and labor history. As I pursued research in these fields, I became convinced that the welfare of American workers in the twentieth century had been closely tied to the global economic and security strategies of American corporations and the U.S. government. Yet, to my surprise, I found that labor and diplomatic historians rarely engaged in meaningful dialogue with one another. My attempt to make sense of the vibrant working-class internationalism I discovered at local levels in the labor movement was inhibited at every turn by the different methodologies of labor and diplomatic historians and by the divergent assumptions that guide them.

Labor historians, preoccupied with rewriting history from the "bottom up," have largely failed to confront the success of business and state leaders in creating a "world system" that exploits workers and limits the power of labor movements in both the industrial core and underdeveloped regions. Diplomatic historians have focused their studies primarily on policymakers, business elites, and trade union officials and have ignored the alternative visions offered by grass-roots labor opponents of U.S. foreign policy. In excluding from their consideration those without direct access to Washington policy-making circles, diplomatic historians have failed to realize that, in the words of Stuart Hall, "hegemonizing is hard work."* Grass-roots activists, even when unsuc-

---

*Stuart Hall, quoted in George Lipsitz, "The Struggle for Hegemony," *Journal of American History* 75 (June 1988): 146.

cessful in creating sustainable political movements, have often played a critical role in preventing government leaders from forming an ideological consensus for their foreign policies within the working class. Often, widespread public opposition to policies has forced political leaders to change their diplomatic tactics, even as their international goals have remained relatively constant.

This book examines foreign policy issues both from the "bottom up" and from the "top down." Utilizing the techniques of a community study, I demonstrate the kinds of local imperatives that helped to stimulate foreign policy activism within municipal labor councils like the Chicago Federation of Labor (CFL) and to make them hotbeds of antiwar and anti-imperialist agitation between 1914 and 1924. Particularly critical in provoking the diplomatic initiatives of the CFL leaders were their close ties to local immigrant communities and their tendency to see debates over foreign policy issues as organic extensions of local class struggles. I also examine the role of CFL leaders in creating the national Farmer-Labor party, a group with a strongly anti-Wilsonian foreign policy agenda, and in rallying dissident city labor councils behind the new party. The story of municipal labor rebellion is juxtaposed with a detailed account of the ways in which American Federation of Labor (AFL) leaders were incorporated into federal bureaucracies during the war and the postwar era and became ambassadors and spokespeople for Wilsonian diplomatic goals and programs in Europe and Latin America. The international visions promoted by local labor dissidents and AFL leaders were fundamentally at odds and helped provoke the AFL's campaign to crush the Chicago insurgency.

My husband, intellectual partner, and fellow outfielder, Nathan Godfried, was most crucial in helping me to develop the analytical frameworks that guide this work. Over the course of many softball seasons, he has patiently assisted me in planning research strategies, analyzing conflicting evidence, and proofreading innumerable drafts. Since his own research and writing draw on the fields of both diplomatic and labor history (among many others), he has helped me link the two in constructive ways. His own dedication to using the past to create a more humane present has inspired me at times when my enthusiasm for this project was at low tide.

I owe deep intellectual debts to my adviser at Northwestern University, Michael Sherry. Special thanks are due David Roediger as well, for first pointing me in the direction of the Chicago Historical

Society and for making invaluable suggestions after reading a draft of the manuscript. Also commenting on early portions of this manuscript and providing important suggestions for revision were Thomas McCormick, Jerry Israel, and Michael Hogan. The two outside reviewers at Cornell University Press, James Barrett and an anonymous second reader, also incalculably improved the manuscript through constructive and incisive critiques that forced me to develop a much clearer conceptual framework for the book. Peter Agree, editor at Cornell, helped to demystify the publishing process and to guide my manuscript with admirable efficiency through the various stages of acquisition, editing, and publication. Thanks are also due Kay Scheuer, Elizabeth Holmes, and other members of the Cornell staff who have assisted with the editing and production of this book, and to Lesley Beneke, the copyeditor.

Northwestern University and the University of Maine helped fund this research project. My colleagues at the University of Maine also provided important encouragement. In particular, I thank Alex Grab for his long conversations with me about U.S. diplomacy and the world economy. Research was also made easier by helpful librarians and archivists at the Chicago Historical Society, University of Illinois, Loyola University, Wisconsin State Historical Society, New York Public Library, University of Maine, and Columbia University. I express my appreciation to the editors at *Diplomatic History* for allowing me to reprint material here which appeared in an earlier article ("The Corporatist Model, World War I, and the Public Debate over the League of Nations" [15 (Spring 1991): 171–97]). I quote from the memoirs of John P. Frey with permission of the Oral History Collection of Columbia University.

Finally, I thank my family and friends for their support. Although sometimes baffled by the process of attaining a Ph.D. and by the academic job market, they have provided practical advice and empathy when I needed to discuss issues with nonspecialists. I thank my brother Mike for sharing his firsthand insights on the labor movement with me, my brother Pat for his sense of humor, and my grandparents for instilling me with a love of history. My deepest intellectual and emotional debts are to my mother, Nancy McKillen, whose resilient spirit and intuitive political insight were the inspiration for this book.

ELIZABETH MCKILLEN

Orono, Maine

Abbreviations

ORGANIZATIONAL NAMES IN THE TITLES OF PROCEEDINGS, MINUTES, REPORTS, AND LETTERS

AALD	American Alliance for Labor and Democracy
AARIR	American Association for the Recognition of the Irish Republic
AFL	American Federation of Labor
CFL	Chicago Federation of Labor
CND	Council of National Defense
FOFI	Friends of Freedom for India
FOIF	Friends of Irish Freedom
IFTU	International Federation of Trade Unions
ILO	International Labor Organization (attached to the League of Nations)
ISCD	Illinois State Council of Defense
ISFL	Illinois State Federation of Labor
NWLB	National War Labor Board
PAFL	Pan American Federation of Labor
PF	Polish Falcons
PNA	Polish National Alliance
PRCU	Polish Roman Catholic Union

NEWSPAPERS

CC	*Chicago Citizen*
GA	*Gaelic American*
IW	*Irish World and American Industrial Liberator*
NM	*New Majority*
NR	*New Republic*
VL	*Voice of Labor*

Translations of Polish newspapers taken from the Foreign Language Press Survey, Works Progress Administration, Chicago Historical Society, are appended with the abbreviation WPA.

Chicago Labor
and the Quest for a Democratic Diplomacy,
1914–1924

❀

Introduction

All forms of secret diplomacy are dead and buried with the past, as far as
the masses are concerned, and the rank and file of the common people all
over the world are determined to speak for themselves and decide what is
the best for the masses.

—Bourke Cochran, speaking before the Mooney
Federal Intervention Committee in Chicago, January 1919

JOHN DEWEY once described the World War I era as a "plastic junc-
ture" in time.[1] By creating a sudden and cataclysmic fissure with the
past, the war exploded traditional assumptions, shook many European
political and social institutions loose from their moorings, and made
the world seem more "malleable." Although most Americans recoiled
in horror at the news of Europeans butchering each other during the
late summer of 1914, many hoped nonetheless that the war would provoke beneficial reform in belligerent nations. Some, predicting imminent American involvement in the European conflict, prophesied that
the war would spur institutional innovation within the United States.
Following the U.S. declaration of war against Germany in April 1917,
a heterogeneous array of groups, from national political caucuses to

Epigraph quoted in David Montgomery, *The Fall of the House of Labor: The
Workplace, the State, and American Labor Activism, 1865–1925* (New York: Cambridge
University Press, 1987), 390.
   1. Quoted in David Kennedy, *Over Here: The First World War and American
Society* (New York: Oxford University Press, 1980), 50. See also John Dewey, "The
Social Possibilities of War," in *Characters and Events: Popular Essays in Social and
Political Philosophy by John Dewey*, ed. Joseph Ratner (New York: Henry Holt, 1929),
2: 551–58.

municipal chambers of commerce and ethnic fraternal organizations, mobilized to promote far-ranging domestic and international reform agendas.[2]

Among those most electrified by the new spirit of change were American workers. As David Montgomery suggests, the World War I era witnessed some of the most militant campaigns and sustained agitation in American labor history. Ignoring government pleas to help promote industrial peace during a time of national crisis, over one million workers struck each year between 1916 and 1922, with four million striking in 1919 alone. Many of the strikes covered vast geographic areas. Others effectively enlisted the support of most major unions and many nonunion workers within a given municipality, spurring general strikes that shut down entire cities. New workplace organizations such as shop committees and systems federations facilitated strike mobilization but also encouraged rank-and-file independence of union leadership, sometimes resulting in spontaneous, unsanctioned work stoppages. The new grass-roots work organizations, while troublesome to trade union leaders, stimulated AFL organizing campaigns among unskilled and semiskilled workers—many of whom were recent immigrants or of immigrant stock—in such previously nonunionized industries as meatpacking, textiles, and the metal trades. New organizing campaigns helped to double AFL membership between 1915 and 1920.[3]

2. Kennedy, *Over Here*, 50. See also Christopher Lasch, *The American Liberals and the Russian Revolution* (New York: Columbia University Press, 1962); John Thompson, *Reformers and War: American Progressive Publicists and the First World War* (Cambridge: Cambridge University Press, 1987); Beth McKillen, "The Corporatist Model, World War I, and the Public Debate over the League of Nations," *Diplomatic History* 15 (spring 1991): 171–97. For an essay that discusses the widespread use of volcano and earthquake metaphors by those who lived through the World War I era, see Stanley Shapiro, "'Hand and Brain': The Farmer-Labor Party of 1920," *Labor History* 26 (summer 1985): 420–21.

3. David Montgomery, "Immigrants, Industrial Unions, and Social Reconstruction in the United States, 1916–1923," *Labour/Le Travail* 13 (spring 1984): 101–13, "New Tendencies in Union Struggles and Strategies in Europe and the United States, 1916–1922," in *Work, Community, and Power: The Experience of Labor in Europe and America, 1900–1925*, ed. James E. Cronin and Carmen Sirianni (Philadelphia: Temple University Press, 1983), 89–110, *The Fall of the House of Labor* (New York: Cambridge University Press, 1987), 426–32; Philip S. Foner, *History of the Labor Movement in the United States: Postwar Struggles, 1918–1920* (New York: International Publishers, 1988), 8:xi, 1–13; Alexander Bing, *Wartime Strikes and Their Adjustment*, ed. Leon Stein and Philip Taft (New York: Arno Press and the *New York Times*, 1971 [1921]); Shapiro, "'Hand and Brain,'" 407; Christopher L. Tomlins, "AFL Unions in the 1930s: Their Performance in Historical Perspective," *Journal of American History* 65 (March 1979): 1021–42.

The new militancy of labor was spurred in part by a desire among workers to share in wartime profits. But many of the unionists of the era considered their organizations to be more than instruments for attaining higher wages and used them as forums for promoting radical change.[4] The loftier aspirations of workers were best expressed in two phrases that gained widespread use during the period: "workers' control" and the "democratization of industry." The two terms meant very different things to opposing factions within the labor movement. Among the most conservative trade unionists, suggests Steven Fraser, workers' control suggested "reassertion by localized work groups of traditional and exclusivist prerogatives over particular skills and workshops." For others, it implied a revitalization of workers' cooperatives. Some revolutionaries associated the term with "democratic mass management of particular industries or even a reconstituted polity and political economy."[5]

"Industrial democracy" was similarly laden with conflicting meanings. For many, it connoted rank-and-file management of the shop floor through work councils and factory committees. Other thinkers also associated the phrase with national management of the economy by a duly elected labor party or socialist government. A number of AFL trade unionists, by contrast, used the term to describe corporatist arrangements whereby labor, government, and business would collectively manage the national economy.[6] If the interpretations given to the terms varied tremendously, they nonetheless reflected a common desire by trade union leaders, rank-and-file workers, and revolutionaries within the labor movement to take advantage of the elasticity of the wartime situation to alter permanently the balance between labor and capital in ways that benefited the working class.

Like the struggles for workers' control and industrial democracy, the quest for a democratic diplomacy energized key groups and individuals within every layer and fragment of the labor movement and spilled out into agitation among unorganized workers. Four interre-

4. Shapiro, "'Hand and Brain,'" 406; Foner, *History of the Labor Movement*, 8:13.
5. See Steven Fraser, "The New Unionism and the New Economic Policy," in *Work, Community, and Power*, ed. Cronin and Sirianni, 173–74; Montgomery, "Immigrants, Industrial Unions, and Social Reconstruction," 101, *Workers' Control in America: Studies in the History of Work, Technology, and Labor Struggles* (New York: Cambridge University Press, 1979); Foner, *History of the Labor Movement*, 8:13.
6. Fraser, "The New Unionism and the New Economic Policy," in *Work, Community, and Power*, ed. Cronin and Sirianni, 173–74; McKillen, "Corporatist Model," 171–97.

lated factors provoked a strong interest among American wage earners and trade union leaders in diplomatic reform issues: the immigrant backgrounds of many, the influence of the international
socialist and labor movements, the displacement of key foreign policy
functions from local government and Congress to the executive
branch, and the military and industrial contribution of the working
class to the war.

In 1920, 13 percent of the U.S. population was foreign-born. The
children of these foreign-born immigrants accounted for another 22
percent, bringing the total of those living within what David Montgomery terms an "immigrant ambience" to 35 percent of all U.S. residents. Within major industrial cities, foreign-born residents and their
children constituted a much greater proportion. In Chicago, for example, approximately 70 percent of the population was immigrant or the
children of immigrants. Not all of those living within an immigrant
ambience were working class, but according to Montgomery "it is safe
to say that the immigrant milieu dominated urban working-class life at
the time."[7]

Interest in foreign policy among immigrants was in part stimulated
by their continued ties with relatives in former homelands. Others had
less emotional reasons for keeping up with world events; they planned
to move back to the old country after earning some money in the
United States. Such plans, however, were disrupted by the war.[8]
Personal connections with Europe spurred a gut-level interest in international affairs that often superseded the interest of immigrants in
domestic events.

A diverse assortment of nationalist groups that mobilized during
the war to gain political freedom for such subject nationalities as the
Irish, Poles, Croats, Magyars, Lithuanians, South Slavs, and Czechs
further piqued the diplomatic awareness of immigrant workers.
President Woodrow Wilson, whose pronouncements about self-determination galvanized such groups into action, criticized many for their

7. Montgomery, "Immigrants, Industrial Unions, and Social Reconstruction," 108.
See also John M. Allswang, *A House for All Peoples: Ethnic Politics in Chicago,
1890–1936* (Lexington: University of Kentucky Press, 1971), 21; Louis Gerson, *The
Hyphenate in Recent American Politics and Diplomacy* (Lawrence: University of Kansas
Press, 1964), 62.
8. See J. D. Gould, "European Intercontinental Emigration, The Road Home: Return
Migration from the U.S.A," *Journal of European Economic History* 9 (spring 1980): 60.

allegedly narrow obsessions with the needs of their former home-lands. Yet these organizations often developed foreign policy pro-grams that included sophisticated plans for reforming American diplomacy and altering the balance of world power to the benefit of oppressed ethnic minorities throughout the globe. Many immigrant workers carried such agendas with them to trade union meetings and activities.[9]

Another impulse generating worker concern with diplomatic reform fed on the international socialist and labor ethos of the era. Many socialists and radicals in the early twentieth century, building on the work of Karl Marx, believed that workers must fight the battle against capitalism simultaneously on the national and international fronts so as to prevent bourgeois states from buoying themselves through impe-rialist exploitation. Marx himself had urged workers to "master the mysteries of international politics, to watch the diplomatic acts of their respective governments" and "to counteract them . . . by all means in their power." An ethos of international labor solidarity pre-vailed among a militant minority within the U.S. labor movement even after European socialist and labor movements pledged their support and loyalty to their respective governments during the war. This mili-tant minority played a key role in organically connecting the struggle for a democratic diplomacy to the struggle for industrial democracy. When labor dissent revived in Europe in 1917 and 1918, U.S. militants joined in efforts to revitalize the international trade union movement

9. For general information on ethnic political mobilization during the war, see John Bodnar, *The Transplanted: A History of Immigrants in Urban America* (Bloomington: Indiana University Press, 1985); Dirk Hoerder, ed., *"Struggle a Hard Battle": Essays on Working-Class Immigrants* (Dekalb: Northern Illinois University Press, 1986); Gerson, *Hyphenate*; Joseph O'Grady, *The Immigrants' Influence on Wilson's Peace Policies* (Lexington: University of Kentucky Press, 1967); Lloyd Ambrosius, *Woodrow Wilson and the American Diplomatic Tradition: The Treaty Fight in Perspective* (New York: Cambridge University Press, 1987), 142–43; Alexander DeConde, *Ethnicity, Race, and American Foreign Policy: A History* (Boston: Northeastern University Press, 1992), 69–127. Wilson's views on nationalist groups are explained in Arthur Link, *Woodrow Wilson: Revolution, War, and Peace* (Arlington Heights, Ill.: Harlan Davidson, 1979), 118. For an interesting example illustrating the truly global aspirations of ethnic leaders, see the material in Chapter 5 on Frank Walsh and the Frank Walsh Papers at the New York Public Library. Walsh was a leading member of the American Commission on Irish Independence and worked after the war to create a League of Oppressed Nationalities. He hoped the organization would enable the fledgling states of the era to form a power-ful new bloc in world politics that would countervail the influence of major industrial-creditor nations.

and to use it as a base for radically transforming international relations.[10]

The same amorphous spirit of change and elasticity that helped to drive the domestic campaigns of labor also fueled diplomatic reform. During the war, the Wilson administration tried to consolidate a number of important foreign policy and military functions in the executive branch of the federal government. Among these was the vital duty of raising and funding the army, a task entrusted during the Spanish-American War to local government and municipal groups. Some local labor organizations, sensing a threat to their power, joined municipal associations in trying to reassert local prerogatives over military mobilization. Others acquiesced in Wilson's plans but seized the opportunity to promote the notion of a democratically officered national army. Still other local labor groups tried to ensure continued grass-roots participation in foreign policy decision making by participating in campaigns to force a congressionally mandated national referendum on all decisions involving U.S. participation in war. Many national labor leaders, by contrast, responded to the consolidation of foreign policy powers in the executive branch by trying to secure a place for trade union representatives in newly evolving federal bureaucracies.[11]

10. Karl Marx quoted in Nathan Fine, *Labor and Farmer Parties in the United States* (New York: Russell and Russell, 1961 [1928]), 94, 303–4; Lewis L. Lorwin, *Labor and Internationalism* (Washington, D.C.: Brookings Institution (Cornwall Press), 1929), 1, and in general. On European labor dissent, see, particularly, Arno J. Mayer, *Political Origins of the New Diplomacy* (New York: Howard Fertig, 1969); Arthur Marwick, *The Deluge: British Society and the First World War* (Boston: Little, Brown, 1966; rpt. London: Macmillan, 1991); Harold Perkin, *The Rise of Professional Society: England since 1880* (London: Routledge, 1989); James Hinton, *Labour and Socialism: A History of the British Labour Movement, 1867–1974* (Amherst: University of Massachusetts Press, 1983), *The First Shop Stewards' Movement* (London: George Allen and Unwin, 1973); Mary Nolan, *Social Democracy and Society: Working-Class Radicalism in Dusseldorf 1890–1920* (Cambridge: Cambridge University Press, 1981); Peter Stansky, *The Left and the War* (New York: Oxford University Press, 1969).

11. Gerald Linderman, *The Mirror of War: American Society and the Spanish-American War* (Ann Arbor: University of Michigan Press, 1974). For local labor initiatives, see the *Chicago Federation of Labor Minutes (CFL Minutes)* in the Chicago Historical Society: 5/6/15, 7–8; 6/20/15, 18–19; 2/6/16, 12–15; 4/16/16, 10–11; 5/16/16, 10–11; 2/18/17, entire session. See also Frank Grubbs, *The Struggle for Labor Loyalty: Gompers, the A.F. of L., and the Pacifists, 1917–1920* (Durham, N.C.: Duke University Press, 1968). Information on AFL initiatives is available in Simeon Larson, *Labor and Foreign Policy: Gompers, the AFL, and the First World War, 1914–1918* (London: Associated University Presses, 1975); and Ronald Radosh, *American Labor and United States Foreign Policy* (New York: Random House, 1967).

A final factor spurring postwar interest in diplomatic reform was the feeling that workers had won a right to a voice in international affairs as a result of their wartime service. Thus a fifteenth-ward mass meeting of the incipient Chicago Labor party in 1919 endorsed a resolution calling for the United States to withdraw all troops from Russia on the grounds that it was the party's duty to assure that "no man in this war shall have died for empty words and worthless phrases and that from this time forward the world may be made forever safe for experiments and new adventures in democracy."[12]

Predictably, given the divergent impulses spurring worker interest in diplomatic reform, the cause provoked fundamental cleavages within the labor movement. Just as the term "industrial democracy" evoked profoundly different meanings among workers, so also the term "democratic diplomacy" became synonymous with movements that were fundamentally at odds with each other.

AFL president Samuel Gompers and his closest colleagues associated democratic diplomacy with trade union participation on corporatist federal councils created to encourage greater collaboration among business, labor, and the state and with the triumph of Wilsonian internationalist principles. Much interested in institutions like the War Emergency Workers' National Committee and Whitley Councils that developed in Britain to promote class harmony after the outbreak of war, Gompers welcomed the creation of a U.S. Council of National Defense in 1916 that solicited input from business and labor leaders on preparedness issues.[13] Appointed to the council in October, Gompers soon came to see it and other evolving war agencies as institutional panaceas that could be used to mediate industrial conflicts at home and to guarantee important labor input on foreign policy and international trade issues. In order to secure a place for the AFL in these institutions, Gompers staged a carefully orchestrated meeting at which leading AFL national and international trade union leaders

12. *New Majority (NM)*, 2/1/19, 6.

13. On the evolution of British corporatist institutions during the war, see Perkin, *Rise of Professional Society*, 202–3, 187; Henry Pelling, *A Short History of the Labour Party*, 3d ed. (New York: St. Martin's Press, 1968), 38–41; F. M. Leventhal, *Arthur Henderson* (Manchester: Manchester University Press, 1989), 49–64; Robert E. Dawse, "The Independent Labour Party and Foreign Politics, 1918–1923," *International Review of Social History* 7 (1962): 33–45; Hinton, *Labour and Socialism*, 96–118. On Gompers's interest in British wartime institutions, see Gompers, *Seventy Years of Life and Labor* (New York: E. P. Dutton, 1925), 2:339, 359; *New Republic (NR)*, 8/11/18, 35; Marguerite Green, *The National Civic Federation and the American Labor Movement, 1900–1925* (Westport, Conn.: Greenwood Press, 1973 [1956]), 379–80.

pledged to support the government in the event of U.S. intervention in the war. In return for their loyalty, AFL leaders and officials from constituent unions were appointed to a number of key war boards and participated in several diplomatic missions to Europe and the Soviet Union in 1917 and 1918. Following the armistice, Gompers joined other participants on the boards in trying to convert them to peacetime use. Proponents of the boards suggested that they held the key to industrial peace in the postwar era and would create a rationalized system for public input on a variety of policy issues, including foreign affairs.[14]

In addition to promoting corporatist institutions designed to give labor more direct access to the executive, Gompers sought to reform diplomacy by encouraging labor representation on the peace commissions that were to convene in Paris, by promoting the League of Nations, and by playing a critical role in creating the International Labor Organization (ILO), a League-sponsored organization. Gompers's request for labor representatives on the peace commissions was a logical outgrowth of the AFL's wartime experience: Just as

14. For Gompers's participation on wartime councils and attempt to extend their mandates, see Chapter 2; Larson, *Labor and Foreign Policy*, 128–52; Ronald Radosh, "The Corporate Ideology of American Labor Leaders from Gompers to Hillman," *Studies on the Left* 6 (1966): 66–88. For general information on the evolution of wartime councils, see Kennedy, *Over Here*, 93–143; Valerie Jean Conner, *The National War Labor Board: Stability, Social Justice, and the Voluntary State in World War I* (Chapel Hill: University of North Carolina Press, 1983); Ellis Hawley, *The Great War and the Search for a Modern Order: A History of the American People and Their Institutions, 1917–1933* (New York: St. Martin's Press, 1979), 20–37.

On the importance of corporatist precepts in the American political tradition, see Gabriel Kolko, *The Triumph of Conservatism: A Reinterpretation of American History, 1900–1916* (Chicago: Quadrangle Books, 1967); Martin J. Sklar, *The Corporate Reconstruction of American Capitalism, 1890–1916: The Market, the Law, and Politics* (Cambridge: Cambridge University Press, 1988); James Weinstein, *The Corporate Ideal and the Liberal State, 1900–1918* (Boston: Beacon Press, 1968). For the application of corporatist precepts to diplomacy, see Thomas McCormick, "Drift or Mastery? A Corporatist Synthesis for American Diplomatic History," *Reviews in American History* 10 (December 1982): 318–30; Michael J. Hogan, "Corporatism," *Journal of American History* 77 (June 1990): 153–60, "Revival and Reform: America's Twentieth-Century Search for a New Economic Order Abroad," *Diplomatic History* 8 (fall 1984): 287–310, *Informal Entente: The Private Structure of Cooperation in Anglo-American Diplomacy, 1918–1928* (Columbia: University of Missouri Press, 1977); Nathan Godfried, *Bridging the Gap between Rich and Poor: American Economic Development Policy toward the Arab East, 1942–1949* (Westport, Conn.: Greenwood Press, 1987).

For negative assessments of corporatist analyses, see Melvyn Dubovsky, "Abortive Reform: The Wilson Administration and Organized Labor, 1913–1920," in *Work, Community, and Power*, ed. Cronin and Sirianni, 197–220; and John Lewis Gaddis, "The Corporatist Synthesis: A Skeptical View," *Diplomatic History* 10 (fall 1986): 357–62.

labor had played an important role in war agencies and on diplomatic missions during 1917 and 1918, so also the AFL president believed that labor delegates to the peace conference could provide valuable counsel. The Wilson administration refused Gompers's request for AFL representation on the American commission, but Gompers and other AFL leaders nonetheless lobbied vigorously on behalf of the peace treaty and the League of Nations. Like President Wilson, Gompers believed that the League would help to eradicate secret diplomacy and war by providing an open forum for the discussion of international issues. The League's Executive Council would promote public international cooperation between major world powers, while the General Assembly would serve a congressional role in giving the larger family of nations a limited voice in the resolution of global conflict.[15]

In return for his support, Wilson appointed Gompers to serve on the Commission on International Labour Legislation, a group charged with creating the proposed labor adjunct to the League. Gompers was subsequently elected president of the commission and played an important role in determining the structure and purpose of the ILO. Gompers took his designs for the ILO from the same institutional blueprints as the Council of National Defense and subsidiary local councils that he promoted. In contrast to other international organizations comprised exclusively of labor representatives, Gompers helped to ensure that the ILO included business, labor, and government delegates. He sought this structure because he believed that business, state, and labor leaders shared a "community of interest" in collaborating to improve the health of the international capitalist system comparable to that which they shared in promoting national economic growth. Because the U.S. Senate failed to ratify the peace treaty, Gompers and other AFL leaders never officially participated in the labor organization they had played such a major role in creating. But Gompers's commitment to corporatist and Wilsonian internationalist principles continued to shape AFL

15. On Gompers's views, see, especially, Gompers, *Seventy Years*, 2: 513, 501–2, *American Labor and the War* (New York: George H. Doran Co., 1919), 75–82. For general discussions of the war boards and League, see Robert Wiebe, *The Search for Order, 1877–1920* (New York: Hill and Wang, 1967), 273; McCormick, "Drift or Mastery?" 218–30; Hogan, *Informal Entente*, 1–2, 13, 37; Melvyn P. Leffler, *The Elusive Quest: America's Pursuit of European Stability and French Security, 1919–1933* (Chapel Hill: University of North Carolina Press, 1979), 363; Emily Rosenberg, *Spreading the American Dream: American Economic and Cultural Expansion, 1890–1945* (New York: Hill and Wang, 1982), 7, 84–85.

diplomacy even after the treaty's demise, profoundly influencing its policies toward revolutionary nationalism, the international trade union movement, and American imperialism.[16]

Although Gompers won the overwhelming support of national and international trade unions for his internationalist agenda throughout the period from 1914 to 1924, he faced bitter opposition from other groups purporting to speak for labor. Among the first to voice discontent with the AFL's internationalist agenda was the Socialist party, which charged the organization with becoming a "fifth wheel on [the] capitalist war chariot."[17] While Gompers tried to gain workers' input on diplomatic issues by participating in war councils during 1916, the Socialist party lobbied on behalf of more direct forms of democracy, proposing that a national referendum should be held on the issue of whether the United States should become involved in the European conflict.[18]

Following the declaration of war against Germany, a minority of Socialists followed Gompers's lead and took up positions in key government agencies to work on behalf of war mobilization. A majority, however, remained firm in their opposition to the war, declaring that as "against the false doctrine of national patriotism, we uphold the ideal of international working class solidarity."[19] They called for continued mass agitation against the war and demanded the socialization of all great industries concerned with military production. Several Socialists took the lead in organizing the People's Council of America,

16. For information on Gompers's plans for the ILO, see, especially, Minutes of the Commission on International Labour Legislation, February 10–March 24, 1919, in *The Origins of the International Labor Organization (ILO)*, vol. 2, ed. James T. Shotwell (New York: Columbia University Press, 1934), 149–322. J. C. Grew to Gompers, 1/29/19; Gompers Memoranda No. 1, 1/30/19; Dictation of Gompers to Miss Lee Guard, 12/30/18; Gompers to Mr. Bowerman, 12/28/18: Correspondence Collection–Gompers Microfilm Collection, University of Wisconsin (CC-GMC). *Proceedings of the AFL*, 1919, 19–31. *American Federationist* 26 (March 1919): 226–31. On the early-twentieth-century concept of a community of interest between business, labor, and the state, see Green, *National Civic Federation*; and Gwendolyn Mink, *Old Labor and New Immigrants in American Political Development: Union, Party, and State: 1875–1920* (Ithaca, N.Y.: Cornell University Press, 1986), 198–200.

17. James Weinstein, *The Decline of Socialism in America, 1912–1925* (New York: Monthly Review Press, 1967), 178.

18. David Shannon, *The Socialist Party of America* (New York: Macmillan, 1955), 86–91; Weinstein, *Decline*, 119–77.

19. Quote from Fine, *Labor and Farmer Parties*, 310–11; Kenneth E. Hendrickson, "The Prowar Socialists, the Social Democratic League, and the Ill-Fated Drive for Industrial Democracy in America, 1917–20," *Labor History* (summer 1970): 304–22.

a group that tried to stir up antiwar sentiment among American trade unions and won Gompers's undying wrath. Although the Socialists failed to develop a fully systematic plan for diplomatic reform, their tactics suggested that the best way to achieve a democratic diplomacy was by giving the public the right to voice their opinions on foreign policy directly through national referenda. If the government refused to implement measures to ensure referenda, then workers must resort to mass political agitation. Many left-wing members even recommended strike action in the event that the government failed to heed their message.[20]

The Socialist party's antiwar activities apparently increased its popularity among the public, for its vote in municipal elections substantially increased throughout the United States. A study by Paul Douglas that examined fifteen cities during the war found that Socialist candidates on average polled quadruple the number of votes they ordinarily received.[21] The party also increased its membership by about thirty thousand between July 1917 and March 1918.[22] But its value as a vehicle for antiwar agitation and opposition to Gompers's brand of labor diplomacy was eroded by government prosecution and by the gradual shift among important sections of the party away from open agitation against the war. The split in the Socialist party in 1919 prevented it from becoming a major actor in the labor struggles to democratize diplomacy during the postwar period.[23]

A more important source of resistance to Gompers's diplomatic programs emerged among city labor councils, also known as central

20. Foner, *History of the Labor Movement*, 7: 17–37; James Weinstein, "The Socialist Party: Its Roots and Strength, 1912–19," *Studies on the Left* 1 (winter 1960), 5–27; Grubbs, *Struggle for Labor Loyalty*; Montgomery, *Fall of the House of Labor*, 371–72. Resolution of the First American Conference for Democracy and Terms of Peace, New York City, May 30–31, 1917, Box 5 (B5), John Fitzpatrick Papers (FP), Chicago Historical Society. Letter from John Sullivan to J. Bogart, Labor Committee of the Friends of Peace, 8/7/15: CC-GMC.

21. Paul Douglas survey cited in Fine, *Labor and Farmer Parties*, 225–26; Foner, *History of the Labor Movement*, 8: 237–38; Weinstein, "The Socialist Party," 5, *Decline*, 145–59; Kenneth Chern, "The Politics of Patriotism: War, Ethnicity, and the New York Mayoral Campaign, 1917," *New York Historical Quarterly* 63 (1979): 291–313. See also Richard Judd, *Socialist Cities: Municipal Politics and the Grass Roots of American Socialism* (Albany: State University of New York Press, 1989), 164–70.

22. Foner, *History of the Labor Movement*, 8: 237–38.

23. Ibid., 7: 28–38, 8: 237–53. See also Weinstein, "Socialist Party," 22–23, *Decline*, x–xi; Shannon, *Socialist Party*, 113–18, 163; Gabriel Kolko, "The Decline of American Radicalism," *Studies on the Left* 6 (September–October, 1966): 9–26.

labor unions. Critical to the evolution of the early labor movement, such organizations were relegated by the AFL in the late nineteenth century primarily to administrative roles. In contrast to national and international unions, which were accorded proportional voting power within the AFL, city labor councils were entitled to only one vote each at the annual convention. But many city labor councils compensated for their weak position within the AFL by building strong bases of local support. As the official representatives of all AFL workers within a given metropolitan area, city labor leaders often forged effective coalitions among local unions that cut across traditional craft rivalries. Such alliances sometimes proved crucial in mounting grass-roots campaigns on behalf of trade union causes and won some city labor council leaders the wary respect of the AFL Executive Council. Equally important, many city labor leaders cultivated close ties with local immigrant leaders and groups, soliciting their support in sustaining strike activities and making the local labor movement "a pole around which a series of ethnic cultural activities" revolved.[24]

Both their militant class consciousness and strong links with immigrant communities compelled many municipal labor leaders to oppose the AFL's internationalist programs in 1916 and 1917. Creatively reconceptualizing ethnic concerns to promote principles of international labor solidarity, city labor council leaders from Seattle to New York played an important role in launching counter-

24. Quote from David Brundage, "Denver's New Departure: Irish Nationalism and the Labor Movement in the Gilded Age," *Southwest Economy and Society* 5 (winter 1981): 18. On the structural strengths and weaknesses of central labor unions, see Montgomery, "New Tendencies," 101, 89–110; Dana Lynn Frank, *Purchasing Power: Consumer Organizing, Gender, and the Seattle Labor Movement, 1919–1929* (Cambridge: Cambridge University Press, 1994), "At the Point of Consumption: Seattle Labor and the Politics of Consumption, 1919–1927 (Ph.D. diss., Yale University, 1988); Julia Marie Greene, "The Strike at the Ballot Box: Politics and Partisanship in the American Federation of Labor, 1881–1916" (Ph.D. diss., Yale University, 1990), 76–99; John Keiser, "John Fitzpatrick and Progressive Unionism, 1915–1925," (Ph.D. diss., Northwestern University, 1965), 77, 166. For an analysis that explores similarities and differences between Canadian and American central labor bodies affiliated with the AFL, see Robert Babcock, *Gompers in Canada: A Study in American Continentalism before the First World War* (Toronto: University of Toronto Press, 1974). For the interplay of ethnicity and class in shaping foreign policy activities, see David Montgomery, "Nationalism, American Patriotism, and Class Consciousness among Immigrant Workers in the United States in the Epoch of World War I," in *"Struggle a Hard Battle": Essays on Working-Class Immigrants*, ed. Dirk Hoerder (Dekalb: Northern Illinois University Press, 1986), 327–51; Eric Foner, "Class, Ethnicity and Radicalism in the Gilded Age: The Land League and Irish America," *Marxist Perspectives* 1 (summer 1978): 32–37.

preparedness efforts and in rallying workers to demand a national labor caucus on the issue of AFL policy toward the war. But AFL leaders, noting privately that central labor unions were centers of pacifism, refused to invite local councils to send delegates to the conference at which trade union leaders pledged their loyalty to the government in the event of war. Following U.S. intervention in the European conflict, dissident central labor unions were pressured by the AFL to conform to national trade union policy on the war, and many municipal councils reluctantly endorsed the AFL's loyalty pledge.[25]

But even while officially supporting the war effort and participating in AFL war campaigns, central labor union leaders often indicted the AFL's collaborationist foreign policy for its dire domestic and international ramifications. Mirroring the arguments of the shop stewards' councils in Britain, municipal labor officials charged that the cozy relationship between national union officials and business and state leaders was preventing the trade union movement from fully utilizing the opportunities war afforded to organize workers and to launch campaigns that would advance the position of the working class. They also hinted that the unwavering loyalty of the AFL leadership to the war effort was inhibiting the chance for a revival of the international trade union movement after the war. The extent of disillusionment among this layer of labor leadership became apparent when city labor councils defied AFL mandates against independent political action and created some forty-five labor parties in the postwar era. Municipal labor officials in places as diverse as San Francisco, Seattle, Minneapolis, Chicago, Butte, and Kansas City also coordinated militant strike and organizing activities in defiance of AFL wishes. Like the British shop stewards' councils, central labor unions threatened for a brief moment in time to become independent bases of rank-and-file

25. Widespread opposition to preparedness among city labor councils in 1916 has been well documented by Foner, *History of the Labor Movement*, 7: 67–68, and Grubbs, *Struggle for Labor Loyalty*. The policies of central labor unions after American intervention in the war are more difficult to trace, but studies on Seattle, San Francisco, and New York City, in addition to my studies on Chicago, suggest a pattern of reluctant acquiescence. See *CFL Minutes*, 4/1/17, 23–44; 4/15/17, 4–5; 5/20/17, 14–20. See also Chapter 2; and Frank, "At the Point of Consumption," 62–63; Foner, *History of the Labor Movement*, 7: 108; Michael Kazin, *Barons of Labor: The San Francisco Building Trades and Union Power in the Progressive Era* (Urbana: University of Illinois Press, 1987), 240–44. On the policy of the AFL toward central labor unions, and on the attitudes of AFL leaders toward the pacifism of local labor leaders, see Chapter 2.

labor initiative, subject neither to the authority of the AFL leadership nor to that of constituent national and international unions.[26]

This book explores the local insurgency launched by one of the most powerful city labor councils in the country—the Chicago Federation of Labor (CFL)—and focuses on its rejection of the AFL's collaborationist foreign policies. Officially an AFL affiliate that represented 350 local unions with a total membership of 350,000 workers, the CFL played a gadfly role in promoting militant trade union tactics throughout the early twentieth century and, according to James Barrett, was "the heart and brain of the two great World War I drives to organize mass-production workers in the steel and meat-packing industries."[27] The CFL also launched one of the strongest labor parties of the postwar era and initiated the drive to organize the national Farmer-Labor party.

The leaders of the Chicago movement for independent labor political action have often been viewed primarily as heirs to the traditions and doctrines of a badly splintered Socialist party.[28] But the Chicago Labor party, like the other labor parties that erupted across the political landscape in 1919 and 1920, represented a new strain in American politics. Born of war, the party exhibited a unique preoccupation with repudiating corporatist forms of power sharing justified in the name of the national interest. Although officially lauding the cooperative spirit behind the war boards and arbitration commissions, Chicago Labor party leaders asked that labor be represented on such councils "in proportion to its voting strength." Similarly, the party demanded that workers should be represented at the peace conference and in any international organizations it created "in proportion to their numbers in the

26. On the political and strike activities of U.S. central labor unions, see Shapiro, "'Hand and Brain,'" 410–13; Theodore Draper, *The Roots of American Communism* (New York: Viking Press, 1957), 139, 319; Robert Morlan, *Political Prairie Fire: The Nonpartisan League, 1915–1922* (Minneapolis: University of Minnesota Press, 1955); Michael Kazin, "The Great Exception Revisited: Organized Labor and Politics in San Francisco and Los Angeles, 1870–1940," *Pacific Historical Review* 55 (1986): 371–402, *Barons of Labor*, 234–69; Fine, *Labor and Farmer Parties*, 363–438; Foner, *History of the Labor Movement*, 8: 101–16; Robert L. Friedheim, *The Seattle General Strike* (Seattle: University of Washington Press, 1964); Harvey O'Connor, *Revolution in Seattle* (New York: Monthly Review Press, 1964); Frank, "At the Point of Consumption," *Purchasing Power*; Montgomery, "New Tendencies," 89–110. On the British Shop Stewards' movement, see Hinton, *First Shop Stewards' Movement*; Perkin, *Rise of Professional Society*, 193–99; Marwick, *Deluge*, 108–26.

27. James R. Barrett, *Work and Community in the Jungle: Chicago's Packinghouse Workers, 1894–1922* (Urbana: University of Illinois Press, 1987), 191. NM, 1/4/19, 4. CFL Minutes, 11/2/17, 10.

28. Weinstein, *Decline*, 224; Fine, *Labor and Farmer Parties*, 378.

armies, navies and workshops of the world." Exhibiting striking political imagination, Chicago Labor party leaders reinterpreted American democratic ideals to justify democratic control of industry, majoritarian political rule by a labor party, and international labor solidarity. These principles would also become critical to the national Farmer-Labor party and would be widely endorsed by the large numbers of central labor unions and local labor parties that rallied behind it.[29]

The diplomatic agendas of the Chicago Federation of Labor, the Chicago Labor party, and the Farmer-Labor party deserve special attention because they illustrate that foreign policy issues played a catalytic role in provoking conflict between the national AFL hierarchy and municipal labor councils and in shaping realignments within the labor movement between 1914 and 1924. Reconfiguring many of the arguments of local Irish and radical groups, the CFL became a center of antiwar agitation after the outbreak of war in Europe. Its opposition to the AFL's preparedness and mobilization policies stimulated a critical controversy between local officials and Samuel Gompers. CFL leaders challenged the AFL's collaborationist foreign policy in part because they recognized that it had enormous repercussions for class relations at home.

Equally important, Chicago activists anticipated the evolution of a global economy and realized that labor's international strategies and diplomatic power would become increasingly critical to protecting the welfare of American workers. Preoccupied on a daily basis with unionizing Chicago's multinational work force, CFL leaders fully understood the implications for workers and the trade union movement of the growing international mobility of capital and labor in the early twentieth century. The carnage of war further illuminated the close interconnections between the well-being of workers and the global economic and security strategies of business and state leaders and impelled Chicago activists to seek more diplomatic influence for the labor movement. But the CFL ultimately promoted radically different forms of international power for workers than did the AFL. Rejecting Gompers's corporatist definition of a democratic diplomacy, CFL leaders instead associated the concept with Labor party politics, the destruction of the manipulative power of international finance and business, anti-imperialism and antimilitarism, and the evolution of international organizations that would express the will of the majority of the world's workers.

29. *Independent Labor Party Platform*, B7–F51: FP. See also Chapter 4.

International and diplomatic reform issues formed a vital component of the platforms of the Chicago Labor and national Farmer-Labor parties and proved crucial both in winning, and in limiting, ethnic group, liberal, and radical support for independent labor politics. Foreign policy thus became a significant part of the "contested terrain" that provoked conflict between local militants and the AFL hierarchy between 1914 and 1924 and critically influenced the ultimate outcome of the battle between them.[30] Labor historians must carefully examine the dynamic interplay between the quest for a democratic diplomacy, labor party politics, and the crusade for democratic control of industry if they hope to understand tensions within the labor movement during the World War I era.

The foreign policy programs of Chicago insurgents and national Farmer-Labor party leaders also deserve attention from diplomatic historians because they demonstrate that the public debate over Wilsonian internationalist principles between 1914 and 1924 has been oversimplified. Wilson himself helped to define the terms of the debate over his foreign policies by characterizing his opponents as small-minded Americans, full of "watchful jealousies" and of "rabid antagonisms." Following Wilson's lead, diplomatic historians have often framed the battle over Wilsonian internationalist principles as one between provincial isolationists and enlightened internationalists. Although revisionist historians have suggested that congressional opponents of the peace treaty objected more to the Wilson administration's tactics than to its internationalist goals, even they have largely failed to question the image of ethnic and working-class opponents of Wilsonianism as provincial and narrow-minded.[31] But many local labor activists opposed Wilsonian foreign policy not because they were shortsighted

30. For the term "contested terrain," I am indebted to the second reviewer at Cornell University press.

31. Link, *Revolution, War, and Peace,* 118. See also Selig Adler, *The Isolationist Impulse: Its Twentieth-Century Reaction* (New York: Abelard-Shuman, 1957); Thomas A. Bailey, *A Diplomatic History of the American People,* 9th ed. (Englewood Cliffs, N.J.: Prentice-Hall, 1974); Thomas G. Paterson, J. Garry Clifford, and Kenneth J. Hagan, *American Foreign Policy, A History: 1900 to the Present,* 3d ed. (Lexington, Mass.: D. C. Heath, 1988), 285–89. For a viewpoint emphasizing the internationalist perspectives of Wilson's Republican opponents, see Hogan, *Informal Entente.* For critical perspectives on the debate among diplomatic historians over Wilsonian internationalism, see Ambrosius, *Woodrow Wilson,* xii, 136, 170; Rhodri Jeffreys-Jones, "Massachusetts Labour and the League of Nations Controversy, 1919," *Irish Historical Studies* 19 (September 1975): 396–416; and Joseph Edward Cuddy, *Irish America and National Isolationism* (New York: Arno Press, 1976).

isolationists, but because Wilson's blueprints for transforming the world order fell far short of realizing their own more radical plans for democratizing diplomacy, achieving an equitable distribution of world wealth and power, and ensuring future peace.

Because workers lived in communities that tended to be segregated along lines of race and national origin, immigrant leaders and local ethnic presses were usually more important than local labor organizations in shaping working-class foreign policy attitudes. But through their strike, organizing, political, and cultural activities during the World War I era, municipal labor leaders impinged on the "insular" communities created by immigrant workers and their leaders in significant ways.[32] In the process, they won a tentative audience for their class-based critiques of American diplomacy, linking immediate ethnic concerns to a broader condemnation of Wilsonianism that stressed its inherently undemocratic and imperialist tendencies. Many ethnic blue-collar workers were likely to see the nationalist programs of their former homelands as intimately intertwined with the class struggle that preoccupied their daily lives. They may have opposed key Wilsonian foreign policies as much to assert principles of international labor solidarity as to vent revenge on the Wilson administration for its failure to deliver on wartime promises to their former homelands. As David Montgomery has written of the immigrant workers of this era, "Apocalyptic visions mingled with clearly articulated programs and demands. Through it all, an idyllic image of life on the land, back home, provided a still irrepressible counterpoint. Intense nationalism, anxiety over the fate of loved ones across the sea, and hopes that a new day was dawning in the old country, as well as in the new, added special poignancy to those themes."[33]

Although it is impossible to gauge the precise influence of municipal labor officials in shaping public political opinion, the Chicago example illustrates that diplomatic historians need to move beyond a bipolar model of working-class foreign policy attitudes that emphasizes corporatist statesmen like Sam Gompers at one extreme and xenophobic ethnic fraternals at the other. A new framework must be developed that treats local labor leaders and their progressive allies within immigrant communities as active agents in shaping patterns of resistance and

32. On the concept of insular ethnic communities, see Lizabeth Cohen, *Making a New Deal: Industrial Workers in Chicago, 1919–1939* (Cambridge: Cambridge University Press, 1990), 30, 1–52.

33. Montgomery, "Nationalism, American Patriotism, and Class Consciousness," 346.

accommodation to American foreign policy initiatives within the working class between 1914 and 1924.

The chapters that follow are arranged in rough chronological order. Chapter 1 explores the roots of labor foreign policy activism in Chicago by examining the city's large Irish and Polish communities and considering how their international ideologies intersected, stimulated, and conflicted with those developed by the CFL between 1914 and 1917. Chapter 2 probes the AFL's collaborationist wartime policies and considers how the CFL and Chicago ethnic groups responded to them. Chapter 3 documents Gompers's neglected plans for using domestic corporatist institutions, the League of Nations, and the ILO to democratize diplomacy after the war and considers how his programs clashed with those of British and European trade unionists. The oppositional international programs of the CFL, the Chicago Labor party, and the national Farmer-Labor party are the subject of Chapter 4. Chapter 5 examines the foreign policies promoted by the Irish and Polish in Chicago after the war and explains why the Chicago Labor and national Farmer-Labor parties were ultimately unsuccessful in courting their favor. Chapter 6 considers the split that occurred between progressives and radicals within the CFL in 1923 and details the demise of the Chicago insurgency. In the Conclusion, I explore the significance of labor's struggle to democratize diplomacy during the World War I era.

CHAPTER ONE

Ethnic and Labor Foreign Policy Ideologies in Chicago, 1914–1917

On the eve of World War I, Chicago was renowned both for its ethnic character and its militant trade union activity. Visitors were impressed first by the hodgepodge of immigrants who resided within city borders and clung tenaciously to old-world traditions. One wealthy Hungarian, for example, wrote to friends back home that "Chicago is the land of promise to all malcontents and emigres." He noted with surprise, "There are whole quarters where nothing but German is spoken. . . . Others are inhabited entirely by Slavs."[1] Some visitors argued that ethnic groups in Chicago seemed to run the city. "My impression," one observer wrote, "is that there are as many governments in Chicago as there are nationalities and . . . that there is no higher or central authority."[2]

If visitors were struck initially by the diverse assortment of nationality groups and ethnic organizations that vied for power in Chicago, many experienced one of the industrial shutdowns for which the city was famous. These experiences also left an indelible impression. The same Hungarian visitor who wrote about immigrants also witnessed a rail strike, finding himself suddenly besieged by "seething, surging masses of humanity" at an area train station. As he struggled to avoid the strikers, the man viewed "workmen and police officers constantly in

1. Monsignor Count Vay de Vaya and Luskod, "The Inner Life of the United States," in *As Others See Chicago, Impressions of Visitors, 1673–1933*, ed. Bessie Louise Pierce (Chicago: University of Chicago Press, 1933), 426.
2. Mary Borden, "Chicago Revisited," in ibid., 495.

conflict and street fights and regular battles" and heard "howls and shrieks mingled with the lugubrious sounds of pistol and rifle."[3]

Like travelers throughout history, early-twentieth-century visitors to Chicago doubtless exaggerated their touring experiences. But their observations nonetheless illuminate key aspects of the local subcultures that critically shaped working-class foreign policy attitudes when the aftershocks of war reverberated through American society. Although Chicago's neighborhoods were nowhere near as ethnically cohesive as tourists claimed, immigrants from the same nationality groups did tend to cluster in residential enclaves when the job and housing markets allowed. Even more important, they formed extensive webs of intragroup social contacts and created ethnic organizations to perpetuate traditions from the old country, to assist each other in adapting to conditions in industrial America, and to promote international agendas that would benefit their former homelands. But the strong local labor movement encroached significantly on ethnic communities, often forcing immigrant workers to reconfigure traditional beliefs and attitudes in ways that promoted class solidarity rather than fragmentation.[4]

Following the outbreak of war in Europe, local ethnic organizations formulated foreign policy ideologies that critically shaped immigrant workers' responses to international events. Michael Hunt and others define ideology as an "interrelated set of convictions or assumptions that reduces the complexities of a particular slice of reality to easily comprehensible terms and suggests appropriate ways of dealing with that reality."[5] The international ideologies of American ethnic groups encompassed more than nationalist goals for former homelands. They also included assumptions about who should have influence over foreign policy decision making, what role the United States should play in international affairs, and how future peace and stability could be achieved.

3. Vay deVaya and Luskod, "The Inner Life of the United States," 417–18.
4. On the ethnic cohesiveness of Chicago neighborhoods, see Dominic A. Pacyga, *Polish Immigrants and Industrial Chicago: Workers on the South Side, 1880–1922* (Columbus: Ohio State University Press, 1991), 8. See also Jonathan Cumbler, *Working-Class Community in Industrial America: Work, Leisure, and Struggle in Two Industrial Cities, 1880–1930* (Westport, Conn.: Greenwood Press, 1979), 5; Cohen, *Making a New Deal*, 27–30, 49–51; James R. Barrett, "Unity and Fragmentation: Class, Race, and Ethnicity on Chicago's South Side: 1900–1922," in *"Struggle a Hard Battle,"* ed. Hoerder, 231–48; Bodnar, *The Transplanted*.
5. Michael Hunt, "Ideology and American Foreign Policy," *Journal of American History* 77 (June 1990): 108–9.

AFL President Samuel Gompers believed that the foreign policy ideologies of immigrant groups posed a threat to his attempts to "weld" the working class into a "solid phalanx in support of Wilson's program."[6] Following U.S. intervention in the European conflict, he participated in a variety of programs designed to "Americanize" immigrants and to inspire patriotism among them. By contrast, CFL leaders, far from viewing immigrant ideologies as hostile to working-class solidarity, incorporated key elements of them into their own foreign policy analyses. Of Irish immigrant backgrounds themselves, several local labor activists proved particularly adept at reformulating Irish-American foreign policy concerns to make them consistent with principles of international labor solidarity.

Attempts by the CFL to create a class-based oppositional foreign policy movement in Chicago before 1917 were undermined both from above and below. Gompers, preoccupied with demonstrating labor loyalty to the government, denied CFL leaders a national trade union forum for advertising their foreign policy agenda. Meanwhile, the CFL's pacifist program failed to elicit enthusiasm among those immigrant groups, like the Poles, whose homelands stood to benefit from U.S. intervention in the war. While the CFL's pacifist programs placed it at odds with some prowar immigrant groups, it nonetheless shared important points of ideological convergence even with these groups. Following the armistice, Labor party leaders used these points of convergence to make significant political inroads into previously hostile or indifferent communities.

On the eve of World War I, Chicago immigrant groups tended to conform to one of two demographic patterns. The Irish and most northern European groups experienced their peak periods of immigration to Chicago before 1900. By 1914 a majority of the members of these older immigrant groups had either lived in Chicago for some time or had been born there. Indeed, the children of immigrants often outnumbered the immigrants themselves in such communities.[7] Many members of older immigrant groups had experienced some social mobility, with a few attaining middle-class status and many more moving from casual, low-paying jobs to secure positions as skilled laborers. Middle-class immigrants forged ties with the area business community, while skilled workers established a foothold for themselves in the local

6. Larson, *Labor and Foreign Policy*, 78.
7. Montgomery, "Immigrants, Industrial Unions, and Social Reconstruction," 109.

labor movement. Immigrants of all socioeconomic levels played a role in building ethnic voluntary associations such as fraternal lodges and benevolent associations. Such groups, in addition to providing a forum for socializing, typically offered basic insurance services to members and were used by ethnic politicians to build constituencies. Many older immigrant groups wielded considerable local and national political power by the beginning of the war.[8]

A second set of nationality groups from southern and eastern Europe experienced their peak periods of immigration after 1900. When war broke out in 1914, a majority of the members of these groups were recent immigrants to Chicago; they held unskilled, nonunionized jobs in the area's mass industries. Such groups lacked a secure base in the labor movement, and had not yet developed political clout comparable to that of older immigrant communities, in part because many new immigrants were not yet naturalized citizens. Political development was also impeded by a high repatriation rate, that is, many members of new immigrant groups returned to Europe after a brief stay in the United States. The outbreak of war, however, stopped the flow of southern and eastern European immigrants back to their homelands, enabling ethnic leaders to develop stronger organizational infrastructures and to begin to contest the political dominance of older immigrant groups.[9]

Both old and new immigrant communities participated in nationalist campaigns during the World War I era and developed foreign policy ideologies that clashed in important respects with those of the Wilson administration. Of the older immigrant groups in the city, the local Irish community probably launched the most sustained and vigorous foreign policy campaigns of the era. Chicago's large Polish community serves as a useful example of mobilization on behalf of foreign policy issues among a new immigrant group. In a rare display of unity, the Irish both in Chicago and in the country at large achieved almost total

8. Barrett, "Unity and Fragmentation," 230–35; Bodnar, *The Transplanted*; and Lawrence McCaffrey et al., *The Irish in Chicago* (Urbana: University of Illinois Press, 1987).

9. Barrett, *Work and Community in the Jungle*, 45; Kantowicz, *Polish-American Politics in Chicago* (Chicago: University of Chicago Press, 1975); Allswang, *A House for All Peoples*; Gould, "European Inter-Continental Emigration, The Road Home," 60.

Many social historians have discarded the model of "old" and "new" immigrant groups, suggesting that it obscures the continuous process of migration that occurred within both types of communities. But for purposes of understanding the respective political and economic power that these groups wielded on the eve of World War I, the models are still useful. See Hoerder, "*Struggle a Hard Battle*"; and Bodnar, *The Transplanted*, xvii.

consensus on nationalist goals and foreign policy programs between 1916 and 1920. Unity proved more elusive within the Polish community, but by 1916 most activists had coalesced around one of two major nationalist campaigns or around an international socialist agenda.[10]

The first Irish settlers came to Chicago in the early 1800s and settled on the south and northwest sides of the city. Chicago's Irish neighborhoods remained small until 1845, when famine brought thousands of new Irish immigrants to the area. Immigration ebbed and flowed for the remainder of the century, depending on the level of economic hardship prevailing in Ireland. The Irish population in Chicago peaked in 1900, with 73,913 foreign-born Irish and 208,728 Chicagoans of Irish stock (the children of immigrants). The Irish population in Chicago declined slightly over the next two decades, and by 1920 census takers recorded only 56,786 foreign-born Irish and 199,956 of Irish stock.[11]

Even as Chicago's Irish population dwindled, its political power increased. The political strength of the Irish in Chicago was rooted in the vast network of Irish voluntary organizations that were created to aid new immigrants and to win their support for the Irish nationalist movement. By 1902, more than 148 such voluntary organizations existed in Chicago. These groups formed a vital organizational infrastructure that ambitious Irish-American politicians used to build patronage machines and to cultivate constituencies within the Irish community. Michael Funchion suggests that "during the half century before 1915 the Irish were clearly the single most important ethnic group in Chicago politics."[12]

Local political success, however, camouflaged deep divisions within the Irish community. Eric Foner argues that Irish-America exhibited bipolar characteristics as early as 1880. One set of Irish organizations

10. For a discussion of the unifying powers of nationalism, see Benedict Anderson, *Imagined Communities: Reflections on the Origin and Spread of Nationalism* (New York: Verso, 1983). For an examination of divisions and factionalism within ethnic communities, see Bodnar, *The Transplanted*, 142.

11. Eric L. Hirsch, "Revolution or Reform: An Analytical History of an Urban Labor Movement" (Ph.D. diss., University of Chicago, 1981), 520–21; Chicago Department of Development and Planning, *Chicago's Irish Population* (Chicago, 1976), 6.

12. Michael F. Funchion, "The Political and Nationalist Dimensions," in *Irish in Chicago*, ed. McCaffrey et al., 69. *Chicago Citizen* (CC), 2/9/17, 1–2; 7/15/18, 5–6. Hirsch, "Revolution or Reform," 520–21, 544. For a sense of the scope of groups existing in Chicago, see Michael Funchion, ed., *Irish-American Voluntary Organizations* (Westport, Conn.: Greenwood Press, 1983), and *Chicago's Irish Nationalists, 1881–1890* (New York: Arno Press, 1976).

coalesced around the Democratic party and the Catholic church and were dominated by the nascent Irish-American middle class. Another set of groups clustered around socially radical Irish leaders and drew their inspiration from the *Irish World and American Industrial Liberator*. However, a cause like the Land League, founded around 1880 to promote peasant ownership of land in Ireland, could occasionally draw the two poles of the Irish-American community together. When Irish-Americans united behind such a cause, suggests Foner, they had a significant impact on both sides of the Atlantic.[13]

In 1914, the Chicago Irish community was probably tripolar. One base of power rested in fraternal and nationalist groups that continued to maintain close ties to the Democratic party and the Catholic church. More socially radical elements in the community coalesced around militant Irish-American labor leaders like John Fitzpatrick and used local labor institutions to conduct ethnic activities informed by a sense of class consciousness. The most prominent members of the Irish-American community, meanwhile, had begun to pull away from the web of social and political connections afforded by traditional voluntary organizations. They formed groups like the Irish-American Fellowship Club that were open only to elites and that professed to be apolitical and nonsectarian.[14]

Complicating these divisions were quarrels within the larger Irish-American community in the United States about the tactics that should be used by the Irish and by Irish-Americans to secure Ireland's independence from Britain. These quarrels typically cut across rather than paralleled basic socioeconomic and political cleavages in Chicago. Some Irish-Americans advocated home rule for Ireland through constitutional agreement with Britain. Irish-America's role in securing home rule was to force Washington to pressure Britain so that it would agree to such an arrangement. Others advocated the violent overthrow of British rule in Ireland and believed that Irish-America's primary role was to supply revolutionaries with money and arms. Still others advocated a policy of

13. Eric Foner, "Class, Ethnicity, and Radicalism in the Gilded Age," 32–37, 46–55. See also Brundage, "Denver's New Departure," 10–21.

14. On local fraternal organizations and their links to the Democratic party, see McCaffrey et al., *Irish in Chicago*, 73–75. Among the most important fraternals existing in the city were the Ancient Order of Hibernians, the Clan na Gael, and the United Irish League of America. On the socially radical Irish faction in Chicago and their activities, see, especially, *CFL Minutes*, 12/12/15, 30, and January–July 1916. On the Irish Fellowship Club, see, especially, letter to Roger Faherty from Mr. McKenna, 4/19/20, B1: Faherty Papers (Fah P), Chicago Historical Society.

passive resistance to British authorities. Within the United States, they promoted boycotts of British goods and joined others in supporting efforts aimed at putting diplomatic pressure on Britain. Disagreements between proponents of these differing views spurred fiery debates at fraternal lodge meetings, important political dinners, Gaelic sporting events, and church and trade union picnics. The local Irish-American press and New York–based Irish newspapers available in Chicago also engaged in spirited debates over nationalist tactics and helped perpetuate local factionalism.[15]

The outbreak of war initially exacerbated nationalist feuds within Irish-America. Much of the debate revolved around Irish parliamentary leader John Redmond's decision to support the British during the war; some Irish-American activists praised Redmond's patriotism, while others denounced him as a traitor to Ireland. Previously friendly fraternals feuded bitterly, and some local branches of Irish-American organizations even split from their executive councils over the issue.[16] Three factors developed in 1915 and 1916 to forge a near total consensus among prominent Irish-Americans on nationalist tactics and foreign policy goals: Wilson's pro-British war policies, the Easter Rebellion in Ireland, and Wilson's attacks on ethnic lobbying. These events also temporarily obscured the socioeconomic cleavages that were tugging at the seams of Irish community life in Chicago: radicals, elites, and mainstream groups were integrated into a revitalized nationwide campaign on behalf of Irish independence and became a part of dynamic intellectual currents shaping an ideological alternative to Wilsonian internationalism.[17]

15. For an examination of these competing viewpoints and the conflicts they created within and between Irish-American organizations, see Funchion, *Irish-American Voluntary Organizations*, and *Chicago's Irish Nationalists*; and Alan Ward, "America and Irish Problems, 1899–1921," in *Irish Nationalism and the American Contribution*, ed. Lawrence McCaffrey (New York: Arno Press, 1976). For primary accounts, see the *Chicago Citizen* (*CC*) and the New York–based papers, the *Irish World and American Industrial Liberator* (*IW*) and *Gaelic American* (*GA*), both of which were available in Chicago and often published stories on Irish-American events in Chicago. See, especially, *IW*, 2/24/17. *GA*, 2/20/15, 7. *CC* 4/26/18, 1; and 7/5/18, 5–6. See also *CFL Minutes*, May–July 1916. Address of Honorable T. P. O'Connor to Irish Fellowship Club, 11/17–3/18, B1; Letter from Faherty to James Connell, 5/11/18, B1; and Minutes of Debate over Irish freedom and American patriotism, 11/17–3/18, B1: Fah P.

16. Funchion, *Irish-American Voluntary Organizations*, 275. *GA*, 8/8/14, 4; 8/15/14, 1; 8/7/15, 14; 11/2/17, 4. *IW*, 9/12/14, 4; 1/16/17, 4; 2/3/17, 4. *CC*, 2/9/17, 5.

17. See, especially, B1: Fah P, 1915–18. *CFL Minutes*, 1915–17. *CC* throughout the war period.

President Wilson's first responses to the war in Europe were to issue a proclamation of neutrality and to appeal to Americans to be neutral in thought, speech, and action. But many critics, including leading Irish-American spokesmen both in Chicago and in the East, thought the president's subsequent actions were anything but neutral. Wilson's problems really started when Britain established an undeclared blockade of Germany's coast in autumn 1914. Subsequently, British naval officers regularly violated the rights of neutral ships sailing to Germany by forcing them to port; staging inspections; and seizing cargoes of munitions, foodstuffs, and textiles. These practices dramatically decreased trade between the United States and Germany. In 1914, American exports to Germany totalled $345 million; by 1915 they had plummeted to $29 million.[18] Germany complained bitterly about American acquiescence in the blockade, proclaiming that America was assisting the British in starving German children. America, advised the kaiser, ought to place restrictions on British trade in retaliation for its violations of neutral rights.

But Wilson, while issuing formal protests, allowed trade between Britain and the United States to continue unabated. The president argued that the U.S. government itself would be perpetrating an unneutral act if it stopped the free flow of goods to Britain. American businessmen took advantage of Wilson's policies and signed several massive munitions contracts with British officials. Thus, while exports to Germany declined, U.S. trade with Britain and France expanded significantly. In 1914, U.S. exports to England and France equaled $754 million; by 1915 they had risen to $1.28 billion.[19]

In February 1915, determined to even the scales, Germany declared a war zone around Britain. Since Britain had blockaded most of Germany's warships, the kaiser announced that he would rely on a new fleet of U-2 submarines to sink enemy vessels. German officers urged neutral passengers not to sail on British commercial ships and also requested

18. Paterson et al., *American Foreign Policy*, 266. See also Link, *Revolution, War, and Peace*, *Wilson the Diplomatist: A Look at His Major Foreign Policies* (Baltimore, Md.: Johns Hopkins University Press, 1957), 31–60; N. Gordon Levin, *Woodrow Wilson and World Politics: America's Response to Revolution and War* (Oxford: Oxford University Press, 1968), 14–49; Daniel Smith, *The Great Departure: The United States and World War I, 1914–1920* (New York: John Wiley and Sons, 1965), 9–66.

19. Paterson et al., *American Foreign Policy*, 266; and Ambrosius, *Woodrow Wilson*, 12. For an excellent account emphasizing Wilson's unneutral reading of international law as it pertained to trade during wartime, see John W. Coogan, *The End of Neutrality: The United States, Britain, and Maritime Rights, 1899–1915* (Ithaca, N.Y.: Cornell University Press, 1981), 16, 249–50.

that American boats stay out of British waters. They suggested that the submarine made previous rules of warfare obsolete. According to maritime law, battleships were supposed to warn commercial vessels of impending attack so that civilians could be evacuated. Yet, once slow-moving submarines surfaced, they risked being rammed by faster British merchant ships. German officials also claimed that neutral vessels in war zones could not realistically be exempted from attack. British sea captains often flew American flags to mislead enemy ship captains. U-2 commanders could not determine from the depths of the sea which were legitimate American vessels and which were British. German officials thus argued that Americans should avoid belligerent waters.[20]

President Wilson responded angrily to German declarations. Britain had interfered with American property rights, but Germany now jeopardized American lives. Neutral citizens, insisted the president, had the right under international law to travel on commercial ships during wartime without fearing for their lives. Wilson subsequently refused to restrict American trade with Britain or to regulate American travel on belligerent ships. He warned that Germany would be held accountable for any American deaths.[21]

Irish-Americans from across the political spectrum suggested that Wilson was committing a gross injustice to Germany by insisting on "old worn out practices of naval warfare." Wilson's notes to Germany, they argued, were "a roundabout way of saying that England is to be allowed to starve the people of Germany by means of her powerful fleet but that Germany shall not be allowed to use her most effective fleet to compel England to come to terms."[22] Irish-American leaders further argued that the president was needlessly endangering the lives of American citizens. They suggested that an embargo ought to be instituted against all belligerents. Americans should also be prohibited from traveling on British ships.[23]

Ill-feeling between Irish-Americans and Wilson intensified when the Germans sunk the *Lusitania* on May 15, 1915, killing 1,198 people—128 of them Americans. Wilson dubbed the act a crime against human-

20. See, especially, Levin, *Woodrow Wilson*, 32–49; Link, *Revolution, War, and Peace*, 31–60; Smith, *Great Departure*, 51–66; Paterson et al., *American Foreign Policy*, 274–87.
21. Link, *Revolution, War, and Peace*, 21–46; Paterson et al., *American Foreign Policy*, 257–97.
22. *GA*, 2/20/15, 4.
23. Ibid. See also *GA*, 5/15/15, 1. *IW*, 5/15/15, 1. *CC*, 2/9/17, 5. Truman Cicero Bigham, "The Chicago Federation of Labor" (Master's thesis, University of Chicago, 1925), 104. *CFL Minutes*, 11/21/15, 7–8.

ity and demanded that the Germans renounce submarine warfare, make reparations to victims' families, and apologize for their actions. Irish-Americans considered Wilson's threats rash. "So it comes to this," wrote the editor of the *Irish World*. "A British ship, which as an auxiliary of the British navy, is virtually a warship, is sunk by a German submarine as she is carrying war material to the British army. After having been warned of the danger to which they are exposing themselves, Americans lose their lives. . . . No one outside of a lunatic asylum would consider the killing of such citizens a sufficient justification for plunging the nation into war."[24] An editor from the *Gaelic American* argued that the *Lusitania* was a "floating arsenal" and a valid target for German submarines. The responsibility for the loss of life, he suggested, lay primarily with the English government "who put noncombatants and children on board an auxiliary cruiser of the British navy." Washington, according to the author, was also culpable for gross negligence; Americans should never have been allowed to sail on belligerent ships.[25]

Early clashes between Wilsonians and Irish-Americans on issues of neutral shipping reflected more than disagreements over wartime tactics; they exposed a growing divergence of opinion between the two groups on America's proper international role. Wilson believed that one of America's primary roles in times of both war and peace was to uphold international law. These laws, he argued, provided the only sound basis for relations and commerce between nations. Without them, the world would regress to barbarism.[26] Irish-American activists, by contrast, implied that international law was simply another tool created and used by large imperial powers to justify the exploitation of weaker nations and colonial peoples. Irish-Americans argued that both Wilson and the American press were obscuring the real issues surrounding the rights of neutral shipping by focusing on pedantic matters of international law. They argued that true freedom of the seas, for large and small nations alike, would come only with the destruction of British naval tyranny.[27]

24. *IW*, 5/15/15, 4. See also Thomas A. Bailey and Paul B. Ryan, *The Lusitania Disaster: An Episode in Modern Warfare and Diplomacy* (New York: Free Press, 1975).

25. *GA*, 5/15/15, 1. See also *CC*, 2/9/17, 5. *CFL Minutes*, 5/16/15, 7–8; 6/20/15, 18–19.

26. See Coogan, *End of Neutrality*, 148–236, 250–54, on Wilson's commitment to international law and on his unneutral reading of it in order to maintain Anglo-American friendship. See also Smith, *Great Departure*, 29–82; Paterson et al., *American Foreign Policy*, 267–70; Link, *Revolution, War, and Peace*, 13, 21–46.

27. See, especially, *GA*, 8/22/14, 7; 8/15/14, 2.

Dissatisfied with Wilson's interpretation of the American diplomatic tradition, Irish-American newspaper editors and politicians scanned American history for themselves and concluded that Wilson was violating George Washington's advice on avoiding entangling alliances by siding with Britain in the current conflict. Some within Wilson's circle, they suggested, actually sought to nullify the Declaration of Independence.[28] They argued that the United States must remain aloof from the clutches of Britain if it was to serve the moral leadership role that the founding fathers intended for it. This role, in contrast to the legal arbiter role promoted by the Wilson administration, required that U.S. policymakers abandon their pro-British biases and give a fair hearing to the appeals of weaker nations and oppressed nationalities.[29]

Irish-American views on assuring a stable postwar world also moved in a direction opposite that of the president between 1914 and 1917. The president believed that one important precondition to a lasting peace was a wartime settlement that restored the status quo antebellum, or the approximate power relations existing before the war. In an unpublished note written in autumn 1916, Wilson suggested that the war must be brought to a close "with the objects of each group of belligerents still unaccomplished and all the magnificent sacrifices on both sides gone for naught. Only then would war be eliminated as in a way to being a means of attaining national ambitions."[30] In advocating a settlement of the war on the basis of the status quo antebellum, Wilson implicitly promoted continued British hegemony for, as he explained to Walter Page, American ambassador to Great Britain, in 1916, the war was ultimately caused by the fact that England dominated the world and that Germany wanted to displace it.[31]

Wilson believed that continued British dominance was important to securing a lasting peace because he thought British support would be crucial in establishing an international league of nations after the war. Wilson promoted an international league as early as fall 1914, arguing that it would provide a neutral forum for creating and implementing international law, thereby preventing future conflicts from careening out of control. Although Britain had committed some violations of interna-

28. See, especially, *IW*, 8/18/14, 12; 1/16/17, 4. *GA*, 12/12/14, 4; 11/27/15, 4.
29. See, especially, *IW*, 2/17/17, 3.
30. Link, *Revolution, War, and Peace*, 26–27.
31. Ibid., 23.

tional law during the war, it had one of the most advanced legal systems on earth and would be a crucial actor in such a league.[32]

Irish-American activists in both Chicago and New York, by contrast, argued it was necessary to shatter the status quo antebellum to assure a stable postwar order. They suggested that as long as Britain continued to wield the lion's share of world power, its closest rivals—apart from the United States—would feel vulnerable and would provoke new wars to even the scales. Some argued that a German victory held the key to postwar stability because it would "bring equality of opportunity to all those who traverse the sea." Others, while not promoting German victory, argued that a more equitable distribution of power and commerce between major industrial nations was essential to a lasting peace. This held true even for Irish-American radicals, who insisted that British capitalists were the driving imperialist force within the international system: until their power was destroyed, fundamental economic reform, and therefore peace, were impossible.[33]

Irish-Americans suggested that postwar stability required the granting of freedom to the world's oppressed nationalities. Wilson himself would later rally behind such a banner but, because of his desire not to alienate Britain, he largely excluded from consideration for political freedom the colonies of the British empire. Irish-Americans of all political persuasions insisted that the colonial peoples of India, Persia, and Ireland must receive their independence in order to prevent violent and destabilizing nationalist rebellions.[34]

The Irish community in America developed a full-fledged indictment of plans for a league of nations only after the war. Nonetheless, hints of their future attitudes emerged in the early war years when they promoted a separate League of Oppressed Nationalities. This organization would be comprised of nationalities from the "nonpredatory class" of the "world family" and would form a powerful "fifth bloc" on the world stage, curbing the exploitative policies of the world's major imperial powers.[35] Such plans suggested that Irish-Americans were skeptical about propaganda emphasizing the value of an international

32. Ibid., 74; and Paterson et al., *American Foreign Policy*, 280–89. See also Coogan, *End of Neutrality*.

33. *GA*, 8/22/14, 7. *IW*, 8/28/14, 4; 3/11/16, 4; 1/16/17; 3/10/17, 4. *CC*, 2/9/17, 5. John Fitzpatrick, Speech to the First Convention of the American Association for the Recognition of the Irish Republic, n.d, B11–F78: FP. *CFL Minutes*, 5/21/16, 18–19.

34. *GA*, 10/16/15, 4. *IW*, 2/24/17, 11. Agnes Smedley (Friends of Freedom for India) to Fitzpatrick, 5/25/19, B8–F60: FP. *NM*, 1/4/19, 5.

35. *IW*, 1/6/17. Frank Walsh, Peace Diary, 34, 29: Frank Walsh Papers (WP), New York Public Library.

league of nations in promoting the interests of colonial peoples. In the postwar period, Irish-Americans claimed that imperial powers would use Wilson's proposed league to strengthen their hold over colonies and weaker states. Such arguments paralleled their views on international law; neither international legal codes nor institutions that promoted them were seen as inherently neutral but were viewed as tools that would be used by the powerful to promote their interests.[36]

The growing chasm between Wilsonians and Irish-Americans on fundamental foreign policy issues provoked a bitter political struggle. Irish-Americans claimed that the president's foreign policies were so at odds with the national interest that an evil cabal of British-Americans must be destroying his capacity for rational analysis. Foremost among these elites were British-American businessmen like Andrew Carnegie.[37] Also influencing the president were treasonous officials within the executive branch.[38] Key British-American labor officials constituted a third important component of this cadre. Samuel Gompers, in particular, was denounced as a pawn of the British and a threat to American neutrality. "When there was no real danger of war," wrote the editors of the *Gaelic American*, "Gompers posed as an advocate of peace, but now when the capitalists want war with Germany to make more money while the working men are getting slaughtered, he is for war."[39] The same editors questioned, "Who is paying Samuel Gompers for the work he is doing for England?" The AFL president, they suggested, was being given money by pro-British employers to help suppress strikes in the munitions industries in Bridgeport, Connecticut.[40] Careful monitoring of British elites and their influence on the Wilson administration prompted some Irish-American leaders to conclude in November 1915 that "England is now running the United States."[41]

Irish-American leaders were astute in singling out big businessmen, executive branch officials, and labor leaders for criticism; these groups later became the crucial players in corporatist networks created by the president. Already by 1915, Wilson had begun to rely on representatives of such groups for advice and to seek their services in winning popular support for his foreign policies.[42] Even as Wilson solicited the advice of key civilian elites and nonelected officials, he became increas-

36. See Chapter 5; and Ambrosius, *Woodrow Wilson*, 91.
37. *IW*, 1/6/17, 4. *GA*, 7/24/15, 4.
38. *GA*, 10/16/15, 4.
39. Ibid., 6/26/15, 4.
40. Ibid., 7/24/15, 4. See also *GA*, 8/30/15, 4; 6/20/15, 4.
41. *GA*, 11/27/15, 4.
42. Kennedy, *Over Here*, 113–14.

ingly critical of ethnic organizations that tried to influence his policies. "There are citizens of the United States," Wilson told Congress in late 1915, ". . . born under other flags but welcomed under our generous naturalization laws to the full freedom and opportunity of America, who have poured the poison of disloyalty into the very arteries of our national life. . . . Such creatures of passion, disloyalty, and anarchy must be crushed out."[43]

Irish-American groups responded to Wilson's attacks by launching zealous campaigns to strengthen their political power. In part, Irish-Americans tried to increase their political influence by forging an alliance with German-Americans. This effort paralleled their attempts to unite oppressed nationality groups abroad. On December 1, 1915, German and Irish groups formed a central legislative committee to work for measures such as the Bartholdt and Hitchcock bill, which authorized an embargo on munitions. Irish-Americans also helped the Germans launch, or strengthen, organizations such as the Teutonic Sons of America, American Independence Union, and Friends of Peace, which were designed to assist with antiwar lobbying.[44] Chicago, because of its central location and large German and Irish populations, became a vital arena for promoting interethnic solidarity.[45]

Irish-American leaders also tried to foster greater solidarity within the Irish community itself. To achieve this goal, leaders of major Irish fraternal and nationalist organizations banded together and formed a new group called the Friends of Irish Freedom (FOIF) in March 1916. Although it stressed unity, the FOIF also encouraged grass-roots initiative. All sectors of the Chicago Irish community lent their support to the new organization, and by the end of the war, twelve chapters existed in Chicago. The new group also fared well nationally, with membership topping 275,700 by 1919.[46] The formation of the FOIF marked a turning point in the Irish community's quest for power, for, as Michael Funchion writes, "the regular meetings of the local chapters

43. Ibid., 24.
44. Cuddy, *Irish America and National Isolationism*, 76–78. See also GA, 3/27/15, 3; 10/2/15, 7; 7/31/15, 2; 7/24/15, 8.
45. IW, 2/24/17, 4. GA, 12/12/14, 6; 2/15/15, 1; 3/27/15, 3; 10/2/15, 7.
46. Funchion, *Irish-American Voluntary Organizations*, 119, 26. CC, 1/2/20, 1; 1/16/20, 6; 1/20/20, 6. Letter from Friends of Irish Freedom (FOIF) to Fitzpatrick, 1916, B5: FP. The tactics of the FOIF were disputed more in the Irish-American Fellowship Club than in the fraternals or among the Irish patriots in the Chicago Federation of Labor. But many Irish-American Fellowship Club members nonetheless supported some of its campaigns. See Address of Hon. T. P. O'Connor to Irish Fellowship Club, B1–F 11/17–3/18; Petition to Wilson, misc. pamphlets of the Irish-American Fellowship Club, B1: Fah P.

[of the FOIF] created an informal and mobilized Irish-American community whose opinion and political strength could be brought to bear on issues in American politics."[47]

The Easter Rebellion, an ill-fated uprising in Dublin against British rule, in April 1916, intensified the feelings of ethnic solidarity flowing through the Irish-American community. Staged by about fifteen hundred members of the Irish Republican Brotherhood and Irish Volunteers, the rebellion initially won little support either in Ireland or Irish-America. Rebels were denounced as "hooligans" and "dirty browsers," while the uprising was perceived as foolhardy and futile.[48] But when the British brutally suppressed the rebellion and executed its leaders, their actions provoked outrage on both sides of the Atlantic and swelled the tide of sentiment favoring immediate political independence for Ireland. Those who remained committed to home rule were discredited, and the distinctions between supporters of passive resistance and physical force blurred as both sides supported independent political initiatives in Ireland that spurred British reprisals and created an escalating pattern of violence. Irish on both sides of the Atlantic, and indeed across the globe, put their differences aside and rallied under the banner of an ill-defined Irish Republic. Irish-America was further united by President Wilson's actions during the crisis; Wilson failed to intervene on behalf of the rebels, and he delayed sending a Senate resolution sympathizing with the rebels to Britain. His inaction received widespread condemnation.[49]

In the wake of the rising, Irish-American groups renewed their campaigns against Wilsonian foreign policy, using the president's handling of the Irish rebellion as evidence of his pro-British tendencies. Wilsonian supporters responded by passing a plank at the 1916 Democratic convention condemning "alliances and combinations of individuals in this country of whatever nationality or descent who agree and conspire together for the purpose of humiliating or weakening the government."[50]

47. Funchion, *Irish-American Voluntary Organizations*, 120.
48. Lawrence McCaffrey, *Ireland: From Colony to Nation State* (Englewood Cliffs, N.J.: Prentice-Hall, 1979), 141.
49. Cuddy, *Irish America and National Isolationism*, 108–14; John Patrick Buckley, *The New York Irish: Their View of American Foreign Policy, 1914–1921* (New York: Arno Press, 1976), 84–85. GA, 4/29/16, 4; 5/20/16, 1; 5/27/16, 4; 6/17/16, 1; 10/21/16, 1; 12/9/16, 6. *IW*, 5/13/16, 4. *CFL Minutes*, 5/7/16, 18–19. Many members of the Irish Fellowship Club still remained critical of radical nationalists in Ireland but they saluted the bravery of the Irish rebels. See *GA*, 12/9/16, 6. Address of Hon. T. P. O'Connor, B1–F 11/17–3/18: Fah P.
50. *GA*, 10/21/16, 4.

To Irish-American leaders, the plank only confirmed that Wilson sought to establish a pro-British oligarchy in the United States. "Wilson," argued the *Gaelic American*, "has gone far to substitute an irresponsible autocracy for the Democratic government founded by the Fathers, and now his henchmen seek to abolish freedom of speech and to abridge the liberty of the citizen."[51] The paper predicted that if Wilson were reelected, "the German-American Alliance, the Clan na Gael, the Friends of Irish Freedom and probably the Ancient Order of Hibernians will be declared to be illegal combinations and attempts will be made to suppress them."[52]

Fearful for their very existence, most Irish-American groups advised their constituencies to abandon the Democratic party in November. As one Irish editor put it, the choice was between "one [Charles Hughes] who attacks you openly in front with a raised club, and the other [Wilson] who stabs you in the back with a poisoned dagger." Surely, he reasoned, Hughes could not be "as bad as Wilson for he is at least a man of honor."[53] Another editor proclaimed that any man who voted for Wilson would be voting for an "anti-Irish, unAmerican and know nothing programme."[54] While traditional Irish fraternals struggled to defeat Wilson by publishing negative propaganda in the papers and staging massive political rallies, FOIF members canvassed door to door to warn their neighbors of the Wilsonian menace. Within Chicago, only one major segment of the community failed to participate in the anti-Wilson campaign: the social radicals clustered around the CFL. For such radicals, support of Hughes was likely the greater evil. Yet, Chicago radicals maintained a venomous opposition to Wilsonian foreign policy and probably undercut the president's campaign in the city.[55]

The efforts of Irish groups helped provoke a heavy Irish-American switchover vote which may have lost Wilson New York, New Jersey, Illinois, and Wisconsin. The president fared particularly poorly in Cook County, Illinois.[56] Irish-Americans also helped elect a large number of Republican congressmen. Although Wilson won the presidential election, Irish-Americans argued that they had triumphed as well. "The

51. Ibid., 10/28/16, 4.
52. Ibid., 11/4/16, 4.
53. Buckley, *New York Irish*, 94.
54. *GA*, 11/4/16, 4.
55. See *CFL Minutes*, July–December 1916. During these months, any mention of the presidential campaign is conspicuously absent.
56. *GA*, 11/18/16, 1.

independence shown by Irish Americans in the presidential election of this year," the editor of the *Irish World* concluded, "cannot fail to increase their influence as political factors in future elections."[57] The *Gaelic American* bannered a headline proclaiming, "Revolting Democrats Made a Historical Demonstration of Their Power, Taught the Bosses a Lesson They Will Long Remember."[58]

The election brought round one of the fight between Irish-Americans and the Wilson administration to a close. In part, the feud had been spurred by a desire among Irish-Americans for political revenge. But it was also provoked by a clash between competing international ideologies. Ideologies, as Michael Hunt has explained, reduce complexities to easily comprehensible terms.[59] Such reductionism does not necessarily preclude sophistication; it is often the necessary first step to arriving at comprehensive solutions to a problem. President Wilson simplified the scope of international problems between 1914 and 1916 by focusing on international law and international institutions as panaceas for resolving conflict. This led him toward more pro-British policies as the war progressed, for the British did not violate international law as heinously as the Germans. The British would also be vital to building international legal institutions after the war. By contrast, Irish-Americans simplified international realities by envisioning the world scene as an ethnic pecking order: The best way to achieve a lasting peace was to redistribute power between nationality groups more fairly. Above all, this meant dismantling the British empire. Until this was done, Irish-Americans placed little faith in the capacity of international law and international institutions to assure peace and justice in the world.

Also provoking ideological conflict between these two groups was the meaning they attached to rhetoric about an open and democratic diplomacy. A longtime defender of executive supremacy in foreign affairs, Wilson disdained both congressional and interest-group meddling in diplomacy. Such meddling subverted the democratic process by giving some groups undue influence. Only the president, he believed, could rise above petty politics to represent the true national interest. Yet, Wilson tried to increase indirectly the diplomatic influence of the public between 1914 and 1917 through two innovations. First, he began to incorporate elite representatives from important economic sectors into newly emerging corporatist executive councils. These representatives not

57. *IW*, 11/18/16, 1.
58. *GA*, 11/18/16, 1.
59. Hunt, "Ideology and American Foreign Policy," 108–9.

only served important government functions but they kept the president informed of changing tides in public opinion. Second, he tried to bring an end to secret treaties between world leaders by promoting international organizations as forums for open negotiations. If treaties were arranged in the open, then the public both at home and abroad could make more informed decisions about their leaders' foreign policies when they voted in national elections. Thus, for the president, the centralization of foreign policy powers—both at the executive level and within international organizations—went hand in hand with the democratization of diplomacy.[60]

Irish-Americans, by contrast, believed that democracy operated best when power was highly decentralized. They defended a Madisonian vision of democracy in which special interest groups mobilized to check each other's influence. If Irish-American groups failed to develop appropriate foreign policy lobbies, then British-Americans would move the executive branch toward a slavish dependence on Britain and would propel the country into war. Just as Irish-Americans perceived the world scene as an ethnic pecking order, so also they envisioned American politics as an unending struggle between nationality groups for dominance. Centralizing power at the executive level was dangerous because it meant that well-placed nationality groups could more easily subvert democratic processes. By 1917, many had become so convinced that a British-American oligarchy was ruling in Washington that they promoted a referendum vote on the issue of American involvement in the war.[61] For Irish-Americans, a democratic diplomacy increasingly became synonymous with a limited executive branch, protections for interest-group lobbying, and direct electoral input by the entire population on key foreign policy issues. Even Irish radicals defended these demands because, even though they ultimately sought to build class-based sources of political power, they believed that traditional democratic rights must be preserved in the interim.[62]

By 1917, then, the intellectual currents swirling through Irish-America had converged to form a compelling ideological alternative to Wilsonian internationalism. Chicago's Irish-American workers and trade union leaders were exposed to this ideology at associational meet-

60. See, especially, Link, *Revolution, War, and Peace*, 14; Kennedy, *Over Here*, 24; Ambrosius, *Woodrow Wilson*, 136; and McCormick, "Drift or Mastery?"
    61. *IW*, 2/24/17, 4.
    62. Ibid. *CFL Minutes*, 2/19/15, 11; 2/8/17. See also Telegram, Fitzpatrick and Nockels to Gompers, 2/4/17: CC-GMC.

ings and church gatherings as well as through the local and national Irish-American press. Certain components of Irish-American ideology—such as its Anglophobia— were clearly incompatible with principles of international labor solidarity. But, as we will see, CFL leaders reconfigured the anti-imperialist strains and strong distrust of centralized authority inherent in Irish-American ideology to promote a class-based analysis of international affairs. Both the local ethnic and labor subcultures that shaped the contours of Irish-American workers' lives bred resentment toward the Wilson administration by 1917 and made Gompers's task of aligning the community behind the president's foreign policy a difficult one.

The changing intellectual currents within Polonia (Polish-America) between 1914 and 1917, by contrast, encouraged a broader range of foreign policy attitudes among Polish immigrant workers. On the eve of the war, the Polish-American community in Chicago rivaled in size that of the Irish, with over three hundred thousand people of Polish stock residing within the city. Because of its large Polish-American population, Chicago was considered to be Polonia's capital and many Polish fraternal organizations were headquartered in Chicago.[63] Yet, Chicago's Polish community lacked the political or economic strength of the Irish because demographically it fit the profile of a "new" immigrant community: Over half of its population had arrived after 1904, most were not naturalized citizens, and a majority were under age thirty-five. As recent immigrants from an overwhelmingly rural country, most Poles lacked industrial skills and qualified only for entry level positions in local businesses. They tended to cluster in the area's meat-packing and steel plants, often replacing Irish and German workers moving up the ladder to skilled positions.[64]

Due to their predominance in unskilled fields that had not been organized by American labor organizations, relatively few Chicago Poles—9.5 percent in 1911—belonged to unions.[65] Yet, more than most city labor councils, the Chicago Federation of Labor tried to organize unskilled, new immigrant workers, creating an ambiguous attitude on the part of Chicago's Polish-American ethnic leaders and

63. *Dziennik Zwiazkowy*, 9/9/16: WPA. Kantowicz, *Polish-American Politics*, 217–18.

64. Barrett, *Work and Community in the Jungle*, 36–45; Kantowicz, *Polish-American Politics*, 28; Pacyga, *Polish Immigrants*, 17; David Brody, *The Butcher Workmen: A Study of Unionization* (Cambridge: Harvard University Press, 1964), 34–58, *Steelworkers in America: The Nonunion Era* (Cambridge: Harvard University Press, 1960), 80–111. *Dziennik Zwiazkowy*, 9/9/16: WPA.

65. Kantowicz, *Polish-American Politics*, 28.

activists toward the labor movement. Some opposed unions entirely, sensing that the German and Irish trade union officials who dominated the local movement posed a threat to their own control over Polish-American workers. But others, although complaining that the union movement was dominated by other nationality groups, still supported its goals. Of the supporters of unionization, some advocated separate Polish locals while others promoted more Polish union officials within existing organizations.[66] Polish-American workers, for their part, sometimes shared the distrust of ethnic leaders toward trade union officials of other nationalities. Yet, they vigorously supported many organizing and strike efforts in Chicago, often displaying a militancy that surpassed that of skilled workers from older immigrant groups. Depending on circumstances, the union movement encouraged either interethnic hostility or cooperation.[67]

Local politics also inspired a confusing mix of attitudes among Polish-Americans toward older immigrant groups. Polish-Americans clearly resented local Irish influence in city government. They protested bitterly about an Irish patronage machine that allegedly gave 75 percent of all city positions to those of Irish heritage, and they registered their strong disapproval of the holiday that was given to city workers on Saint Patrick's day. Polish-Americans even implied that the judiciary was biased in favor of the Irish. One editor summarized a local case with a banner headline reading: "I'll Kill That Polak Said the Irish— The Jury Freed the Irishman."[68]

Even though Poles objected to older immigrant political dominance, they imitated their tactics, trying to encourage ethnic solidarity in voting and to develop ethnic lobbies. This held true even for most Polish

66. *Narod Polski*, 1/4/11: WPA. *Dziennik Zwiazkowy*, 11/9/10, 1–2: WPA. *Dziennik Zjednoczenia*, 12/7/21; 7/24/22: WPA. Montgomery, "Nationalism, American Patriotism, and Class Consciousness," 332; Barrett, "Unity and Fragmentation," 233. Interview by David Saposs of Edward J. Evans, Chicago District Organizing Committee of Iron and Steel Workers, 12/7/18, B26–F6: David Saposs Papers (SP), Wisconsin State Historical Society. Pacyga, *Polish Immigrants*, 184–85.

67. Saposs interview with Evans, 12/27/18, B26–F6; fragment of Letter on Overland Situation and the Poles, B22–F3; Interview with Saposs, 11–13 (introductory material); and Saposs interviews with the steel strikers, 1919–20: SP. Barrett, "Unity and Fragmentation," and *Work and Community in the Jungle*; Montgomery, "New Tendencies," 91; and Robert Asher, "Union Nativism and the Immigrant Response," *Labor History* 23 (summer 1982): 325–48; Pacyga, *Polish Immigrants*, 235, 158–257.

68. Quote from *Dziennik Zjednoczenia*, 9/24/21, 1: WPA. See also *Dziennik Zjednoczenia*, 3/20/22, 1: WPA. *Dziennik Zwiazkowy*, 2/26/15: WPA. *Narod Polski*, 1/12/21, 1; 6/8/21, 1: WPA. Pacyga, *Polish Immigrants*, 204.

socialists, who established a Polish language section within the American Socialist party and used ethnic ties and rivalries to solicit political support for their campaigns. Like their Irish counterparts, then, Polish-American activists seemed to envision American society as an ethnic pecking order. Yet, while the Irish were obsessed with the power of British-Americans, the Poles feared the influence of Irish- and German-Americans.[69]

These fears helped to shape initial Polish-American attitudes toward the war. As German- and Irish-Americans mobilized to proclaim their opinions on the conflict, Polish-Americans feared that their failure to do the same would leave Poland out of Wilson's wartime calculations.[70] Polish-American mobilization on behalf of Polish independence proved more complicated than in the case of Irish-America for two reasons. First, at the time of the war, Poland was occupied by three different powers: Germany, Austria, and Russia. Irish-America united around a shared hatred of Britain, but no common enemy bound Polonia together. Some believed that Poland's salvation lay in joining the German-Austrian war effort, while others argued that it was better to side with Russia and her allies. Also complicating the question of Polish independence within Polonia was a broader spectrum of nationalist political thought than existed among Irish-Americans: A radical right wing favored the creation of an aristocratic and imperialistic Poland while the political left promoted a socialist government for the homeland.

For these reasons, a fully unified nationalist campaign never emerged within Polonia. Yet, by 1916, most fragments of the community would coalesce around one of three movements. It was a group of Polish-American socialists who initially took the lead in trying to organize a campaign on behalf of Polish independence. Responding to nationalist stirrings within the section of Poland dominated by Austria in 1912, representatives of one of the three major socialist traditions in Polonia (the Alliance of Polish Socialists, or ZSP), called on interested groups to establish a national committee on behalf of Polish independence. In a meeting held in December, spokespeople from all the major socialist factions and from key fraternal organizations formed the KON, or Committee for National Defense. The committee purported

69. *Dziennik Zwiazkowy*, 8/1/16, 1–4: WPA. *Narod Polski*, 5/12/17, 1: WPA. Kantowicz, *Polish-American Politics*, 10, 93–4; Pacyga, *Polish Immigrants*, 204.

70. See, especially, *Dziennik Zwiazkowy*, 4/7/17, 4; 4/27/17, 1–4; 5/19/18, and undated article, circa World War I: WPA.

to represent all shades of the Polish-American political spectrum, but the socialist leaders who founded the organization soon aligned it closely with the policies of the Polish socialist and independence leader Joseph Pilsudski.[71]

Pilsudski's wartime strategies were later portrayed as pro-German. According to Mary Cygan, however, the Polish leader's policies were more complicated and encompassed a two-step plan. Initially, Pilsudski believed that Poles should raise a separate army to fight with the Austrians and Germans against Russia. Pilsudski predicted that after Russia was defeated, America would enter the war. At this point, Pilsudski believed that Poles should reverse their allegiances and fight against the Austrians and Germans so as to assure political freedom for the remainder of Poland.[72]

The pro-Pilsudski orientation of the KON soon cost it defections from both the right and left. As detailed by Cygan, two of the three Polish socialist factions in the United States continued to support the KON. These two factions merged to form the Polish Federation of the Socialist Party (ZPSP) in 1913. This group comprised the Polish section of the American Socialist party until 1916, when it was expelled for supporting the German-Austrian war effort. Its place was taken by a small group of Polish socialist internationalists who attacked the KON's Polish nationalist campaign as a distraction from the class struggle. The Socialist party of America helped to sow the seeds of its own destruction by accepting the new group in place of the nationalist faction; the internationalists proved to be pro-Bolshevik and rallied against more conservative Socialist leaders at war's end.[73]

A more serious defection from the KON occurred when many Polish fraternal organizations, including the prestigious Polish Roman Catholic Union and the Polish National Alliance, withdrew from the organization. A portion of the Polish Falcons, a paramilitary organization that trained Polish youth in military techniques, also left the KON.

71. Mary Cygan, "Political and Cultural Leadership in an Immigrant Community: Polish-American Socialism, 1880–1950" (Ph.D. diss., Northwestern University, 1989), 73–90, 155. Cygan provides excellent detail on the three socialist traditions in Polonia. See also Louis Gerson, *Woodrow Wilson and the Rebirth of Poland, 1914–1920* (New Haven, Conn.: Yale University Press, 1953), 51–61.

72. Cygan, "Political and Cultural Leadership," 73–119; Gerson, *Woodrow Wilson,* 50–51.

73. Cygan, "Political and Cultural Leadership," 73–119, 155; Gerson, *Woodrow Wilson,* 50–51.

Some of these defectors supported a new conservative political coalition developing in Poland under the rubric of the National Democrats. Others, although dissatisfied with Pilsudski's forces, lacked firm allegiances toward other Polish political parties. Both groups of defectors came together in 1916 to form the Polish National Department. This organization, like the KON before it, claimed to represent a broad spectrum of nationalist opinion. But it almost immediately allied itself with pro-entente Polish organizations dominated by the National Democrats.[74]

These conservative allegiances might have generated conflict within the National Department but for the unifying power of its leading spokesman, Jan Paderewski. An accomplished concert pianist and fervent Polish nationalist, Paderewski was living in Switzerland when the war broke out. He came to America in 1915 and successfully organized a broad network of relief efforts for Poland. The flamboyant pianist also obtained an audience with Col. Edward House, the president's closest advisor, and won his and Wilson's public sympathy for Polish independence. In return for his accomplishments, Paderewski was appointed the National Department's official representative to a Polish Committee in Paris that acted as a kind of government in exile for pro-entente forces. Subsequently, Paderewski became a symbolic leader of Polonia, uniting both moderates and conservatives—despite occasional disagreements over tactics—within the National Department.[75]

The relative strengths of the three diplomatic positions that emerged by 1917 are hard to determine. Clearly, the least popular of the foreign policy factions was the socialist internationalists, but this was to some degree offset by the influence they derived from their connection with the Socialist party of America after 1916. In assessing the battle between the KON and the National Department, most scholars have suggested that the National Department was the undisputed winner, since it gained the allegiances of all the major fraternal organizations defecting from the KON. Others have questioned these conclusions, arguing that the KON actually gained strength and focus after the defections from the right-wing groups. Some place support for the

74. Cygan, "Political and Cultural Leadership," 113; Louis J. Zake, "The National Department and the Polish-American Community, 1916–1923," *Polish-American Studies* 38 (autumn 1981): 16–25; M. B. Biskupski, "Paderewski as Leader of American Polonia, 1914–1918," *Polish-American Studies* 43 (spring 1986): 37–56; Gerson, *Woodrow Wilson*, 50–52.

75. See, especially, Biskupski, "Paderewski"; and Gerson, *Woodrow Wilson*, 46–110.

KON during the World War I era at around one hundred thousand. Thus, all three groups must be seriously examined when considering Polish-American foreign policy attitudes.[76]

Not surprisingly, the National Department was the most pro-Wilsonian in its views. Members of this group openly expressed their gratitude to the president for his support of Polish independence and urged Poles to vote for Wilson in the 1916 election. In Chicago, Poles seemed to heed their advice, with approximately two-thirds of the city's Poles voting for Wilson.[77] This group also quickly rallied to the president's side when he began promoting American preparedness, declaring that the United States must have a "strong sword" with which to defend itself. The president, they suggested, could also be assured that there would not be a "single citizen or foreigner [within Polonia] who would not answer his call."[78] When Wilson actually declared war, many Poles hailed his decision. One editor proclaimed that "we must joyfully welcome the fact that the United States has finally tossed the musty Monroe Doctrine to the four winds" and become "a free and equal citizen of the world." Another declared that "in the destruction of the audacious Teutonic Knights of the Cross and in the victories of democracies of the world lies our [America's] deliverance and through it freedom will be granted to Poland." The editor further argued, "He would be a criminal and malefactor who would not combat the plots or intentions of the enemies of the country."[79]

Even though Polish groups coalescing around the National Department expressed gratitude to Wilson for championing Polish freedom and endorsed his war policies, they did not give unqualified support to his larger plans for reforming the world order. In particular, leaders of the Polish National Department were skeptical about Wilson's plans for an international organization to enforce international law, implying that it would not prove to be the magic cure-all for the world's problems that Wilson believed. After a long meeting with the president, Roman Dmowski, a colleague of Paderewski's, complained that Wilson had a "great faith in the possibility of settling international

76. Cygan, "Political and Cultural Leadership," 86–87; Gerson, Woodrow Wilson, 50–52.
77. Dziennik Zwiazkowy, 9/25/16, 1: WPA. Kantowicz, Polish-American Politics, 115; Gerson, Hyphenate, 68–69.
78. Dziennik Zwiazkowy, 3/3/17: WPA.
79. Dziennik Zwiazkowy, 4/7/17, and undated article, circa, World War I: WPA.

problems on the basis of justice enforced upon all" but that he "did not know much about Polish affairs, that he did not much understand European politics, [and] that he simplified too much their most complex aspects."[80] Leaders of the National Department insisted that the key to achieving postwar peace and stability lay in creating three states of approximately equal power in Central Europe: Russia, Poland, and Germany. This plan, of course, would require not only that Poland be given its freedom but that some German and Russian territories be ceded to Poland.[81] In many respects, the international ideology of the leaders of the National Department more closely resembled that of Irish-Americans than the Wilson administration. Both Polish National Department leaders and Irish-American ethnic officials were unimpressed with plans for an international league of nations and instead emphasized the need to establish a relative balance of power between nationality groups. To this end, a few Polish-American leaders supported the liberation of Ireland, believing that British and German power must be diffused if lasting peace were to be achieved.[82]

Polish socialists were on an even more dangerous ideological collision course with the president. The KON alienated the president by its early support of the Germans. Paderewski also supplied the Wilson administration with negative propaganda about the KON in his many meetings with Colonel House. Leaders of the organization hoped the president's attitude would change when in 1917 it followed Pilsudski's original plan and changed its position to one of support for the entente powers. Yet, to Wilsonian critics, this policy change only confirmed that the organization could not be trusted. After the war began, the Wilson administration engaged in extensive surveillance and censoring activities against the KON. For its leaders, Wilsonianism became associated with the suppression of democratic rights at home and the promotion of reactionary governments abroad.[83]

The socialist internationalists joined the crusade of the Socialist party against the war. The party focused on the role of big business in fomenting militarism, and it joined other pacifist, ethnic, and labor groups in calling for a referendum vote on the war. It also evoked the

---

80. Roman Dmowski quoted in Gerson, *Woodrow Wilson*, 95.
81. Gerson, *Woodrow Wilson*, 52–80.
82. *Dziennik Zwiazkowy*, 4/27/17, 1–4: WPA.
83. See Cygan, "Political and Cultural Leadership," 111–17; Gerson, *Woodrow Wilson*, 51.

spirit of labor internationalism and called for a worldwide labor campaign against the war. After the United States entered the European conflict, the party continued its pacifist activities and faced widespread prosecution. In 1918, many Polish socialist internationalists would rally behind the Bolshevik banner, signaling their ultimate rejection of Wilsonian internationalism.[84]

The varying foreign policy ideologies circulating within Polonia encouraged an ambiguous set of attitudes among Polish-American workers toward Wilsonian internationalism. Many were grateful to the president for his declarations on behalf of Polish independence and supported U.S. intervention in the war as a way to ensure a German defeat and Polish independence. But neither socialists nor nonsocialists in Polonia vigorously embraced his larger international plans. Like Irish-Americans, Poles were skeptical of the value of an international league of nations in the absence of a fundamental redistribution of world power. Their extensive foreign policy activities and defense of special interest group lobbying were also suggestive of a decentralized vision of American political power incompatible with Wilson's—and Gompers's—evolving corporatist mentality. By contrast, such attitudes intersected in critical respects with the anticollaborationist agenda of the postwar Chicago Labor party and helped it to win surprising support in heavily Polish neighborhoods. However, because Poles were poorly represented in the CFL before the stockyard- and steel-organizing campaigns of 1918 and 1919, the council's wartime foreign policy programs proved insensitive to Polish nationalist sentiment and won it no apparent adherents within the community.

The foreign policy activism of the Chicago Federation of Labor during World War I can be understood only by examining the other war that still lingered in American memories in 1914: the Spanish-American War. Cuba's revolt against Spain in the mid-1890s aroused much sympathy among the American public. Subsequently, many special interest groups demanded American support for the Cuban rebels. Although several historians have argued persuasively that President William McKinley intervened in Cuba primarily for strategic and economic reasons rather than as a result of public pressure, many grass-roots groups

84. Cygan, "Political and Cultural Leadership," 96–111, 117–19. Fine, *Labor and Farmer Parties*, 310–16; Foner, *History of the Labor Movement*, 7: 17–37; and Weinstein, "The Socialist Party," 5–27.

nonetheless believed that they played an important role in forcing
McKinley to declare war against Spain.[85]

Grass-roots groups proved crucial to the actual conduct of the war.
McKinley relied heavily on battalions of the Volunteer National
Guard that were funded primarily by local organizations or local
branches of national associations and were staffed almost exclusively
by men from the same hometown. Gerald Linderman suggests that
because grass-roots groups and local battalions played such an important role in funding and fighting the war, the American victory rekindled a sense of local spirit. There was a resurgence of boosterism
throughout the nation, and local organizations boasted loudly of the
role they played in helping their country win the war. The Spanish-
American conflict lived in the memories of many Americans as a time
when both they and the nation at large benefited from popular
involvement in foreign policy decision making and in war mobilization
efforts. This spirit of local self-congratulation was diminished but not
destroyed when U.S. forces brutally suppressed Filipino independence
and severely curtailed political freedom in other areas they occupied
during the war.[86]

Popular conceptions about mobilization during the Spanish-American
War influenced American reaction to World War I. Because many anticipated that municipal government and grass-roots groups would once
again play a key role in shaping war policy, they viewed America's
response to the European conflict through strangely local prisms. Supporters of military readiness launched preparedness parades not only to
demonstrate loyalty to the president but also to show municipal patriotism. Because business groups figured disproportionately in such
parades, they reinforced perceptions among local labor militants that
the owning class was trying to railroad the country into war. Local
labor councils and state federations throughout the country staged
demonstrations to offset municipal preparedness activities. City streets
became theaters in which class alignments on issues of war policy were
played out, doubtless influencing the thinking of area workers far more
than simple newspaper accounts. Local business and labor groups also

85. Linderman, *Mirror of War*, 60–75. For an interpretation of the war that stresses
McKinley's strategic motivations, see Paterson et al., *American Foreign Policy*, 1:
197–207.
86. Linderman, *Mirror of War*, 60–75; T. H. Breen et al., *America Past and Present*,
3d ed., vol. 2 (New York: Harper and Collins, 1991), 637–43; Richard E. Welch,
Response to Imperialism: The United States and the Philippine-American War, 1899–1902
(Chapel Hill: University of North Carolina Press, 1979).

clashed over military preparedness in the schools and over munitions contracts entered into by area businesses.[87]

For city labor councils and state labor federations, then, conflicts over war policy became an organic extension of local class struggles. The CFL's foreign policy programs between 1914 and 1918 were in part designed to thwart and offset the initiatives of some of the same groups that consistently opposed unionization in Chicago. Yet, CFL foreign policy activities cannot be understood within an entirely local context because they were also geared toward influencing the foreign policy programs of the AFL. Because city labor councils and state federations were entitled to only one vote each at national conventions, they wielded little influence over policy-making processes within the AFL. In 1915, eighty-six national and international unions controlled 18,825 votes, while local and state organizations wielded only 130. But the CFL's president, John Fitzpatrick, was committed to democratic reform within the AFL, and he used the Chicago council as a base from which to launch his efforts, thereby transforming it into one of the most powerful local labor bodies in the country.[88]

Born in Athlone, Ireland, Fitzpatrick immigrated to the United States as a child. His parents died when he was eleven years old, and he began working in the Chicago stockyards, doing a brief stint on the killing floor before taking up horseshoeing. While still an adolescent, Fitzpatrick became active in the Horseshoer's Union and was appointed a stockyards organizer. The young Fitzpatrick soon gained a reputation as a man of exceptional intellect, idealism, and integrity, and in 1895 he was elected president of the CFL, a position he held until 1901.[89]

---

87. CFL Minutes, 4/16/16, 10–11; 5/21/16, 14–16; 1/7/17, 11–17. Illinois State Federation of Labor (ISFL) Proceedings, 1915, 292, and 1916, 289. For a general account of labor antipreparedness activities, see Foner, History of the Labor Movement, 7: 67–77. Foner cites Cleveland; New York; Allentown, Penn.; Milwaukee; Minneapolis; and San Francisco as cities in which strong local labor organizations or groups of militants opposed preparedness. On New York, see Grubbs, Struggle for Labor Loyalty. Montgomery ("New Tendencies," 101) notes that a variety of central labor bodies began reasserting themselves during the war, among them those in Philadelphia and Seattle. In his autobiography, James Maurer details the antiwar activities of the Pennsylvania State Federation of Labor. See James H. Maurer, It Can Be Done: The Autobiography of James Hudson Maurer (New York: Rand School Press, 1938), 222–56.

88. Keiser, "John Fitzpatrick," 77, 166. Fitzpatrick to Officers and Delegates of the American Federation of Labor, 11/22/15: CC-GMC.

89. David Saposs Interview, introductory materials, 1: SP. Keiser, "John Fitzpatrick," 7–8, 166; Fine, Labor and Farmer Parties, 381; Barrett, Work and Community in the Jungle, 191–93.

Following a short absence, Fitzpatrick returned to the CFL presidency in 1906, this time retaining it until his death in 1946. On assuming the presidency for the second time, Fitzpatrick moved to rid the council of the corruption that had flourished under his predecessor Skinny Madden. Fitzpatrick also instituted procedures to give more control of the CFL to locals, opened the weekly Sunday meeting to rank-and-file workers, and began holding referendum votes on major issues. Fitzpatrick coupled these local innovations with a campaign to democratize procedures within the AFL. In particular, he lobbied to restore full contract powers to locals, to institute the referendum election of officers, and to liberalize parliamentary procedures at the AFL convention.[90]

The depth of Fitzpatrick's emotional commitment to union democracy can be gauged by a scathing letter he sent to officers and delegates of the AFL regarding cancellation of a local printer's contract. In sharply angled, deeply engraved penmanship suggestive of anger, Fitzpatrick wrote Gompers that "through misrepresentation distortion of the laws and through juggeling [sic] and trickery a resolution which had for its purpose fulfillment of that [the printer's] contract was nonconcurred in by [the] . . . convention." Fitzpatrick concluded, "I demanded a hearing and I have been denied. I came to this convention an absolute beliver [sic] in the democracy of the Labor Movement and my faith is not weakened, it is strengthened and I know that justice will prevail."[91]

The CFL president's advocacy of democratic reforms won him the support of a talented group of labor militants. Of these, some—like Fitzpatrick himself—fell within a "progressive union" tradition, advocating moderate, evolutionary change within the labor movement and American society. Foremost among this group were Ed Nockels, CFL secretary; Robert Buck, a former alderman and future editor of the CFL's insightful paper, the *New Majority*; and Margaret Haley and Lillian Herstein, both of the Chicago Teachers Federation. Another set of CFL activists was associated with radical socialist and syndicalist groups that advocated a policy of boring from within traditional union movements as a means of promoting class revolution. Some of these

90. Keiser, "John Fitzpatrick," 166, and in general; Eugene Staley, *The History of the Illinois State Federation of Labor* (Chicago: University of Chicago Press, 1930), 332. Letter from the Secretary of CFL to Members of the Executive Council of the AFL, 2/22/16, B4: FP. NM, 9/10/21, 6.

91. Fitzpatrick to Officers and Delegates of the American Federation of Labor, 11/22/15: CC-GMC.

radicals, in particular the future communist leader William Z. Foster, later sabotaged the political efforts of the progressive element within the federation. In the interim, they proved invaluable as organizers and helped spur the CFL to champion causes, such as the unionizing of unskilled workers, that were not promoted by the AFL. The combined efforts of the progressive and militant wings within the CFL won it unprecedented support; by 1917, the Chicago council boasted one of the largest memberships in the country.[92]

Fitzpatrick's position as head of such a large and militant city council afforded him a limited but important kind of influence. Although the CFL lacked voting power commensurate with national and international unions, it derived strength from the fact that it was not officially aligned with them and could claim to speak for workers from a variety of trades. John Keiser writes of Fitzpatrick that "since figuratively he represented the rank and file of many local unions, he could advocate reforms without feeling the immediate hostile reaction of an unsympathetic hierarchy of national offices and multitude of . . . officials."[93]

Labor council leaders tended to promote reforms that were unpopular with national and international union officials because structural imperatives within the labor movement were pushing the two groups in opposite directions. Most nonsocialist national and international union leaders tried to centralize power within their unions in the early twentieth century and to limit rank-and-file initiatives. The reasons for this trend toward centralization were numerous and complex. Some union leaders were concerned with their own self-aggrandizement, seeking to limit democratic input in order to assure a perpetuation of their own power or to prevent disclosure of fraudulent dealings. Others believed that centralization was a necessary prerequisite to guaranteeing labor legitimacy in arbitration proceedings with businessmen: A union's power would be undercut if it could not control its own membership or if it constantly needed to consult with the membership in the process of negotiation. This was particularly true of unionists who worked with the National Civic Federation, a group that promoted conciliation

92. Barrett, *Work and Community in the Jungle*, 192; William Z. Foster, *Pages from a Worker's Life* (New York: International Publishers, 1939), 141–79, *American Trade Unionism: Principles and Tactics* (New York: International Publishers, 1947); Fine, *Labor and Farmer Parties*, 381; *CFL Minutes*, 11/2/17, 10. On Lillian Herstein's involvement in the CFL, see especially, B1–F1: Lillian Herstein Papers (Hr P), Chicago Historical Society.
93. Keiser, "John Fitzpatrick," 20.

between businessmen and union leaders. Still others sought to win the support, and enforcement powers, of the federal government by demonstrating a high level of industrial discipline and professionalism within their unions.[94]

But city labor council leaders were not so enamored of the trend toward centralization. Such centralization often undercut their power by placing more functions in the hands of national and international union executives. Equally important, the leaders of city labor councils were strategically well placed to witness the negative results of centralization. For John Fitzpatrick, one of the consequences of centralization was worker apathy. This apathy bred corruption by preventing workers from taking an active interest in their union's affairs. As the leaders of a broad spectrum of the working class, city labor leaders also disdained the narrow craft-consciousness that a focus on arbitration between individual unions and business leaders encouraged. Thus, beginning in 1910 with the Philadelphia General Strike, city labor leaders began to reassert themselves and to demand more power for city labor councils. State federations, which sometimes worked in alliance with municipal labor leaders, also lost influence as a result of centralizing tendencies within the labor movement. As war loomed, the issue of how labor's attitudes toward foreign policy would be determined became an important part of the "contested terrain" provoking tension between different layers of labor leadership. Longtime proponents of union democracy, CFL leaders quickly proved critical actors in the dispute.[95]

94. Foner, *History of the Labor Movement*, 3: 136, 66; James Green, *The World of the Worker: Labor in Twentieth-Century America* (New York: Hill and Wang, 1980), 36–42, 100–101; Philip Taft, *The AFL in the Time of Gompers* (New York: Octagon Books, 1970), 150–55, 307; Green, *The National Civic Federation*; Andrew Dawson, "The Paradox of Dynamic Technological Change and the Labor Aristocracy in the United States, 1880–1914," *Labor History* 20 (summer 1979): 325–51. For a study of the diverging attitudes of socialists toward the war, see David J. Saposs, *Left Wing Unionism: A Study of Radical Policies and Tactics* (New York: Russell and Russell, 1967 [1926]).

95. Not much has been written on city federations, but see Montgomery, "New Tendencies," 101; Shapiro, "'Hand and Brain,'" 410–13; Dubofsky, "Abortive Reform: The Wilson Administration and Organized Labor 1913–1920," *Work, Community, and Power*, ed. Cronin and Sirianni, 197–220. See also *Proceedings of the AFL*, 1915, 436–37, and 1916, 208, 269; and Keiser, "John Fitzpatrick," 20, 166. On state federations, see Letter from John Walker to John Fitzpatrick, 2/9/16: FP. See also Staley, *The Illinois State Federation of Labor*, 200–204, 307–13; *ISFL Proceedings*, 1915, 246–47; Greene, "The Strike at the Ballot Box," 3, 13, 75–84; Frank, "At the Point of Consumption." For the term "contested terrain," I am indebted to the second reviewer of this book for Cornell University Press.

Also catapulting the CFL toward a leadership role in forging an oppositional foreign policy were the Irish immigrant backgrounds of many CFL leaders, their organic connections with the local Irish community, and their intuitive acceptance of the labor internationalism of the era. Nationalist loyalties and sympathy for an international brotherhood of labor are often viewed as incompatible tendencies. But John Fitzpatrick and other Irish patriots within the CFL welded their sympathy for Irish freedom to a broader critique of international capitalism, implying that the struggle for Irish independence was at its roots a class struggle. Following the Easter Rebellion, one resolution proclaimed that

> Whereas for centuries past the Celtic population of Ireland has been dominated and governed against its consent by that same ruling class which, for a still greater period of time, has dominated and exploited the working class of England and has made use of the working class of England to hold Ireland in military and political subjugation. . . .
> Be it therefore resolved that the Chicago Federation of Labor hereby places itself on record as asserting the inherent injustice of the domination of the Celtic people of Ireland by alien people and powers and therefore as protesting against the consequent unjust and illogical appeal to the doctrine of treason as a ground for the summary execution of Celtic persons taken as prisoners of war.[96]

Such proclamations clearly drew inspiration from Irish-American internationalist ideologies, but they also transcended them. For CFL leaders, British imperialism was but one part of a larger story: that of an international capitalist economy and the divisions of wealth and power it encouraged within the world community. Fitzpatrick and other Irish patriots within the CFL thus linked British imperialism not only to the sufferings of the Irish working class but to the oppression of British workers. They also implied that British capitalists were indirectly undermining the economic well-being of U.S. laborers. "The same imperialistic British capitalists who are grinding down the Irish workers into subjection," wrote Fitzpatrick, "through alliance with the pro-British New York House of Morgan Company and other supposed American money concerns are exploiting the workers of the United States."[97] CFL leaders additionally recognized that Americans were imperialists in their own right, and they frequently sponsored Mexican

96. *CFL Minutes*, 5/21/16, 18–19.
97. Fitzpatrick, Speech to the First Convention of the American Association for the Recognition of the Irish Republic, n.d., B11–F78: FP.

nationalists to speak on American financial, political, and military interventionism in Mexico.[98]

For Fitzpatrick and other key CFL leaders, then, nationalist rebellions were a part of the class struggle, not a distraction from it. Under their tutelage, the CFL became a center of nationalist activity that was used by such varied ethnic groups as the Irish, Mexicans, Indians, and Russians to win working-class support for independence campaigns and revolutionary struggles in their homelands. Since many CFL officials played leading roles in the founding of local Friends of Irish Freedom councils, the relationship between the local Irish-American community and the CFL was particularly close.[99] Irish nationalist activities in turn nurtured a strong anti-imperialism among CFL leaders that likely helped sustain their opposition to U.S. intervention in the war after the AFL became an avid promoter of Wilson's preparedness campaigns.

Not surprisingly, the first response of the CFL to the war was to frame numerous resolutions condemning it as a capitalist plot and urging the American people to fight the impulse toward war. "We feel and believe," proclaimed one typical resolution, "that wars are unnecessary and caused by the exploiters of labor for the express purpose of advancing the position of large capitalists whose interest is solely commercial and . . . call upon all the working people of America who must do the fighting if war occurs to register their emphatic protest against the

98. See especially, *CFL Minutes*, 8/16/16, 2–3; and Bigham, "The Chicago Federation of Labor," 104.

99. On the participation of CFL leaders in FOIF activities, see, especially, Friends of Irish Freedom to Fitzpatrick, 1916, B5; Agnes Smedley to Fitzpatrick, 5/25/19, B8–F60; Receipt from the Commission on Irish Independence, B9–F63; Resolutions Passed at the Mass Meeting of the Friends of Irish Freedom, General John Stark Branch at St. Anne's, B9–F56: FP. On other Irish activities of the CFL, see, especially, *CFL Minutes*, 5/21/16, 18–19; 7/16/16, 16–18; 5/7/16, 18–19. For information on the CFL and Mexico, see, especially, *CFL Minutes*, 8/16/16, 2–3; Bigham, "The Chicago Federation of Labor," 104. Aspects of the Indian campaigns of CFL and other labor activists are illuminated in Agnes Smedley (Friends of Freedom for India) to John Fitzpatrick 5/25/19, B8–F60: FP, NM, 4/19/19, 8–9. Taraknath Das to Frank Walsh, 1/19/21, B10: WP. Speech of Basanta Koomar Roy, Fraternal Delegate from the Friends of Freedom for India, *Proceedings of the First National Convention of the Labor Party of the U.S.*, Chicago, November 22, 1919, 32–37. For a sense of the Russian activities of CFL activists and their close ally Frank Walsh, see Joseph Manley of Trade Union National Committee for Russian Relief to Walsh, n.d. circa March 1922; Manley to Walsh 3/8/22, B11; Nockels to Walsh, 9/30/22, B11; Treasurer, Friends of Soviet Russia to Walsh 5/31/22, B9: WP. Walsh to Mr. A. B. Martin of Friends of Soviet Russia, 5/31/22, B9: WP. Foner (*History of the Labor Movement*, 8: 60–62) estimates that central labor unions in seventy-two cities supported the Alliance for Trade Union Relations with Russia.

same."[100] Initially, the CFL tried to convince President Wilson to mediate an end to the European conflict. After the administration's negotiating efforts failed, CFL leaders geared their energies toward maintaining neutrality. In August 1914, replicating the activities of local Irish groups, Fitzpatrick sent a letter to the president asking him to impose an embargo on American shipments to Europe in order to prevent incidents between American sea captains and European belligerents. When the president failed to respond, CFL leaders became disheartened and began to doubt Wilson's commitment to keeping the nation out of war.[101]

These suspicions were confirmed by Wilson's handling of the *Lusitania* affair. Following the incident, the CFL sent a resolution to the AFL Executive Council asking that it convene a congress of labor groups in the United States to take a vote on workers' positions on the war. If the vote was against American involvement, the AFL should develop effective methods of labor resistance to the Wilson administration's foreign policy. Gompers responded that he would submit the resolution to the Executive Council for a vote "if it becomes necessary," but he refused to take any immediate action.[102]

Disappointed with the AFL's response, local labor activists joined with Rep. Frank Buchanan to form Labor's National Peace Council. This organization, which promoted strict American neutrality, brought together local and national trade union officials throughout the country who opposed U.S. intervention in the war. By the summer of 1915, it claimed a membership of over one million. But leaders of the council were soon indicted on charges of conspiring with German naval officials to prevent the shipment of munitions to the Allies. Although most of the charges subsequently proved to be false, they damaged the council's reputation. Many labor activists, fearful of being charged with treason, abandoned the organization.[103]

Unable to forge an effective national coalition, the CFL devoted itself to promoting foreign policy activism within Chicago. In November 1915, CFL leaders commissioned several local delegates to study the preparedness issue. After a three-month investigation, the committee declared its opposition to preparedness as advocated by President Wilson. Committee members argued that the way to prevent war was not

100. *CFL Minutes*, 5/16/15, 7–8.
101. Bigham, "The Chicago Federation of Labor," 104.
102. *CFL Minutes*, 5/16/15, 7–8; 6/20/15, 18–19.
103. Gompers, *Seventy Years*, 2: 340–41, 347, 349; Foner, *History of the Labor Movement*, 7: 50–63.

to be militarily prepared but to develop a humane world society. In a well-educated society where all were adequately fed and clothed, workers would refuse to participate in war. Committee members proposed an alternative preparedness program that included passing the Keating child labor bill, supporting legislation abolishing strikebreaking, extending trade union power to its greatest possible limit, developing a democratically officered and controlled military system, and opposing an increase in the standing army.[104] The writers of the preparedness report argued that the Chicago labor movement had a peculiar responsibility to fight the headlong rush to war because it was situated "in the very center of America, feeling the life of both the East and West" and was therefore especially suited to "counteract the hysteria and speak for the international spirit of labor which we hope will revive when the guns of Europe have been stilled and we are able to start to build upon the ruins of a better civilization."[105]

Following release of the committee report, the CFL became one of the first city councils to stage boycotts and counterdemonstrations of preparedness parades at which they especially denounced the prowar gestures of business groups like the Illinois Manufacturers' Association. The CFL also kept tabs on munitions production and sales by local businesses and ultimately concluded that such enterprises were engaging in treasonous activities by selling to belligerents. They suggested that public ownership of war-related industries was the only way to prevent a dangerous economic dependence on the Allied powers. John Fitzpatrick personally led an unsuccessful campaign against the introduction of military training in the schools. Labor opponents of military training argued that it would eventually become compulsory and encourage a "hunt for enemies." It would also contribute to a decline in internationalist spirit and, according to one particularly dramatic campaigner, carried with it the curse of death.[106]

104. CFL Minutes, 2/6/16, 12–15. To compare the CFL's activities to other groups, see, especially, the debate in the New Republic on preparedness: 6/10/16, 137–38; 2/24/17, 92; 3/3/17, ii, 145; 3/10/17, 26. Resolutions of the First American Conference for Democracy and Terms of Peace, New York City, May 30–31, 1917, B5: FP. Letter from John Sullivan to John Bogart, Labor Committee of the Friends of Peace, 8/7/15: CC-GMC. See also Fite and Peterson, Opponents of War; Grubbs, Struggle for Labor Loyalty; Larson, Labor and Foreign Policy; Lasch, American Liberals; Weinstein, "The Socialist Party," 5–27; Montgomery, Fall of the House of Labor, 371–72.
105. CFL Minutes, 2/6/16, 17.
106. On boycotts of parades and antibusiness activities, see CFL Minutes, 4/16/16, 10–11; 5/21/16, 10–11, 14–16. For the military training issue, see, especially, CFL Minutes, 1/7/17, 10–17.

One of the CFL's most vigorous antipreparedness campaigns was an attack on the local presses, which the CFL suggested represented big business interests and were trying to drive the country into war. CFL activists wrote letters to the local papers and engaged in preparedness debates in order to publicize the "real sentiments of the people."[107] But they soon recognized that these campaigns were insufficient, and they endorsed plans for a labor paper and public ownership of the cable, telegraph, and telephone lines. One CFL resolution proclaimed that "the moneyed interest's control of the press news through associations such as the Associated and United press is not only a menace to a free press but also to a unified and efficient means of communication in war as well as peace." In the postwar era, these plans would culminate in the CFL-sponsored paper, the New Majority, and in a labor press service, the Federated Press, with extensive networks in Europe.[108]

Following the German decision to commence unrestricted submarine warfare, the CFL renewed its efforts to provoke AFL action on the war. On February 4, 1917, the CFL reaffirmed its old antiwar declaration of August 2, 1914, and called on Gompers to demand that American citizens be prevented from entering war zones. But when they received no reply, they joined other area ethnic and radical groups in calling for a referendum vote of the people on the issue of the war.[109]

By the time the United States intervened in the European conflict, the CFL had gone a long way toward creating a class-based foreign policy ideology that clashed fundamentally with that of the Wilson administration and the AFL. The local council blamed profit-seeking businessmen rather than German autocracy for the war. Its leaders believed that a lasting peace would be achieved only when the working classes of the world developed sufficient power to thwart the greed and militarism of the owning class. Like Irish- and Polish-American groups, the CFL demonstrated no visible enthusiasm for international law or international organizations of nations as solutions for resolving conflict. Their long-term plans for transforming American foreign policy and international relations included schemes for educating workers on foreign policy issues, developing alternative sources of international

107. CFL Minutes, 4/16/16, 10–11; 5/16/16, 10–11; 5/21/16, 14–16; 6/18/16, 4; 1/7/17, 10–17. See also draft of Fitzpatrick letter, intended recipient unknown, 3/21/17, B4: FP.
108. CFL Minutes, 10/11/16, 23; 10/1/16, 25–26.
109. Telegram, Fitzpatrick and Ed Nockels to Gompers, 2/4/17: CC-GMC. CFL Minutes, 2/8/17.

news, opposing imperialism, supporting political reforms that would give the American people more direct control over foreign policy, and cultivating the power of the labor movement.

The CFL's campaigns illustrate both the potential and limits of city labor councils as vehicles for promoting working-class opposition to U.S. foreign policy initiatives prior to American intervention in the war. Deeply involved in the nationalist activities of the local Irish community, CFL leaders borrowed from Irish-American foreign policy ideology in ways that promoted rather than undermined principles of labor solidarity. But their class analysis of the roots of imperialism and war, while attractive to many trade unionists from old immigrant backgrounds, won no apparent support among groups like Polish-Americans whose homeland stood to gain from U.S. intervention in the European conflict and whose relations with the local labor movement were often strained. The CFL's antiwar agitation was also undermined by the AFL, which helped to prevent the development of an effective national labor coalition to oppose U.S. intervention in the European conflict. Yet, resentment among local militants toward Gompers and Wilson would simmer during the war, ultimately culminating in a Labor party offensive with far broader potential appeal to Chicago's workers. In building support for the postwar Labor party movement, Chicago labor leaders drew on the strong distrust of centralized power, international law, and international leagues of nations common to the foreign policy ideologies of the CFL and the city's Irish and Polish organizations.

CHAPTER TWO

Samuel Gompers, Wartime Diplomacy, and the Struggle for Labor Loyalty in Chicago, 1917–1918

THE spirit of AFL president Samuel Gompers's wartime diplomacy, and the obstacles he faced in implementing his foreign policy programs, were perhaps best captured by President Woodrow Wilson at the 1917 AFL convention. The president, who attended the convention to rally labor behind the war, characterized Gompers as a man who knew how "to pull in harness" during a time of national crisis. Ominously, the president warned that there were others within the labor movement who sought to "kick over the traces" and would have "to be put in a corral." So impressed was Gompers with the president's comments that he published them in full in his autobiography and noted the "thrill of pride" he felt in "the manner of man who was our nation's chief in that critical period."[1]

The AFL president unswervingly supported the administration's foreign policies between 1916 and 1918 in part because he agreed with Wilson that Germany was primarily responsible for the war and must be defeated. But equally significant, Gompers hoped to seize the opportunity afforded by the war to promote corporatist institutions like those that had evolved in Britain after the outbreak of the war. A longtime promoter of the National Civic Federation, Gompers believed that collaboration between labor and capital was essential in modern industrial

---

1. Gompers, *Seventy Years*, 2: 284. See also John Frey, "The Reminiscences of John P. Frey," 1957, Columbia University History Collection, Butler Library Columbia University, New York (Frey, *Reminiscences*), 2: 307. Foner, *History of the Labor Movement*, 7: 159; Larson, *Labor and Foreign Policy*; Montgomery, *Fall of the House of Labor*, 330–410.

societies and hailed the development of institutions in Britain that for-
malized this cooperation under the auspices of state commissions.
Beginning in 1916, Gompers tied AFL support for a U.S. war effort to
labor participation on evolving corporatist defense councils. The AFL
president also argued that corporatist alliances ought to be extended
into the international sphere, suggesting that the commissions to any
future peace conference should include functional representatives from
groups like labor. These civilian representatives, he argued, afforded the
best hope of preventing the secret diplomacy that had caused the war.

Gompers quickly won the overwhelming support of AFL national
and international union leaders for his wartime policies, but he faced
bitter opposition from the international labor community and from
local militants within the United States. Ironically, many British and
European labor leaders became disillusioned with corporatist alliances
in their own countries just as Gompers was beginning the tedious task
of building similar networks in the United States. When the AFL president tried to promote his corporatist brand of labor diplomacy abroad
in 1917 and 1918, he faced the combined opposition of key British and
European labor leaders who were instead preoccupied during the final
two years of the war with revitalizing the spirit of international labor
solidarity and using international labor organizations to negotiate an
end to the war.

At the same time, Gompers was battling local labor leaders who were
undercutting support for his programs at home. At first, Gompers effectively routed oppositional local labor forces by using parliamentary procedures to deny them a vote on the issue of whether labor should
support the war. But the dissenting spirit of city labor councils quickly
revived, and their leaders became the vanguard of a movement that
challenged AFL collaborationism in ways that mirrored the British shop
steward committees' attacks on British labor leadership. If Chicago is a
representative example, then Gompers's attempts to win support for a
corporatist diplomacy were also impeded by ethnic organizations, which
systematically opposed his efforts to Americanize immigrants and continued to provide viable ideological alternatives to Wilsonian internationalism.

Distant observers of Sam Gompers's career were likely surprised
when he became an avid promoter of President Wilson's preparedness
programs and war policies. A self-proclaimed pacifist, Gompers had
participated in a variety of peace congresses and activities designed to
ensure more democratic control over international relations during his

long tenure as AFL president. Gompers also gained a reputation as an anti-imperialist during the Spanish-American War when he opposed the annexation of the Philippines and Hawaii.[2] In his memoirs, Gompers reminisced that "from early boyhood vanquishment of war was an ultimate dream which I earnestly expected." He also told of his participation in programs designed to establish peaceful mechanisms for eradicating "secret diplomacy and territorial and industrial aggrandizement."[3]

Gompers's abandonment of his pacifism in World War I was in part a result of his firm conviction that Germany was ruled by a brutal and aggressive autocracy that must be defeated if freedom anywhere were to be preserved. "The time had come," he concluded in 1915, "when the world could no longer exist part democratic and part autocratic." The AFL president argued that "it was an issue on which there could be no real neutrality."[4] Florence Thorne, Gompers's devoted personal secretary, noted of his policies that "he was quite oblivious to Great Britain's invasion on the high seas but . . . recounted vividly damages to our shipping and losses of lives by German submarines. He seemed personally committed to aid Great Britain."[5]

Antipathy toward the German government was only one factor influencing Gompers's war policies. The AFL president's attitudes were also shaped by his evolving vision of the labor movement's role in American society and world affairs. The AFL rode to ascendancy over the Knights of Labor in the 1880s and 1890s on the crest of a highly successful strike wave. But by the turn of the century Gompers had joined other union leaders in trying to curtail strikes and promote arbitration as a means of resolving industrial disputes. Gompers and a handful of other AFL trade unionists began to participate actively in the National Civic Federation, a group created in 1900 to bring together representative

2. Gompers, *Seventy Years*, 2: 326; Rhodri Jeffreys-Jones, "Massachusetts Labor, Henry Cabot Lodge, and the Abortion of Empire," in *Anglo Saxonism in U.S. Foreign Policy: The Diplomacy of Imperialism, 1899–1919*, ed. Serge Ricard and Helene Christol (Aix-en-Provence: Université de Provence, 1991), 25–26; William Whittaker, "Samuel Gompers, Antiimperialist," *Pacific Historical Review* 38 (1969): 429. See also Delber Lee McKee, "The American Federation of Labor and American Foreign Policy, 1886–1912," (Ph.D. diss., Stanford University, 1952); Welch, *Response to Imperialism*; Paul Tallion, "The American Federation of Labor and Expansionism, 1890–1910" (Senior thesis, Northwestern University, 1985). On a surprise reaction to Gompers's shift in foreign policy orientation, see Maurer, *It Can Be Done*, 246.
3. Gompers, *Seventy Years*, 2: 322, 326.
4. Ibid., 339.
5. Foner, *History of the Labor Movement*, 7: 44. NR, 8/11/17, 35; 7/24/15, 294.

labor leaders and businessmen under the auspices of neutral third parties and convince them that they shared a "community of interest" in promoting the economic health of particular industries and of the country as a whole. The organization launched campaigns against socialists and antiunion employers, insisting that capitalism was fundamentally sound but that it was threatened by extremists on both sides of the political spectrum. Because the National Civic Federation was a voluntary organization and could arbitrate only those disputes submitted to it, the organization resolved very few industrial conflicts in the twentieth century. But among its members it reinforced an essentially corporatist vision of society in which business and labor would voluntarily work together under the auspices of disinterested expert observers to resolve their differences and achieve industrial harmony.[6]

One could overestimate Gompers's commitment to this corporatist vision, for he never entirely abandoned the strike as a necessary instrument of last resort in achieving labor goals. Nonetheless, his emphasis in the early twentieth century shifted away from violent confrontation with businessmen and toward arbitration under the direction of neutral parties. By 1912 Gompers even seemed ready to accept that the state had a role to play in achieving industrial harmony. During the presidential election of that year, Gompers and several other key AFL officials vigorously supported Woodrow Wilson, hoping to seize what some have called a political "opening to the middle."[7]

According to Gwendolyn Mink, AFL leaders forged ties to the Democratic party not because they sought state welfarism for workers but because they wanted to preserve the AFL's autonomy. In part, AFL leaders hoped to protect the organization from the antilabor court injunctions that were sapping labor's strength and threatened to destroy the right of workers to organize. They also desired protection from below in the form of anti-immigration measures, for Gompers believed that the new immigrants from southern and eastern Europe were lowering labor standards and bringing dangerous socialist and anarchist ideas to America's shores.[8] But most importantly, the AFL allied itself with the Democratic party to institutionalize voluntary mediation between busi-

6. Green, *National Civic Federation*, ix, 58, 90–132, 466–67; Mink, *Old Labor*, 206.
7. Mink, *Old Labor*, 18. Greene, "The Strike at the Ballot Box," 582–84.
8. Mink, *Old Labor*, 236–39, 10; Dubofsky, "Abortive Reform: The Wilson Administration and Organized Labor, 1913–1920," in *Work, Community, and Power*, ed. Cronin and Sirianni, 197–212.

ness and labor under federal auspices, thereby preventing more extensive and potentially repressive state intervention in industrial affairs. Wilson did not disappoint AFL leaders in this last respect. Shortly after assuming office, he created the Labor Department and the Commission on Industrial Relations, both of which were consciously modeled on the National Civic Federation.[9] Thus, by 1914, AFL leaders were poised to use their contacts within the Wilson administration to implement a federalized version of corporatism.

Gompers also drifted toward a corporatist-oriented diplomacy during the prewar era. As Gompers began to emphasize conciliation and mediation in the early twentieth century, his foreign policy underwent a subtle transformation. According to Delber McKee, he came to a "tacit compromise" with the State Department, toning down his opposition to imperialistic and militaristic policies in return for free reign in pursuing labor initiatives in foreign countries and in American protectorates. In the aftermath of the Spanish-American War, Gompers officially endorsed ward status for the Philippines and Puerto Rico and focused his initiatives there on building unions modeled on those of the AFL. In rationalizing his emphasis on union organizing rather than independence for these protectorates, Gompers argued that "we realized that in order to protect our standards within the states we must help the island workers to develop their own higher political, social and industrial problems [sic]."[10]

Gompers's position suggested that he was now willing to acquiesce in American imperialism if the AFL could play a role in shaping it in ways that benefited American trade unions. In general, American workers shared a community of interest with businessmen in promoting trade expansion because it contributed to the economic health of industries at home. By contrast, business investment abroad fostered competing industries that sometimes undersold American companies and hurt American workers. AFL leaders hoped by establishing AFL-styled unions in the Philippines and Puerto Rico to improve wage rates for native workers, thereby giving them more capital to buy American goods. They further sought to preempt revolutionary politics that might result in extensive state-sponsored restrictions on trade. Higher wage rates in American protectorates would also work to the advantage of AFL trade unionists by making investment in these areas less profitable

9. Mink, *Old Labor*, 243–46.

10. Gompers, *Seventy Years*, 2: 326–28; McKee, "The American Federation of Labor," 134.

for American businessmen and by raising the prices of goods from such protectorates on the world market.[11]

These same kinds of considerations led Gompers to promote AFL-styled unions in Canada and Latin America. Concerned about the establishment of U.S. branch plants in Canada, Gompers launched organizing campaigns there that dwarfed those of the Canadian national trade union center, the Trades and Labor Congress (TLC). Robert Babcock suggests that the TLC eventually became so dependent on its stronger and wealthier American counterpart that it was reduced to the level of an American state federation of labor. Gompers's efforts in Latin America would culminate in the postwar era in the establishment of the Pan-American Federation of Labor, an organization designed to bring together moderate trade union movements and to discourage the growth of socialism and anarchism in the Americas.[12]

Prior to 1914, the AFL president took a particular interest in Mexico, cultivating extensive contacts with trade unionists there. When revolution enveloped the neighboring country, Gompers tried to use his labor contacts to promote Wilsonian foreign policy goals. The AFL president's moment of glory came when the Carranza regime imprisoned several American soldiers after they clashed with Mexican forces at the port of Veracruz. Wilson demanded their immediate release and a diplomatic standoff ensued. Gompers, then meeting with Mexican labor delegates in Washington, sent a telegram from the conference to Carranza appealing for the release of the soldiers. Carranza subsequently granted the soldiers' freedom and Gompers, with customary modesty, took credit for himself and the conference in breaking the impasse between the two countries.[13]

If Gompers's dealings with Mexico were in part motivated by inflated perceptions of his own personal influence, they also envisioned an important emissarial role for the AFL in promoting U.S. foreign policy

11. Jeffreys-Jones, "Massachusetts Labor," 25–47; Frey, Memoir, 3: 425. Dawson, "The Paradox of Dynamic Technological Change," 340; McKee, "The American Federation of Labor," 141–52, 237.

12. Babcock, Gompers in Canada, 98–110; Gompers, Seventy Years, 2: 310; McKee, "The American Federation of Labor," 141–52, 237; Harvey Levenstein, Labor Organizations in the United States and Mexico (Westport, Conn.: Greenwood Press, 1971); Rosenberg, Spreading the American Dream, 83.

13. Gompers, Seventy Years, 2: 310; McKee, "The American Federation of Labor," 141–52, 237; Levenstein, Labor Organizations in the United States and Mexico; Rosenberg, Spreading the American Dream, 83; Gregg Andrews, Shoulder to Shoulder? The American Federation of Labor, the United States, and the Mexican Revolution, 1910–1924 (Berkeley: University of California Press, 1991), 34.

goals. At home, Gompers became increasingly enmeshed during the early twentieth century in activities designed to promote a business-state-labor partnership in achieving national economic health. Gompers's diplomatic activities during this same period suggest that he wanted to extend this partnership into the international realm. By encouraging nonrevolutionary forms of trade unionism in underdeveloped regions and by acting as a state emissary to defuse disputes between the United States and other countries, the AFL could help promote American economic expansion. Business, labor, and the state shared as much of a community of interest in promoting such expansion as they did in encouraging national economic efficiency. Economic growth could improve material standards for everyone and undermine the popularity of socialist schemes calling for a radical redistribution of wealth.[14]

It is uncertain whether a majority of trade union leaders and rank-and-file unionists in the AFL shared the increasingly corporatist vision of Gompers and his closest colleagues prior to 1914. Many historians of "business unionism" have emphasized that corporatist values did extend beyond Gompers's inner circle and were pervasive among the leaders of the most powerful constituent national and international unions within the AFL. Yet the extent of these union leaders' allegiance to corporatist precepts is almost impossible to determine before 1914. Social historians, meanwhile, have documented rank-and-file resistance to corporatist values in the early twentieth century. But the scale of this resistance is also difficult to gauge. Support for Gompers's foreign policies is even more unclear, since the AFL president conducted many activities without official authorization and thoroughly dominated the AFL International Relations Committee that assured funding for his ventures.[15] But war helped to clarify alignments over Gompers's corporatist orientation by accelerating the pace of change and casting a floodlight on newly evolving corporatist bureaucracies in Washington.

President Wilson first began to prepare for possible U.S. involvement in the war in 1915, when he appointed two efficiency engineers to study the problem. Gompers, stimulated both by his observations of British

14. See, especially, Gompers, *Seventy Years*, 2: 303–21; Andrews, *Shoulder to Shoulder*, 5–6.

15. Foner, *History of the Labor Movement*, 3: 136–69; Green, *World of the Worker*, 36–42, 60–133; Dubofsky, "Abortive Reform," in *Work, Community, and Power*, ed. Cronin and Sirianni, 122–97; Montgomery, *Workers' Control*; Larson, *Labor and Foreign Policy*, 33–37; Mink, *Old Labor*; Conner, *National War Labor Board*.

society and by his contacts within the National Civic Federation, took an immediate interest in the little-known research project. Of British origin himself, Gompers seemed fascinated by the wartime partnership that developed in Britain between the trade union movement, the government, and business.[16] In some respects, the alliance was an unlikely one. Between 1888 and 1914, economic and social divisions between the classes in Britain had grown, provoking a resurgence of trade unionism and culminating in a major strike wave after 1911. These developments were accompanied by the evolution of a labor party that introduced distinctly class themes into British politics and threatened to reshape fundamentally property relations in the country.[17]

But if British labor leaders wielded unprecedented power by the turn of the century and spoke the language of class conflict, they had no more interest than their American counterparts in shattering entirely the economic and political systems that had borne them. As Harold Perkin has demonstrated persuasively, many British labor leaders embraced a professional and corporatist ethos in the prewar years, stressing the value of negotiations between expert representatives of the business and labor classes in achieving an industrial paradise. British union leaders, like their AFL counterparts, also increasingly sought to involve the state as a third party in arbitrating disputes. This held true even for some socialists, who hoped to achieve public ownership of the means of production via bureaucratic innovations by industrial and political experts rather than by fomenting class antagonism. But efforts at accommodation between business, labor, and state leaders before 1914 were often halfhearted and were always threatened from below by rank-and-file workers who believed their leaders had sold them out.[18]

War, however, afforded what Perkin has called a "short cut" to an "enforced corporatism by the state."[19] At first critical of their government's declaration of war, most British labor leaders—with a few prominent exceptions like James Ramsey MacDonald—reversed their position after the invasion of Belgium and gave their support to the war effort. British workers, for their part, enlisted in the military services in num-

16. Harold C. Livesay, *Samuel Gompers and Organized Labor in America* (Boston: Little, Brown, 1978), 5; Gompers, *Seventy Years*, 2: 339, 359; NR, 8/11/18, 35; Green, *National Civic Federation*, 379–80.

17. See, especially, Perkin, *Rise of Professional Society*, 27–115; Pelling, *Labour Party*, 1–34; Hinton, *Labour and Socialism*, 95, *First Shop Stewards' Movement*, 13.

18. Pelling, *Labour Party*, 1–4; Perkin, *Rise of Professional Society*, 27, 104–30, 183.

19. Perkin, *Rise of Professional Society*, 186.

bers proportionately equal to that of other classes.[20] On August 24, 1914, the Joint Board of Trade Unions Congress, the General Federation of Trade Unions and the Labour Party aligned labor solidly behind the government by urging "both employers and workers to abandon all strikes and lockouts for the duration" of the war.[21] Trade union leaders also assisted government officials in forming the War Emergency Workers' National Committee, a group that brought the labor movement into direct collaboration with the government in resolving business-labor conflicts. Industrial harmony was further promoted by the evolution of extensive state-sponsored arbitration machinery that included the industrywide Whitley councils and national bodies such as the Arbitration Department of the Ministry of Labor and the Industrial Conference. The alliance between labor, the state, and business was cemented with the appointment of key businessmen and labor M.P.s to cabinet positions.[22]

To keep abreast of developments in Britain, Gompers periodically sponsored British trade unionists to come to the United States to speak at AFL functions. The AFL president generally praised the wartime partnership in Britain but criticized the British for moving too slowly in mobilizing for war. Gompers also attacked British labor dissidents for disrupting production. The AFL president sought to avoid the organizational problems faced by the British in the early years by aligning American labor behind the mobilization effort even before actual U.S. participation in the war.[23]

Gompers's contacts with prominent National Civic Federation organizer Ralph Easley proved crucial to achieving this end. In 1915, Easley and Gompers had worked together investigating allegations that strikes in the American munitions industry were a product of German sabotage. To finance the investigation, Easley solicited the financial help of Henry P. Davidson of the J. P. Morgan investment firm, thus illustrating the extraordinary community of interest that developed between busi-

20. Ibid., 111, 186; Pelling, Labour Party, 35–38; Dawse, "The Independent Labour Party," 35–46.

21. Perkin, Rise of Professional Society, 187.

22. Ibid., 202–3, 187; Pelling, Labour Party, 38–41; Leventhal, Arthur Henderson, 49–64; Dawse, "The Independent Labour Party," 33–45; Arthur Henderson, The League of Nations and Labour (Oxford: Oxford University Press, 1918); J. Ramsey MacDonald, National Defence: A Study in Militarism (London: George Allen and Unwin, 1921); Hinton, Labour and Socialism, 102; Montgomery, "New Tendencies," 93–94.

23. Gompers, Seventy Years, 2: 339, 359; NR, 8/11/18, 35; Green, National Civic Federation, 379–80.

nessmen and AFL leaders in destroying labor militancy during the war. Easley also put Gompers in touch with Howard Coffin, one of the engineers appointed by Wilson to study the issue of economic mobilization. Gompers subsequently worked closely with Coffin on the industrial survey and requested a position on the Council of National Defense proposed by the survey.[24]

As Gompers waited for word on the fate of the council and his appointment, he began to promote preparedness more aggressively. In a speech in March 1916, Gompers claimed that "preparedness must be the attitude of a nation toward all relations of life and all lines of development." According to the AFL president, preparedness was "something very different from militarism." Both left an "indelible impression upon the nation" but one was "for freedom and the other for repression." The best way to assure that American preparedness promoted freedom, he suggested, was to give wage earners representation on all government councils.[25] Thus, while Gompers agreed with CFL leaders that preparedness should not be used as a rationale for destroying humanitarian safeguards, he insisted that the best way to protect human rights was to cooperate with the government in formulating policy.

The AFL president's preparedness campaign paid off: In October 1916, he was granted a position on the Civilian Advisory Commission of the Council of National Defense. The council was comprised of the secretaries of the Departments of War, Navy, Agriculture, Commerce, Labor, and the Interior. The commission included civilian representatives from finance, general industry, merchandise, medicine, and labor. These two bodies were charged with preparing the nation for war by opening up "a new and direct channel of communication between business and scientific men and all departments of the government."[26] Gompers's role on the advisory commission was a small one: He was empowered to develop a labor subcommittee to study the potential impact of mobilization on workers. But despite the limitations of the new position, Gompers believed it afforded him a unique opportunity to advance the cause of trade unionism. "I can say candidly and not to be over vain," he told his colleagues in an Executive Council meeting, "that I have had some influence with the Commission and Council in helping to guide their policies." He believed he had won respect from business-

24. Larson, *Labor and Foreign Policy*, 44–45; Gompers, *Seventy Years*, 2: 350–53.
25. *American Federationist* 23 (March 1916): 176–78; Samuel Gompers, *American Labor and the War*, 75–82, 59.
26. Gompers to Newton Baker, 10/31/16: CC-GMC. Kennedy, *Over Here*, 115.

men who "never dreamed that any labor man would have anything more than a fighting, biting snarling struggle for five cents more," and paved the way for the "voice of labor" and the notion that a labor man could be a "humanitarian and a liberty loving citizen."[27]

So enamored with the new spirit of cooperation did Gompers become that he promoted labor representation on a variety of other executive councils, ranging from those concerned with military service to those focusing on Pan-American relations.[28] The AFL president also began to promote aggressively the notion that labor representatives should be included on the national commissions to a postwar peace conference. In the early years of the war, Gompers had recommended a meeting of organized labor at the same time as a future peace conference. Such a meeting, he hoped, would serve as "an organized channel through which the interests of the masses of the population of all countries could be represented." But Gompers's participation on the Council of National Defense convinced him that labor should seek representation on the peace commissions themselves. The AFL Executive Council concurred, suggesting in its 1916 report that "the influence which a representative group of workers of the world could wield in such a [Peace] Congress, was appreciated by all those who had an understanding of human rights and freedom." The report concluded that "the people have a right to do things for themselves . . . they need no longer look up to others to do things for them . . . even the things that pertain to government and international relations."[29]

But if Gompers was to achieve his plans he needed first to demonstrate to other members of the Council of National Defense that labor was a reliable partner in newly evolving corporatist coalitions. As opposition to possible U.S. involvement in the war increased in early 1917, the council asked Gompers to secure a pledge of labor's loyalty.[30] In response, Gompers wrote a letter summoning the Executive Council to Washington. The AFL president suggested that "the whole world is afire and there is imminent danger that at any time the United States may be involved." He argued that there were two ways in which the matter could be approached, "either with Labor's representatives maintaining

27. Minutes, Conference in Executive Council Room, 3/6/17: Con C-GMC. Gompers to Advisory Commission, 4/12/17 and 4/5/17; Gompers to Walker, 6/1/17: AFL Letterbooks (LB)-GMC.
28. NR, 6/10/16, 137–38.
29. Gompers, Seventy Years, 2: 393; Proceedings of the AFL, 1916, 54–55.
30. Gompers, Seventy Years, 2: 359; NR, 5/26/17, 98; Frey, Memoir, 2: 306; Larson, Labor and Foreign Policy, 84–88; Foner, History of the Labor Movement, 7: 103.

certain ideals of human welfare" or "if labor should hold aloof from the entire situation, plans . . . [would] be adopted by those out of touch with the labor movement and out of sympathy with the needs and ideals of workers."[31]

Gompers asked for the council's help in constructing a position paper to express labor's views on the war. Yet when Executive Council members arrived at the meeting, they were told that a statement of labor's position had already been "cooked up." A labor congress on the AFL's position during wartime had also been planned and invitations sent to national and international trade union officials.[32]

Some council members probably hoped that a more open discussion of the war issue would ensue at this meeting. But they were to be disappointed for Gompers carefully manipulated the meeting to prevent any substantial dissent. Gompers avoided much controversy over his statement on the war by excluding central federated bodies like the CFL from the meeting. Noting to close advisors that these organizations were centers of pacifism, Gompers instead made plans to send representatives around after the Washington Trade Union Conference to persuade local and state leaders of the efficacy of supporting the labor report on the war. Gompers also prevented dissent by allowing little time between the date on which he sent out the memo (March 2) and the date on which the meeting was held (March 12). Ten days was insufficient for any union to call a referendum on the issue or to elect representatives to attend the meeting. To protest what they perceived as an effort by Gompers to circumvent democratic procedures, five AFL unions refused to appoint delegates to attend the meeting. Most others, however, sent well-entrenched members of their national bureaucracies. Gompers carefully drafted the war statement, entitled "Labor's Position in Peace or War," to fit the temperament of these kinds of established union officials.[33]

"Labor's Position in Peace or War" declared that "whether we approve it or not, we must recognize that war is a situation with which we most reckon." The immediate problem, according to the report, was "to bring upon war conditions instructive forethought, visions and prin-

31. Gompers to Executive Council, 2/28/17: CC-GMC.

32. Ibid. See also Minutes, Conference of the Executive Council, 3/7/17: Con C-GMC.

33. Minutes, Conference of the Executive Council, 3/6/17, 18–31; and 3/7/17, 1–15. William Z. Foster, *History of the Communist Party in the United States* (New York: International Publishers, 1952), 132. E. G. Scott to Gompers, 3/8/17; John White to Gompers, n.d.: CC-GMC.

ciples of human welfare and conservation." It asked that in both peace and wartime the government ensure that union standards were observed, recognize the trade union movement as labor's representative, and grant labor equal representation on defense boards. Labor's "earnest hope" was "that our Republic may be safeguarded for peace." But "despite all our endeavors and hopes . . . should our Country be drawn into the European conflict, we with these ideals of liberty and justice herein declared as the indispensable basis for national policies offer our services to our country in every field of activity."[34]

Of the 168 delegates who attended the conference, only five publicly criticized the document. These delegates eventually withdrew their objections to the report, and it was endorsed unanimously.[35] One of the initial critics of the report later wrote Gompers complaining about the way the meeting was handled. "When I arrived there [at the conference]," wrote Daniel Tobin of the Teamsters, "I found you had a program already prepared: cut and dried to be adopted by the gathering of the so-called labor leaders and that we would not be allowed to change one word of that declaration." Tobin also claimed that officials at the meeting did not have authority from the rank and file of their unions to act on the proposition. But Tobin was the exception rather than the rule among national and international officials. Shortly after the special conference in Washington, a regular meeting of the AFL convention also overwhelmingly endorsed "Labor's Position in Peace or War."[36]

Much historical debate has raged over the support given by a very large majority of national and international union leaders to Gompers's war program. Noting the opposition of many trade union leaders to American involvement in the war prior to the Washington conference, some have emphasized the importance of Gompers's strong-arm tactics in forging unity on the issue of AFL support for the war effort. As Simeon Larson argues, "those who openly defied Gompers found that the entire machinery of the Federation was mobilized in an effort to defeat them."[37] Gompers wore down his opponents through smear campaigns that questioned their patriotism and often linked them to German sabotage. Since the AFL president controlled all appointments to convention committees, he also had the power to deny his opponents

34. AFL, "Report of the Executive Council," in *Labor and the War*, 64–68.
35. *Proceedings of the AFL*, 1918, 412. Duncan to Gompers, 3/17/17: CC-GMC.
36. Daniel Tobin to Gompers, 3/30/17, CC-GMC. *Proceedings of the AFL*, 1917, 318–19. Frey, Memoir, 2: 306. NR, 5/26/17, 38.
37. Larson, *Labor and Foreign Policy*, 45.

any real voice in shaping AFL policy. Moreover, by March 1917, it was clear that President Wilson would rely on Gompers in determining appointments to future war and industrial councils. Such considerations, suggest some historians, led most union leaders to accept passively the war program offered up at the Washington Trade Union Conference. Initial critics of Gompers's policies abandoned their opposition for similar reasons.[38]

But such accounts assume an excessive timidity among trade union leaders. Many opponents of the war, while disagreeing with Gompers about the morality and necessity of U.S. intervention in the conflict, nonetheless shared the AFL president's trade union philosophy and believed that his war program would serve the best interests of American labor. Although many still thought that U.S. intervention in the war was a mistake by the time of the March conference, few were willing to promote the militant forms of mass action that would have been necessary to prevent its occurrence by this late date. As Perkin has commented of their British counterparts, top union leaders by 1917 viewed themselves as an integral part of the industrial system and had a "professional interest" in seeing that it did not "drift too near the brink of disastrous confrontation."[39] To invite serious class discord on the war issue would have been suicidal because it might have opened the door to a revolution from below and would certainly have destroyed the fragile business-labor partnerships that many had devoted their lives to creating. By contrast, trade union leaders could advance the cause of industrial harmony by joining with Gompers and supporting the war effort. Even some former antiwar socialists like Sidney Hillman likely abstained from opposing Gompers's programs because they hoped to be strategically well placed to influence the evolving state-business-labor partnership. Thus, in supporting Gompers's war programs, many national and international union leaders were likely rendering a yes verdict for corporatist forms of power sharing.[40]

Following Wilson's declaration of war, Gompers solidified his support among national and international union leaders by expanding labor's role in war agencies and appointing key trade union representa-

38. Ibid., 25, 71–87, 146–56; Foner, History of the Labor Movement, 7: 106; Lorwin, Labor and Internationalism, 145–48.
39. Perkin, Rise of Professional Society, 174.
40. On socialists and IWW members and the war, see Foner, History of the Labor Movement, 7: 108–11. See Montgomery, Fall of the House of Labor, 422, on progressive unionists and their fear of revolution.

tives to fill new positions. The AFL president first created a system of subcommittees within the labor commission attached to the Council of National Defense. Labor, public, and business representatives were invited to serve on the committees in equal numbers. As Gompers readily admitted, "practically every international labor officer served on one of the councils."[41] Many of the business and public representatives, meanwhile, were drawn from Gompers's contacts within the National Civic Federation. The new committees drew up guidelines on wages and hours, welfare work, mediation and conciliation, industrial training, and the draft. One of the most controversial reports called for the maintenance of existing industrial standards during the war. Neither employees nor employers, it argued, should take advantage of the wartime situation to gain benefits for themselves at the expense of the other side. If changes in wages or working conditions were necessary, they should be arbitrated by the war boards and adjustment commissions. Vigorously supported by Gompers, the report failed to gain the endorsement of the AFL Executive Council. Gompers nonetheless worked privately to convince union leaders to avoid strikes and to submit their grievances to the labor commission or its subsidiary bodies for arbitration.[42]

But as Gompers expanded the system of labor subcommittees and tried to increase their functions within the Council of National Defense, power over actual wartime mobilization began to shift to newly created war councils like the War Industries Board, Air Craft Production Board, Food Administration, Fuel Administration, and Emergency Fleet Corporation. As originally planned, the Council of National Defense was to be the coordinating center of a vast system of state and local councils of defense charged with organizing war mobilization in their regions. But members of the council soon realized that economic organization needed to occur along lines of industrial function rather than geography and they mandated the creation of the new executive boards. The new boards proved remarkably efficient in achieving economic mobilization within particular industries and preempted many of the functions of the Council of National Defense.[43]

41. Gompers, *Seventy Years*, 2: 360–62. Gompers, Letters to Advisory Commission, 4/5/17; 4/13/17; Gompers to Walker, 6/1/17: LB-GMC.
42. W. Gifford to Gompers, 4/9/17; and Gompers to Daniel Tobin, 4/17/17: CC-GMC. Larson, *Labor and Foreign Policy*, 77–89; Montgomery, "New Tendencies," 92; NR, 6/16/17, 172.
43. Kennedy, *Over Here*, 93–143; David Noble, *America by Design: Science, Technology, and the Rise of Corporate Capitalism* (New York: Alfred Knopf, 1979), 150, 207–98.

To avoid being isolated in an increasingly obsolete agency, Gompers became more directly involved in negotiating industrywide agreements between trade unions and prominent corporations. In summer 1917, Gompers negotiated an agreement with Secretary of War Newton Baker for the construction of cantonments. The AFL president was not given authority by the building trades to act on their behalf, but he claimed a role as a member of the Council of National Defense. The agreement called for the establishment of an adjustment commission that was to include one army representative, one public representative, and one labor representative appointed by Gompers. Wages were to be determined by the union scale in force in each locality, with due consideration to increased costs of living. Controversy arose over the issue of "open," nonunionized shops. According to some, Gompers agreed orally to accept open shops wherever they already existed but then changed his mind after a popular backlash. Whatever the case, Gompers later refused to confirm the agreement. The document nonetheless became the framework shaping the construction of cantonments and was used as a model for a number of other such agreements. These contracts gave Gompers immense power, for in many cases he appointed the labor representatives to adjustment commissions.[44]

Gompers and the labor commission also formulated plans for a National Labor Adjustment Committee. The Council of National Defense acted on the labor commission's plans in January 1918 and created the National War Labor Conference Board, which in April reconstituted itself as the National War Labor Board (NWLB).[45] The new body consisted of five labor representatives appointed by Gompers, five employee representatives, and two public representatives. It was designed both to coordinate the efforts of industrywide adjustment commissions and to resolve intractable disputes appealed to it. The board had no powers of coercion and thus became a testing ground for the principles of voluntary mediation, revealing both their strengths and weaknesses. At first the board scored some successes, due largely to its two charismatic public representatives, the fiery labor lawyer Frank Walsh and former president William Howard Taft. Both had previously worked for the Commission on Industrial Relations and played an

44. Foner, *History of the Labor Movement*, 7: 167; Montgomery, *Fall of the House of Labor*, 375; Gompers, *Seventy Years*, 2: 373; NR, 9/15/17, 176; Nockels to Walsh, 8/11/17: WP; Montgomery, "New Tendencies," 92–93.

45. Gompers, *Seventy Years*, 2: 367; Montgomery, *Fall of the House of Labor*, 374; Foner, *History of the Labor Movement*, 7: 173.

important role in encouraging compromise between business and labor representatives on the NWLB. As one observer commented, "there never was a team of vaudevillians who did their act more in harmony than Taft and Walsh in conducting the affairs of the War Labor Board."[46] The two became particularly famous for resolving disputes at Bethlehem Steel and General Electric, where they "painstakingly translated the right to bargain collectively from principle to practice."[47]

Yet the limits of the board soon became obvious. Labor and business board members clashed frequently because of their incompatible goals. Walsh and the labor representatives, according to Valerie Conner, sought to use the NWLB as a "clarion call to reform" and to "lead other adjustment agencies and the public at large toward permanent higher standards." By contrast, the employers viewed the board as an "instrument established to maintain the status quo."[48] Complicating this internecine strife was the board's lack of enforcement powers. Thus, by mid-1918, both employees and trade unions were evading the board's edicts. Much disillusioned, Walsh resigned from the board at the end of the war, arguing that as then constituted "it could not be anything but a disappointing mirage to the working people of the country."[49]

Gompers's faith in corporatist forms of power sharing, by contrast, seemed to grow as the war progressed. In early 1918, he proposed to "democratize" all cabinets within the executive branch by creating advisory adjuncts to their main offices, modeled on the war boards. Gompers also laid plans for a permanent system of adjustment commissions in industry.[50] Of most immediate significance, the AFL president moved to formalize a business-labor-state partnership in foreign affairs. Committed since 1916 to trade union participation on the peace commissions, Gompers's appetite for diplomatic power was further whetted by Wilson's use of labor representatives on diplomatic missions during

46. Conner, *National War Labor Board*, 185.
47. Ibid., 108–9.
48. Ibid., 50. Walsh speech, n.d., B4; Resolution of the NWLB, 11/20/18, B7; Victor Olander to Walsh, 11/25/18, B7: WP.
49. Walker to Olander, 12/4/18; Employers Association to Members, 11/28/18, B7: WP. Conner, *National War Labor Board*, 126–41. Walsh, in contrast to Gompers, also resigned from the American Alliance for Labor and Democracy (AALD) at war's end. See Gompers to Walsh, 12/31/18, B7; Walsh to Basil Manley, 12/20/18, B7:WP. For the growing disillusionment of liberals with war boards, see NR, 6/16/17, 172; 7/7/17, 263–64; 9/15/17, 176.
50. Mr. Clarkson to Gompers, 3/28/18; Gompers to Wilson, 11/37 [sic 27?]/18; W. B. Wilson to Clarkson, 3/26/18; Gompers general letter, 11/5/19; Gompers to Walker, 7/1/17: CC-GMC. Gompers to Fitzpatrick, 3/29/18, B6–F46: FP. Gompers, *Seventy Years*, 2: 523.

the war. Of particular importance, Wilson appointed AFL vice-president James Duncan to serve on the Root Commission, an emissarial council whose major purpose was to encourage Russia to stay in the war. While traveling through the revolution-racked country, Duncan sent glowing reports back to the AFL praising the commission's work and boasting of his role in steeling the determination of Russian workers to continue fighting.[51]

Labor's apparently successful diplomatic debut on the Root Commission reaffirmed Gompers's belief that after the armistice labor would play a key role in the shaping of American foreign policy. Following the return of the Root Commission, Gompers campaigned more vigorously for labor participation on the peace commissions, arguing that organized labor saw no reason why the government should stray from its well-established policy of "recognizing the constructive and representative character of the American Labor Movement." Many, according to Gompers, assumed "as a matter of course" that he would be named to the American Peace Commission.[52]

But the AFL leader feared his international initiatives might be threatened by renewed British and European interest in a labor-negotiated peace settlement. In the forefront of the movement was British Labour party leader Arthur Henderson. Initially an avid supporter of the war effort, Henderson journeyed to Russia at the British government's behest in June 1917 and became convinced that the country was in imminent danger of withdrawing from the war. Upon his return, Henderson endorsed plans for a meeting of all belligerent labor and socialist parties to negotiate an end to the war.

The British labor leader's support for an interbelligerent labor meeting was propelled both by a desire to bolster Russian morale and to buoy his own sagging political fortunes. Henderson hoped that by promoting the labor meeting, he would convince Russian political leaders that the Allies were bargaining in good faith to bring an end to the war. Such a gesture might help to keep the Kerensky government in the war until a peace could be negotiated. Henderson also sought to quiet growing opposition to his collaborationist foreign policies at home. In particular, Henderson's unequivocal support for the war effort had incurred wrath from a powerful shop steward movement with roots in the militant Clydeside region of Scotland. The new movement took inspiration

51. *Proceedings of the AFL,* 1917, 322–47.
52. Gompers, *Seventy Years,* 2: 476.

from the Russian revolution and from Irish syndicalism. It objected to the growing business-state-labor partnership, arguing that the independence of trade union and Labour party officials was being undermined. The movement's leaders were particularly incensed when Henderson promoted a government initiative to impose conscription. They subsequently pledged to support the trade union leadership "just as long as they rightly represent the workers," but to "act independently immediately [as] they misrepresent us."[53] To Henderson prolonged warfare thus invited the specter of revolution at home as well as abroad.

Although Henderson's new policies were designed more to quell than fan the flames of class discord, they outraged British cabinet members who looked with horror on a labor-negotiated peace. Prime Minister David Lloyd George officially rebuked Henderson for traveling to Paris to make arrangements for the labor and socialist conference, thereby provoking Henderson's resignation. Relieved of governmental responsibilities, the British labor leader devoted himself full-time to developing a viable labor alternative to the government's foreign policy and to building labor's political strength. Henderson worked with longtime war opponent James Ramsey MacDonald and with economic theorists Sidney and Beatrice Webb to formulate a labor statement on war aims which unequivocally endorsed the League of Nations, called for an international trusteeship of African colonies, and demanded international action to achieve a fair distribution of the world's raw materials.[54]

The foursome also continued to lobby vigorously on behalf of the international socialist and labor conference. Apart from their stated purpose of negotiating an end to the war, European labor leaders hoped to rekindle the spirit of international labor solidarity that had been destroyed in 1914. According to leading dissidents like MacDonald, an international league of state leaders would not by itself ensure peace because it was just such leaders who had provoked the current war. Only "corporate action of the workers of Europe" would ensure future international security and justice. The future prime minister argued that an "organization of international democracy" was needed that would "control the action of the various nations so that the official diplomacy,

53. Perkin, *Rise of Professional Society*, 197–98, 193–99; Hinton, *First Shop Stewards' Movement*; Leventhal, *Arthur Henderson*, 80–92; Pelling, *Labour Party*, 42–44; Marwick, *Deluge*, 16–17.

54. Pelling, *Labour Party*, 42–43; Hinton, *Labour and Socialism*, 100–101; MacDonald, *National Defence*; Henderson, *League of Nations and Labor*; Dawse, "The Independent Labour Party," 35–46.

if disruptive and aggressive, will be deprived of its backing from public opinion."[55]

Gompers, by contrast, vigorously opposed the forms of labor action promoted by MacDonald because war had taught him that "one had to be an effective nationalist before one could be an effective internationalist." The AFL president argued that German governmental leaders were behind the initiative for a labor-negotiated peace because an early settlement would leave them in control of occupied territories. Denouncing the notion that class solidarity must take precedence over patriotic commitments, the AFL president argued that "we did not feel that we had to connive with wage earners of other countries to forge a club against our own republic."[56]

The proposed conference thus laid bare more than a difference in wartime tactics: It suggested that Gompers's agenda for diplomatic reform was fundamentally at odds with that of European labor leaders. For Gompers, a democratic diplomacy meant labor participation in equal numbers with business and state leaders on government councils and in international organizations. British and European labor leaders, by contrast, had moved away from a corporatist-oriented diplomacy by 1917 and sought to make labor an international force in its own right. These differing attitudes toward labor's proper diplomatic role provoked a bitter clash between the truculent American labor leader and his British counterparts.

Although Gompers publicly opposed the Stockholm meeting throughout the autumn of 1917, the first sign of a serious split between British and American labor leaders came in the wake of the Interallied Labor Conference of February 1918. The AFL failed to send delegates, claiming that the invitation had arrived too late. Shortly thereafter, however, Gompers sent a five-man mission to Britain, prompting the liberal media to speculate that Gompers was trying to mend fences over Stockholm.[57] But the mission was actually constituted in response to a request by Lloyd George, who hoped to use AFL representatives to dissuade British Labour party and trade union leaders from proceeding with the interbelligerent conference. As mission member John Frey later admitted,

---

55. MacDonald, *National Defence*, 15–17. See Hinton, *Labour and Socialism*, 100–101, for the importance of rhetoric regarding a "democratic diplomacy" to European and British trade unionists.

56. Gompers, *Seventy Years*, 2: 405.

57. Ibid., 2: 403–4. *NR*, 5/25/18, 96–97; 3/23/18, 218–19; 3/2/18, 126–27, 226; 6/15/18, 193.

"Lloyd George intended to use us for propaganda purposes in every way that was legitimate."[58] The U.S. labor group soon gained a reputation for arrogance and intransigence, with one observer commenting that its members behaved "as if their mission was to convince the misguided foreigners how wrong it is to differ with Americans."[59]

Not surprisingly, the group made little headway in convincing British labor leaders to abandon the Stockholm conference and Gompers soon determined to lead personally a second American delegation to Britain. The highlight of Gompers's trip came in September 1918, when another Interallied Labor Conference was held. Determined to prevent the conference from endorsing a Stockholm meeting, Gompers maneuvered to ensure that AFL trade unionist John Frey was appointed to the War Aims Committee. As Frey later reminisced, Gompers urged him to remain unbending in his opposition to the interbelligerent meeting, advising him that "when you get into the committee start the fight from the drop of a hat. Don't call a spade a spade. Call it a son-of-a-bitch. Fuck them."[60]

Frey's efforts helped ensure that the committee accepted most of American labor's war aims, but they still endorsed plans for an interbelligerent conference. Gompers subsequently entered the fray, battling against the interbelligerent conference on the floor of the convention. Whether the committee actually withdrew the provision for a conference is uncertain, but Gompers succeeded in amending to the report a statement that the Allied labor movements pledged to assist their governments in winning the war until such time as the Central Powers withdrew from occupied territories and were no longer a military menace. European trade unionists would later accuse the AFL of running a "steam roller" over the conference.[61]

Gompers's and Frey's strong-arm tactics temporarily threw the forces promoting an international labor conference into disarray, preventing any renewed action before the armistice was signed in November. Yet the two AFL leaders ultimately failed to quell the spirit of labor interna-

58. Frey, *Reminiscences*, 2: 326–27; Gompers, *Seventy Years*, 2: 408–9.
59. NR, 5/25/18, 96–97; 6/15/18, 191.
60. Frey, *Reminiscences*, 2: 362–64. Gompers, *Seventy Years*, 2: 414–45; NR, 9/28/18, 240.
61. Gompers, *Seventy Years*, 2: 434–35. For more information on the labor missions and interallied conferences, see *American Federationist* 25 (1918): 294. *Proceedings of the AFL*, 1918, 54, 142–51, 334; 1919, 25, 263–67. AFL, *Labor and the War*, 2, 81–90. Report on the Labor Mission from W. T. Buckler to Gompers, 10/29/18: CC-GMC. Radosh, *American Labor and United States Foreign Policy*, 150–55.

tionalism that was gathering momentum throughout Europe. Thus when the peace conference commenced in January 1919, Gompers would find himself isolated from the great body of the European trade union movement. Gompers's international initiatives would also be undercut by a growing rebellion among local labor councils.

The AFL president first antagonized local militants by failing to invite them to the Washington Trade Union Conference. In the wake of the conference, dozens of angry local activists complained bitterly about the undemocratic way in which the affair was handled. "I am directed by this lodge in regular meeting assembled," wrote E. J. Bicket of I.A.M. Lodge 379, "to say to you that you did *not* speak for the members of this lodge when you assured President Wilson that organized labor was with him in any action he might take in the present German-American difficulty." Another worker questioned indignantly, "I would like to ask you 'et tu Brutus?' . . . With what right do you recommend to the poor wage earners to shed their blood?" In response to a claim made by Gompers and other AFL officials that to be disloyal in wartime was analogous to being a scab in a strike, one local labor leader wrote that the comparison was a false one because "in a strike the membership was at least given a chance to vote." The man claimed that the decision to declare war in the United States was made in as undemocratic a fashion as Germany had declared war against Belgium and France.[62] Several other workers, more puzzled than angry, simply inquired of the AFL Executive Council how their national and international unions could have voted to support "Labor's Position in Peace or War" when they had not yet solicited the opinion of constituent locals.[63]

In Chicago, city federated leaders at first chose to ignore "Labor's Position in Peace or War," instead sending a telegram directly to the president two weeks after the conference informing him that:

> The common people do not want war. We believe they will vote against war if given the opportunity—the trust owned press to the contrary not withstanding. The strong defense policy along the line of armed neutrality already laid down offers every protection that could be obtained through a declaration of war. . . . If we refuse to be guarantors to the aims of belligerents or war bonds held by American bankers, we believe peace nego-

62. E. J. Bicket, IAM Lodge 379, to Gompers, 3/14/17; Jim Rothberg, Wage Earner, to Gompers, 3/14/17: CC-GMC. Ostho Herman to John Fitzpatrick, 10/11/17, B6–F42: FP.

63. See, for example, St. Paul Lodge 112 to Gompers, 3/20/17; Thomas McGowan, Division 118 AASERE of Pottsville, Pennsylvania, to Gompers, 3/15/17: CC-GMC.

> tiations will come before July. No nation that allows itself to be driven into War by the reactionary elements is acting along the line of real courage.[64]

But while CFL officials preferred to ignore the AFL statement on the war, representatives from local trade unions continued to file into the weekly meetings demanding to know who had authorized the Washington Trade Union Conference and whether the CFL supported its decision. In response, the CFL had its Executive Council investigate both its own record on the war and the records of the Washington Trade Union Conference.[65] On April 15, two weeks after the U.S. declaration of war, the council reaffirmed that it was on record as opposing the war but deferred further action until locals could confer with their internationals about their positions on the European conflict.[66] After stalling on the issue for yet another month, the CFL Executive Council finally advised its membership to endorse "Labor's Position in Peace or War."[67]

But the council's report suggested that officials endorsed the document for pragmatic reasons and continued to have misgivings about its content. The authors of the CFL report argued that "some criticism of Labor's position as enunciated might have been made inasmuch as it was in recognition of war in place of a protest against war and that a demand for peace should have been made." But they argued that nothing could be found in "Labor's Position in Peace or War" that would be "detrimental" to the current interests of organized labor. The council thus recommended that CFL members endorse the statement by voting in favor of its report.[68]

In a vigorous debate that followed, no executive board member defended the CFL report on the grounds that the AFL had taken a correct moral position on the war. Some board members recommended accepting the CFL report because most other central bodies that considered opposing AFL policy on the war had decided against pursuing the issue; if the CFL chose to oppose the AFL's position, it would be without partners. Victor Olander, secretary of the Illinois State Federation of Labor, argued in defense of the report on the grounds that it "would

64. *CFL Minutes*, 4/15/17, 4–5.
65. Ibid., 4/1/17, 23–44.
66. Ibid., 4/15/17, 4–5.
67. Ibid., 5/20/17, 14–15.
68. Ibid., 5/20/17, 14–15.

serve to keep this central body and the organized labor movement of this community in the proper light before the citizens of this city, state and nation." John Fitzpatrick, when pressed for his views, said that he would support the report but offered no explanation for his decision. Later, Fitzpatrick rationalized his vote by using Gompers's analogy of a scab during a strike. According to Fitzpatrick, it was both unethical and unwise to scab on a nation during wartime regardless of whether one supported the original goals of the war or not. The CFL finally voted 140 to 59 to endorse "Labor's Position in Peace or War."[69]

Events in Chicago illuminated the dilemmas faced by previously anti-war city federateds in the wake of the Washington conference. Denied a voice in the conference, city federated leaders could do nothing to prevent it from unanimously endorsing "Labor's Position in Peace or War." And once the overwhelming majority of national and international unions officially pledged their loyalty to any future American war effort, continued opposition to American involvement in the war by local labor groups seemed increasingly futile. Had more time lapsed between the conference and American intervention in the war, city labor councils might have been able to regroup and launch a new antiwar offensive. But with war following quickly on the heels of the conference, city labor leaders faced the undesirable choice of "pulling in harness" with the rest of the AFL or incurring its wrath and persecution. In a show of independence, the CFL delayed endorsing "Labor's Position in Peace or War" for a full two months. Ultimately, however, the pragmatic majority within the organization abandoned their opposition to the war because they believed it would serve no purpose but seriously to weaken the local labor movement. The strong antiwar city labor councils in New York, Seattle, and San Francisco followed a similar pattern.[70]

Official support for the war effort, however, did not necessarily translate into approval for the evolving corporatist order in Washington. In spring 1917, the Chicago Federation of Labor launched an attack on the adjustment commissions created by Gompers. Ed Nockels, secretary of the CFL, best summarized the objections of local activists to the commissions in a telegram he sent to Gompers. "Great many representatives of labor unions here," he cabled, "express themselves as fearful of the creation of the labor adjustment commissions claiming that the three to be appointed for the government would give the employeers [sic] a

69. Ibid., 5/20/17, 17–20; 10/7/17, 22–25.
70. See Frank, "At the Point of Consumption," 62–63; Kazin, Barons of Labor, 240–44; Foner, History of the Labor Movement, 7: 107–8.

decided advantage and be used to destroy and obstruct organized labor."[71]

Nockels's telegram exposed a major ideological chasm that had opened between local union leaders and AFL officials. Gompers and other AFL leaders presumed that government officials on war boards and commissions would ordinarily support labor demands. These beliefs were a product of their favorable experiences with the Wilson administration both before and during the war. By contrast, many local leaders argued that government officials would more frequently promote business interests. Far removed from the nation's political power centers, municipal labor leaders experienced little of the wartime euphoria felt by national and international union officials who traversed Washington corridors for the first time during 1917. Local leaders were instead preoccupied during the early months of the war with the spiraling inflation that sapped the paychecks of rank-and-file workers and provoked continuous grumbling at city labor meetings. Likewise, they were mired deep in local feuds over food and coal shortages. To such leaders, Wilson's advisers seemed as much the puppets of prominent capitalists as had officials from the Taft administration. By entrusting the fate of America's workers to these men, they suggested, AFL leaders were dooming any chance for labor advancement during the war.[72]

The views of local labor men like Nockels were reinforced when Gompers submitted his report to the Council of National Defense calling for the maintenance of existing labor standards. Local labor leaders throughout the country widely attacked the report as a no-strike order. Lacking Gompers's faith in the war boards, they suggested that if the trade union movement could not resort to strike activity, then it would be unable to assure that workers' wages kept up with inflation. They also argued that the war situation would be an ideal time to press for the eight-hour day but that Gompers's proclamation forced labor to give up its most effective tool for assuring this victory.[73] Still others criticized

71. Telegram from Ed Nockels to Gompers, 8/10/17: CC-GMC. See also Herbert Merrill, Schenectady Trades Association, to Gompers, 4/9/17; Telegram from Gompers to Merrill, 4/10/17; R. Ham, Electrical Workers 262, to Sam Gompers, n.d.; and June–July 1917 correspondence: CC-GMC. Maurer, *It Can be Done*, 246–56; Shapiro, "'Hand and Brain,'" 405–22.

72. For an example of local attitudes, see Note 71 and Fitzpatrick to Gompers, 12/4/17; Gompers to Fitzpatrick, 12/7/17: CC-GMC. See also Frank, "At the Point of Consumption," 62–68; Kazin, *Barons of Labor*, 234–75.

73. For interpretations of the report as a no-strike order see, June–July correspondence in CC-GMC, especially Herbert Merrill, Schenectady Trades Association, to

Gompers's report because they feared it would keep labor from using wartime to unionize workers in major industries such as steel and the packing industry. In a typically sarcastic letter, John Fitzpatrick wrote Gompers asking for a copy of his statements about "preserving the status quo" so that he would know whether he had AFL approval for organizing packing-house workers.[74]

The complaints from city federated leaders and local activists became so voluminous that in summer 1917 Gompers began to devise new plans to encourage greater labor loyalty. Initially uninterested in the programs of those who sought to create local and state institutions modeled on the National Council of Defense, Gompers now determined that these bodies might be helpful to him in winning the support of labor dissidents. Too busy to assist in the formation of these programs himself, Gompers enlisted the aid of trusted state labor leaders. These men helped state and municipal defense council executives win the support of key local leaders. Likewise, they developed local programs for inspiring rank-and-file patriotism.[75] Gompers further tried to promote labor loyalty in 1917 by launching a special labor propaganda agency known as the American Alliance for Labor and Democracy (AALD). The AALD, funded in part by George Creel's Committee on Public Information, sought to assist its benefactor in "Americanizing" the working class. To achieve this goal, it conducted patriotic campaigns and also sabotaged the activities of socialist and ethnic groups.[76]

The success of Gompers's plans to win labor loyalty at local levels can be gauged by a careful look at the response of Chicago workers to Gompers's campaigns in Illinois. Gompers relied on two principal men in Illinois to implement a statewide system of corporatism and bring labor leaders into this system: Illinois Federation of Labor President John Walker and his secretary, Victor Olander. Early in the war,

---

Gompers, 4/9/17; Telegram from Gompers to Merrill, 4/10/17; R. Ham, Electrical Workers 262, to Sam Gompers, n.d.: CC-GMC. See also Foner, *History of the Labor Movement*, 7: 165. For fears about the influence that the report would have on the eight-hour day, see Gompers to Maisel, 4/10/18; and Gompers to Fitzpatrick, 12/7/17: CC-GMC. On dissenting attitudes toward Gompers's wartime activities in Pennsylvania, San Francisco, and Seattle, see Maurer, *It Can Be Done*, 248–56; Kazin, *Barons of Labor*, 234–69; Frank, "At the Point of Consumption," 62–68. ·

74. Fitzpatrick to Gompers, 12/4/17; Gompers to Fitzpatrick, 12/7/17: CC-GMC.

75. Gompers to Walker, 5/25/17; Gompers to Walker, 7/1/17: CC-GMC. Gompers to Fitzpatrick, 3/29/18, B6–F46: FP.

76. See, particularly, George Creel to Gompers, 7/26/17; Maisel Report to Gompers, 10/6/17, 1–11; AALD Fliers, 1/4/18: CC-GMC. Shannon, *Socialist Party of America*.

Gompers cultivated Walker's support by offering him a position on one of the national labor subcommittees. Shortly thereafter, Gompers also asked Walker to serve on the labor mission to Great Britain and assigned Olander to a post on a mediation commission. In 1918, Gompers solicited Walker's and Olander's aid in a campaign to establish a labor committee subsidiary to the Illinois State Council of Defense.[77]

Chaired by the utilities mogul and organizational genius Samuel Insull, the Illinois council was one of the most dynamic of its kind. Following the lead of the national council, Insull created a central coordinating commission that included Illinois's most prominent businessmen, politicians, and labor officials. Walker and Olander failed to convince Insull to establish a replica of the national labor subcommittee, but he did appoint the two to several commissions designed to investigate specific problems in the state's industries. One such commission uncovered evidence of the extensive importation of black strikebreakers by businessmen in southern Illinois. The commission blamed the businessmen for fomenting a race riot in East Saint Louis and subsequently the Illinois Defense Council began to monitor immigration into the area. Another commission reported extensively on profiteering in the local coal industry and requested that a federal commission be created to investigate the industry. Partly in response to their request, the Wilson administration created the Fuel Administration.[78]

But Insull's concern was not primarily with economic coordination, which lay mostly in the hands of national war boards and industry-wide commissions, but with fund-raising and propaganda. These functions were partly entrusted to adjunctory committees that reported directly to the central coordinating commission and organized activities like the selling of patriotic cookbooks, the staging of allied bazaars and movie expositions, and the establishment of Americanization programs for immigrants. Yet these committees primarily oversaw rather than imple-

77. Gompers to Walker, 5/25/17; Walker to Gompers, 2/23/18; Gompers to Walker, 6/1/17: CC-GMC. For Walker's personal views on the war, see Ed Wieck to Walker, 5/21/17, 40:16; Walker to Wieck, 6/6/17, 42:6; Walker to Germer, 11/23/17, 48:6A; Walker to Germer, 11/13/17, 48:6: John Walker Papers (Wal P), Illinois Historical Survey Library, University of Illinois, Urbana-Champaign. Walker's positive attitudes toward the war boards are apparent in ISFL Proceedings, 1918, 29. On Olander, see Conner, National War Labor Board, 28, 96. Walsh to Olander, 12/4/18, B7; Walsh to Walker, 6/23/24, B13: WP.

78. Illinois State Council of Defense (ISCD) Letterbook, 90–91, 111–15, B74; ISCD Recordbook, 340, 456, B75; Samuel Insull, Memoirs, 12, B17: Samuel Insull Papers (IP), Loyola University Library, Chicago. ISFL Proceedings, 1917, 46. Forrest McDonald, Insull (Chicago: University of Chicago Press, 1962), 172.

mented patriotic campaigns. Insull's real bureaucratic innovation, suggests his biographer, Forrest McDonald, was not in creating the "mountaintop" but in building a "mountain under it." To assure that patriotic campaigns were supported within individual localities, Insull formed a separate division whose duty it was to recreate the "central organization" of the state council "in miniature in almost every neighborhood, in every community in the state."[79]

Harold Ickes, future advisor to President Franklin Roosevelt, was appointed to lead the new division. Although Insull disliked him, Ickes proved adept at organizing neighborhood defense councils. Under his guidance, over 1,079 committees with a membership of at least eight thousand were established.[80] Not surprisingly, Ickes was particularly concerned with establishing councils in the turbulent multiethnic neighborhoods of Chicago. On Walker's advice, Ickes solicited the aid of John Fitzpatrick in his Chicago campaigns. Ickes urged Fitzpatrick to help him form neighborhood committees because "the end will come earlier or later just in the proportion that the patriotic intelligence of this country understands the issues of the war." Ickes advised CFL leaders to organize councils around local schools, churches, and the courthouses. As mandated by the state defense board, representatives to the neighborhood councils were to come from a variety of classes. The neighborhood bodies were to sponsor weekly assemblies that would be modeled on the old New England town meeting. But Ickes cautioned that "academic discussions as to whether or not the country should be at war would not be helpful at the present time." Instead, the assemblies would publicize Herbert Hoover's food relief programs in Europe and promote the Liberty Loan Campaign and state fund-raising activities.[81] Like Insull, Ickes hoped to create a state war administration that operated like a smooth-functioning corporation, carefully regulating worker input in a manner the board of directors found constructive.

Ickes appeared to be successful in soliciting Fitzpatrick's aid, for the CFL president not only assisted him in forming neighborhood committees but also spoke at mass meetings of the Neighborhood Defense Campaign. Fitzpatrick additionally recruited a number of socialists and

79. McDonald, *Insull*, 109. ISCD Letterbook, 11, B74; ISCD Recordbook, 230–44, 301, 441–47, 450–57, B75: IP.

80. McDonald, *Insull*, 171. ISCD Recordbook, 441–47, B75: IP. State Council of Defense Chart, n.d. circa 1917, B6–F41: FP.

81. Harold Ickes to Fitzpatrick, 9/21/17, B6–F41: FP. ISCD Letterbook, 111, B74; ISCD Reportbook, 441–47, B75: IP.

radicals to work for Ickes. Even more surprisingly, Fitzpatrick accepted positions on the Liberty Loan Committee, the District Exemption Board, and the Citizen's War Board.[82] Indeed, such a stalwart of labor patriotism and prudence did Fitzpatrick seem to become that even conservative, business-dominated groups such as the National Patriotic League and the National Security League asked him to speak at meetings.[83]

Yet, a closer look at Fitzpatrick's wartime activities suggests that he was extremely selective about the patriotic campaigns in which he participated. Fitzpatrick, for example, failed to support the AFL campaign to destroy the socialist People's Council because he believed that this group was entitled to free speech. Despite the disapproval of Victor Olander, secretary of the Illinois State Federation of Labor, Fitzpatrick allowed People's Council representatives to speak at CFL meetings. When the governor banned a People's Council meeting, Fitzpatrick sent a letter of protest.[84] Worries about free speech additionally led Fitzpatrick to criticize government and AFL interference with radical and ethnic newspapers in Illinois and to renew the CFL's campaign for public ownership of the press.[85]

Interestingly, Fitzpatrick also showed his independence by stalling on an order from AFL officials to form a branch of the AALD in Chicago. In a CFL debate, Fitzpatrick initially supported formation of a local chapter.[86] After seeing the AALD in action, however, Fitzpatrick became concerned about its repressive and covert activities. Fitzpatrick subsequently ignored all correspondence coming from AALD headquarters in New York, provoking an angry reaction by AALD president Robert Maisel who demanded to know how plans for the local branch were coming.[87] In response, Fitzpatrick finally admitted that he had taken no steps to launch an AALD organization in the area. But he vigorously defended his procrastination, arguing that AALD officials had not suffi-

82. State Council of Defense to Fitzpatrick, 8/31/17, B6–F41; Harold Ickes to Fitzpatrick, 10/12/17, B6–F42; L. Meyers to Fitzpatrick, 3/29/18, B6–F46; G. Thompson to Fitzpatrick, 3/22/18, B6–F46; E. Cliffort to Fitzpatrick, 6/11/17, B6–F41; Telegram from L. T. McArthur to Fitzpatrick, 10/25/17, B6–F42: FP. See also Cyrus McCormick to Gompers, 8/3/17: CC-GMC.
83. See, for example, Florence King to Fitzpatrick, 7/30/17, B5; and Mr. Byllesby to Fitzpatrick, 9/13/17, B6: FP.
84. CFL Minutes, 9/2/17, 8–12.
85. Letter from George Edmund Ross to Fitzpatrick, 4/3/18, B6–F47: FP.
86. CFL Minutes, 10/7/17, 22–25; and Fitzpatrick to Gompers 8/31/17: CC-GMC.
87. See, especially, Gompers to Perkins, 4/2/18: CC-GMC. Letter from Herman Robinson to Fitzpatrick, 10/9/19, B6–F42: FP.

ciently answered his questions about the organization's covert activities. A bitter correspondence ensued, but Fitzpatrick refused to yield in his opposition to the AALD and officials eventually abandoned their attempts to create a Chicago branch.[88]

In defiance of the national industrial truce, Fitzpatrick and other CFL officials also continued to encourage strikes and to launch new organizing campaigns. When accused of disloyalty, they noted their impressive record of war work and claimed that it was businessmen who behaved in an unpatriotic fashion by trying to cheat their workers.[89] The most significant initiative undertaken by the CFL during the war was an organizing campaign in the stockyards where Fitzpatrick had labored as a boy.

Unionization campaigns in the local packing houses had made little headway since an unsuccessful strike in 1904 and 1905. But war brought shortages of labor and rekindled militance among the industry's workers. Activists associated with the CFL responded by creating the Stock Yards Labor Council, an innovative body that included representatives from a variety of local trade unions. By the end of 1917, the council had unionized between one-quarter and one-half of all employees in the area's stockyards. When the "big five" packers in the area refused to negotiate with the council, it responded by threatening a strike. The Wilson administration intervened, sending a federal mediation team led by Judge Samuel B. Alschuler to arbitrate the dispute. In March 1918, Alschuler granted what one council member described as "85 percent of the union's demands," including an eight-hour day, overtime pay, and enforced lunch breaks.[90]

Fitzpatrick was initially euphoric over the commission's decision, telling a meeting of stockyard workers, "It's a new day and out in God's sunshine you men and women, black and white, have not only an eight-

88. Gompers to Perkins, 4/2/18; Director, AALD, to Fitzpatrick, 4/11/18: CC-GMC. Maisel to Fitzpatrick, 4/11/18, B6–F47: FP. Fitzpatrick to Maisel, n.d. circa 1918: CC-GMC. See also *CFL Minutes*, June–August, 1917. So desperate did AALD leaders become that they even tried to solicit Frank Walsh's help in encouraging the CFL to form a local branch. Walsh was a good friend of Fitzpatrick. No record exists of whether Walsh tried to use his influence to sway CFL leaders. See Wright to Walsh, 8/30/17, B5; Gompers to Walsh, 12/2/18, B7: WP.

89. See, especially, *CFL Minutes*, 4/21/18, 22; 9/1/18.

90. Foner, *History of the Labor Movement*, 7: 236, 234–37; Fitzpatrick to Gompers, 4/17/17, 12/7/17, 12/9/17, 12/25/17: CC-GMC. *CFL Minutes*, 2/3/18, 6; Barrett, *Work and Community in the Jungle*, 191–202; Montgomery, "Unity and Fragmentation," 233–40; Brody, *Butcher Workmen*, 81–83, 75–127; Montgomery, *Fall of the House of Labor*, 383.

hour day but you are on an equality."[91] In a CFL meeting, Fitzpatrick claimed that seven key labor demands had been met by Alschuler's presidential commission. When some members criticized AFL policies surrounding the strike, Fitzpatrick argued that Gompers and other AFL leaders had rendered every possible assistance. For a short period thereafter, Fitzpatrick made a point of praising the system of war boards and arbitration commissions.[92]

But the cynicism of CFL leaders soon returned. Wartime inflation quickly negated wage increases in the stockyards. Alschuler responded slowly to the new problems: only in November 1919 did the presidential commission finally grant a new wage increase to packing-house workers. The commission refused even to consider labor demands for a forty-four-hour week, the abolition of piece rates, and double pay for overtime during 1918 and 1919. Perhaps most important, union officials realized, in the words of Jim Barrett, that "arbitration not only gave authority and legitimacy to the union, but also took away the right to strike and drew union officials into the effort to discipline workers and maintain production."[93] Such authoritarian roles ill-befitted promoters of union democracy like John Fitzpatrick and Ed Nockels.

Disillusionment with the war boards and government arbitration systems intensified when the National Labor Board rendered judgments in several other area disputes that local unions widely perceived as more favorable to business than labor interests. In October 1918, a member from the local machinist factory reported that he had personally lost confidence in the arbitration councils and did not know of "a better method for killing off a strike" than to refer a dispute to the National War Labor Board for settlement. Fitzpatrick concurred, commenting that "just as the boys of the tank corps motto is 'treat them rough,' I say it is our duty to treat the National War Labor Board rough. . . . The Board is not composed of supporters of labor but of labor baiters and labor crushers." Fitzpatrick's attitudes were probably reinforced by the increasing disillusionment of his good friend Frank Walsh with the work of his own board.[94]

As CFL leaders grew increasingly skeptical of the domestic utility of war boards, they also came to doubt that these boards could guarantee

---

91. Barrett, *Work and Community in the Jungle*, 200.
92. See, especially, *CFL Minutes*, 4/7/18, 15–16; 8/4/18.
93. Barrett, *Work and Community in the Jungle*, 200–201.
94. *CFL Minutes*, 11/3/18, 22; 12/15/18, 6–9. Walsh to Olander, 11/20/18, B7; Walsh to Fitzpatrick, 11/19/18, B7: WP.

labor significant input on foreign policy issues. For many, Irish independence was the litmus test of Gompers's programs for using war boards
to democratize diplomacy. In May 1917, the CFL passed a resolution
requesting that the U.S. government demand that the British government grant to "the Irish nation full and complete independence." The
CFL further asked that these demands be made a part of "any and all
agreements and that Ireland be named with Belgium and other small
nations in the demand for protection and freedom." The AFL convention, however, failed to act on the Irish issue in 1917.[95]

At the 1918 convention, Irish advocates introduced two new resolutions calling on the AFL to demand that Wilson immediately negotiate
complete independence for Ireland. The committee on resolutions subsequently proposed substitute legislation that asked convention delegates
to endorse President Wilson's war principles and requested that he bring
the question of home rule for Ireland before the peace conference. The
substitute fell far short of the demands made in the original resolutions.
"Do I understand," asked a sponsor of one of the initial resolutions,
"that the Executive Council will take no part in urging upon the
President of the United States and upon Congress to immediately put
into effect what the Allies are all fighting for—the freedom and independence of small nations?" He continued later, "I think the American
Federation of Labor can do no less than the British Labor Party, that has
come out flat-footed for the independence of Ireland." A vigorous
debate followed, but officials refused to allow a vote on the original resolutions and instead included only the substitute home rule legislation
on the ballots of convention delegates.[96] No account of the CFL's
response to the fate of the Irish issue in the AFL convention exists, but it
doubtless dismayed Irish advocates and likely contributed to a growing
alienation with the AFL hierarchy.

In autumn 1918, the CFL broke openly with the AFL and announced
its intention to form a labor party. In several special sessions, CFL officials developed a declaration of party principles that demonstrated that
they had come to perceive industrial, political, and diplomatic democracy in vastly different terms than AFL officials. Gompers sought to
assure fairness in industry by establishing adjustment commissions composed of equal numbers of business, government, and labor leaders. He
tried to guarantee political democracy by assuring that labor was given

95. *CFL Minutes*, 5/6/17, 31. Friends of Irish Freedom to Fitzpatrick, 3/20/17, B5;
Bulletin, Friends of Irish Freedom, B7–F51: FP.
96. *Proceedings of the AFL*, 1918, 336–39.

an equal voice on war boards. CFL leaders endorsed the principles behind the war boards and arbitration commissions but made its provocative demand that labor deserved representation on these bodies "in proportion to its voting strength." CFL leaders also asked for the "elimination of autocratic domination of the forces of production and distribution either by selfish private interests or bureaucratic agents of government" and called for the "democratic control of industry and commerce for the general good by those who work with hand and brain."[97]

The statement of party principles also revealed differences in the ways the CFL and AFL sought to rid the world of secret diplomacy. In addition to asking for worker representation on the peace commissions and in future "international tribunals" in proportion to "their numbers in the armies, navies and workshops of the world," CFL leaders requested that labor delegates be "democratically designated" rather than handpicked by Samuel Gompers. Chicago activists also demanded a separate worker supplement to the League that would be "pledged and organized to enforce the destruction of autocracy, militarism and economic imperialism throughout the world, and to bring about world-wide disarmament and open diplomacy, to the end that there shall be no more kings and no more wars."[98]

Determined to snuff out the incipient movement, AALD leaders sent a team to Chicago to investigate. They reported that CFL officials were unduly influenced by two foreign political philosophies: Bolshevism and radical Sinn Feinism.[99] But while CFL leaders drew some inspiration from Russian and Irish revolutionaries, their militancy was ultimately bred not by outside agitators but by centralizing and corporatist tendencies within the labor movement. During the early twentieth century, AFL officials had dramatically increased the voting power of national and international officials while reducing the number of votes given city federateds to one each. To compensate for his lack of voting power, Fitzpatrick developed a strong base of local support among rank-and-file workers. He tried to use his popularity to pressure AFL officials into instituting democratic reforms. His efforts, however, proved largely unsuccessful. These failures frustrated CFL leaders and led them to iden-

97. *Independent Labor Party Platform*, B7–F51: FP.
98. Ibid.
99. See Maisel to Gompers, 2/26/19; J. Hendrick to Gompers, 12/6/19; Wm. Hutcheson to Gompers, 12/4/19, J. M. Cline to Gompers, n.d. circa winter 1919: CC-GMC.

tify more closely with rank-and-file workers than with the AFL hierarchy. Strong ties to ordinary workers from a variety of industries bred a sense that labor could achieve more through militant class action than by pursuing the business unionist methods then popular among many national and international leaders.

These feelings were reinforced during the war. Local officials shared the sense of betrayal felt by many rank-and-file workers at not being consulted on the important issue of whether labor should support the war. Many were also annoyed at Gompers's excessive reliance on war commissions over which they had little control to arbitrate disputes. These experiences convinced CFL officials that workers must break with the AFL and take their fates in their own hands. By the time Gompers belatedly tried to solicit the support of local labor officials, CFL leaders had already developed too acute a sense of class consciousness to be easily co-opted into corporatist networks. CFL leaders judged the new wartime institutions not by whether they promoted good relations between different sectors of society but by how much they improved the conditions of rank-and-file workers. Gauged according to these standards, the war boards seemed a failure. Meanwhile, CFL leaders assessed AFL programs for democratizing diplomacy by determining how much AFL officials had been able to help fellow workers abroad, particularly in Ireland. Again, Gompers's initiatives seemed to fall short. Disillusionment over wartime programs spurred CFL leaders to act on their longtime desire to break with official AFL policy and launch a labor party. The CFL was not alone in its drift toward independent labor political action. Similar labor party movements would sprout in at least forty-five other cities by the end of 1918. Twenty-three states would boast labor parties by 1920. Among the strongest of the new parties were those in Kansas, Washington state, Minnesota, and downstate Illinois.[100]

This new oppositional strain within the American labor movement can perhaps be best understood by comparing it to rank-and-file resistance movements that developed in Britain during the war. The shop steward committees offer the closest parallel. These committees, like the new labor parties, were led by local labor militants who were upset by the decline in union democracy during the early twentieth century. Such

100. *CFL Minutes*, 5/6/17, 31; 11/3/18, 22; 12/15/18, 6–9. Walsh to Olander, 11/20/18, B7; Walsh to Fitzpatrick, 11/19/18, B7: WP. *Independent Labor Party Platform*, B7–F51: FP. Foner, *History of the Labor Movement*, 8: 259–62; Shapiro, "'Hand and Brain,'" 408–13.

militants vigorously opposed corporatist forms of power sharing because they threatened to erode further rank-and-file control over the labor movement. Like their American counterparts, they were also more distrustful of business and state participants in corporatist alliances than national and international union leaders. These suspicions eroded their support for the war effort and fueled the drive to force Labour party and trade union leaders toward more independent domestic and foreign policies.[101]

Both Arthur Henderson and Samuel Gompers were suspicious of local militants and initially incurred their wrath by collaborating unquestioningly in government war policies. But Labour party politics forced Henderson to come to an accommodation with local militants. As James Hinton writes, "Labour politics in the last eighteen months of the war were about the balance between working-class ambition aroused by the struggle for participation in the war economy and fuelled by growing war weariness on the one hand, and on the other, the commitment to class collaboration both for its own sake and in the interests of national victory." Henderson's new political agenda in 1918, by focusing on ending the war, reviving international labor solidarity, and increasing labor's political strength at home, brought most local militants back into the Labour party fold.[102]

By contrast, Gompers grew more out of touch with city federated leaders during 1918 and 1919. Thus, as he moved to institutionalize corporatist structures at home and abroad at war's end, he faced rebellion within the ranks. The new American labor parties drew inspiration from the British Labour party but, because they were led by local militants, also reflected their peculiar concerns with issues of industrial democracy, workers control, and direct involvement by workers—as distinct from trade union leadership—in the process and substance of foreign policy decision making. This emphasis on rank-and-file assertiveness alienated national and international union leaders who might otherwise have supported a labor party movement. Thus, while labor party politics in Britain helped to mediate conflicts between local militants and national union leaders, in the United States it exacerbated differences between them.

101. Hinton, First Shop Stewards' Movement, Labour and Socialism, 103; Perkin, Rise of Professional Society, 193–99. See also the comparative essays on labor movements in Europe and North America at war's end in Cronin and Sirianni, Work, Community, and Power.

102. Hinton, Labour and Socialism, 103; Pelling, Labour Party, 42–45; Perkin, Rise of Professional Society, 204–17.

The revitalized nationalist campaigns of ethnic organizations like those in Chicago's Irish and Polish communities also threatened to fragment the labor movement by war's end. To the surprise of some, a number of Irish-American groups and newspapers pledged their support for the U.S. war effort only a few days after the declaration of war. Like CFL officials, they argued that working against one's country during wartime was both immoral and imprudent—regardless of whether the reason for entering the conflict seemed suspect. "There can be no doubt," proclaimed the editors of the *Chicago Citizen*, that ". . . Irish-Americans stand now where they have always stood—heart and soul for the flag and constitution of the United States." They argued that Irish-Americans had enjoyed "the privileges and blessings of freemen" under the "colors" of the American flag and ought now to support the United States in its times of trouble even if they had previously disagreed with Wilson over war policy.[103] Several older fraternals followed suit a few days later and announced their intent to remain loyal to the United States.[104]

The leaders of the FOIF and revolutionary Clan na Gael, by contrast, initially remained more critical of the Wilson administration's decision to enter the European conflict. "If our government had insisted upon England abandoning her illegal and indefensible blockade," proclaimed one FOIF official, "no American ships would have been the victims of German torpedoes." The official concluded, "It is well that we should not lose sight of the real cause of a war in which thousands of American lives will be lost."[105] Others criticized the new wartime institutions created by President Wilson, in particular, the Food and Fuel Administrations. Members of these two bodies, argued FOIF and Clan na Gael leaders, had not been democratically elected yet had almost unlimited power to establish price levels and to requisition food and supplies.[106]

Many FOIF and Clan leaders had similar reservations about the new Selective Service System. According to one observer, this institution would make "any European militarist green with envy." The same individual criticized the administration for suppressing free speech.[107] Editors of the *Irish World* ably summarized the collective worries of

103. CC, 2/9/17, 1.
104. Ibid., 9/28/17, 1; 10/12/17.
105. IW, 4/7/17, 4.
106. Ibid., 6/2/17, 4; 9/8/17, 4.
107. Ibid., 7/28/17, 4; 6/2/17, 4; 9/7/17, 12.

most Clan na Gael and FOIF members when they proclaimed that "whilst American blood and American treasure are poured out, democracy at home is . . . being supplanted by a species of dictatorship which will place the property and liberty of the citizen at the absolute mercy of one man and his agents."[108] Yet, when President Wilson began to promote his plans to win freedom for oppressed nations in late 1917, Clan and FOIF leaders threw their reservations to the wind and pledged to support the administration. If Irish freedom was one of the fruits of war, they reasoned, then the lives of American soldiers would not have been lost in vain.[109]

Most Polish-American groups and newspapers also pledged their support for the U.S. war effort within the first nine months after the decision to intervene. Their declarations of patriotism were of a sentimental character similar to that of Irish-Americans. The Polish Roman Catholic Union (PRCU), for example, pledged in a telegram to President Wilson that "we will do everything possible to help defend the honor and dignity of Old Glory." In its newspaper, the PRCU exhorted fellow Poles to "stand by the President of the United States" and "gather under the Star Spangled Banner, our adopted flag, the flag that represents liberty so dear to our hearts."[110] Similarly, the Polish National Alliance welcomed American entrance into the war and pledged its undying support to the Wilson administration.[111] An independent paper, *Polonia*, also affirmed the loyalties of area Poles, arguing that "the Poles will be ever loyal to America, and especially at this time can America depend on them."[112] Even the socialist KON vowed its support for the U.S. war effort, leaving the tiny Polish Socialist Language Federation as the only major Polish-American organization in Chicago to oppose American involvement.[113]

While Chicago's Irish and Polish groups urged members of their respective communities to support the war, they nonetheless suggested that ethnic Americans should carefully choose the types of war activities in which they became involved. In particular, they argued that their members ought not to participate in generic war campaigns when an

108. Ibid., 6/2/17, 4; 8/27/17, 4.
109. Cuddy, *Irish America and National Isolationism*, 134–35.
110. *Narod Polski*, 4/18/17, 1; 2/21/21, 1: WPA.
111. *Dziennik Zwiazkowy*, 4/7/17: WPA.
112. *Polonia*, 4/12/17, 2: WPA.
113. Norman Oliver Jung, "Chicago's Foreign Language Press in World War I," (Master's thesis, University of Chicago, 1959), 51–56; Cygan, "Political and Cultural Leadership," 113–14.

ethnic counterpart was available. Irish groups, for example, staged their own patriotic parades and encouraged members to participate in these gatherings rather than in ones sponsored by the community.[114] Polish groups established their own branches of the Liberty Loan Campaign and requested that all Polish contributors "mark your nationality in the square in the application where it reads Polish." Subsequently, leaders of the Polish National Alliance and Polish Roman Catholic Union used these forms to claim that they had raised more money for the campaign than any other ethnic group.[115] In rationalizing these kinds of ethnocentric practices, one editor argued, "If we are to show our gratitude, love and affection for our adopted country . . . then let us do it in a way that all America knows about it."[116]

Irish and Polish groups wanted "all America" to know about their war efforts partly because they wished to show that they could be loyal to the United States without losing their ethnicity. The Polish National Alliance, for example, had argued prior to American involvement that, contrary to popular press reports, not a single foreign-born citizen would be disloyal to America in the event of war.[117] The Alliance later pursued this argument by suggesting that, at least in the Polish case, ethnicity only reinforced American patriotism. Thus, Polonia's leaders promoted a proposal to allow Polish-Americans to enlist in a special Polish fighting force rather than the regular army on the grounds that the new recruits would "carry our Polish eagle beside the American Stars and Stripes with pride, and, as Poles from America, we shall enter mortal combat on the side of the Allies and the United States." When President Wilson approved the initiative, it was widely applauded throughout the Polish-American community despite the official opposition of the KON.[118]

Many Irish groups simultaneously took care to outline the useful and patriotic role ethnic organizations could play even when the interests of their old homelands and those of the United States conflicted. One issue over which American and Irish interests seemed fundamentally at odds was Irish conscription. Desperate for troops in 1918, the British vowed to end voluntary recruitment in Ireland and instead institute a draft

114. CC, 1/11/18, 1; 9/21/17, 1; 7/12/18, 1.
115. *Dziennik Zwiazkowy*, 5/8/18, 10; 9/24/18: WPA. On the success of the Polish liberty bond campaign and its implications, see Cohen, *Making a New Deal*, 77–78.
116. *Dziennik Zwiazkowy*, 2/7/17, 2: WPA. See also Pacyga, *Polish Immigrants*, 188, 196.
117. *Dziennik Zwiazkowy*, 3/3/17, 1: WPA.
118. Ibid., 8/6/17, 8. Cygan, "Political and Cultural Leadership," 113–14.

comparable to that in Britain. The proposal outraged the Irish separatist party Sinn Fein, which immediately launched an anticonscription campaign. A few radical Irish groups in America also sided with Sinn Fein and denounced British actions in unqualified terms. The activists who clustered around the *Chicago Citizen*, on the other hand, adopted a different tact. They announced that an American citizen could not publicly "support the Sinn Fein cause without disloyalty to his country, for part of this policy is to keep Irishman [*sic*] out of the army. . . . [and] such conduct is treason to the United States." It added, however, that "this of course does not mean that Ireland has not the right to decide this matter for itself. If self determination is alienable to nations it belongs to Ireland among others."[119]

Meanwhile, officials from the Irish Fellowship Club sent a petition to Wilson asking him to counsel Britain against instituting conscription in Ireland. They argued that if Britain drafted Irish citizens, American interests would be threatened; Britain would be forced to withdraw troops from the European front to quell the rebellion that would result in Ireland.[120] Whether Wilson actually followed their advice is unclear. But when Britain abandoned its conscription plans, local activists claimed partial credit and asserted that well-organized lobbying by Irish-Americans had once again worked to the benefit of both Ireland and America.[121]

By demonstrating that ethnic groups were playing a positive role in American society during the war, Chicago's Irish and Polish leaders hoped to undercut the initiatives of "Americanizers" like Gompers. Ethnic leaders also sought to use their record of wartime service to ensure that Wilson fulfilled his obligations to their homelands. Thus, a banner headline in the *Chicago Citizen* boldly proclaimed that "Ireland's Hope is in America—President Wilson's Famous Motto: Make the World Safe for Democracy—Gives Irish Men Here and the World Over Reason to Rely on the Friendship of the United States in the Peace Conference—Citizens of Irish Ancestry Stand Proudly on Record of Faithful Duty and Bravery in Service of Uncle Sam just now."[122]

Yet throughout the late fall of 1918, Wilson ignored the Irish issue while frequently denouncing German violations of the rights of small

119. CC, 10/18/18, 1.

120. "Petition to President Woodrow Wilson by the Irish Fellowship Club of Chicago on the Present Situation Between England and Ireland as Affecting the Interests of America, April 20, 1918," Misc. Irish Fellowship Club Pamphlets: Fah P. CC, 4/26/18, 1.

121. CC, 4/26/18, 1; 10/18/18, 1; 4/19/18, 4; 10/18/18, 1; 7/5/18, 4.

122. Ibid., 8/30/18, 7. See also Peter J. Peel to Wm. P. J. Haley, 12/2/18: Fah P.

nations. Wilson's silence bred renewed suspicion among Irish-Americans. As one editor from the *Chicago Citizen* noted, Wilson had recently told reporters that "the central powers have convinced us that they are without honor and do not intend justice." He questioned whether Wilson was aware that "the self same words can be applied to the British government's dealings with Ireland."[123] The *Chicago Citizen*'s editors also argued that Wilson's famous "fourteen points," enunciated in January 1918, demanded "a reconstruction of the world" and pointedly suggested that they should apply not just to the vanquished but also to the victor.[124] Irish groups also noted a pro-British bias in the press and went so far as to accuse the major daily papers of a well-coordinated "conspiracy of silence on the issue of Ireland."[125]

To redress the continued pro-British bias of the Wilson administration and U.S. newspapers, ethnic leaders urged the Irish-American press to launch a new publicity campaign on Ireland's behalf.[126] They also argued for better political coordination among Irish-Americans so that they could punish those who failed to fight for Ireland's cause. "People say that Mr. Wilson thinks that the Irish-American has been married to the Democratic party," wrote one paper, "and since no Irish man believes in divorce there is no danger to the Democratic party. We do not think he is right in this latter conclusion."[127]

The continued rapid growth of the FOIF bore witness to the success of the new political campaigns. Their popularity was also apparent in the large turnouts for Irish-American meetings, some of which drew between forty and seventy thousand people.[128] By the end of the war, Chicago's Irish-American community was mobilized and ready to launch a renewed attack on the Wilson administration if it failed to grant self-determination to Ireland. The purpose of such a campaign, they perceived, would be twofold: punish Wilson for his failure to deliver on wartime promises and reassert the political powers that Wilson had tried to take from them during 1917 and 1918.

Polish-Americans also sought to use their record of wartime service as a political bargaining chip and seemed poised to lead a charge against the president if he failed to live up to his pledge to support Polish inde-

123. CC, 11/8/18, 4.
124. Ibid.
125. Ibid., 9/6/18, 1.
126. Ibid.
127. Ibid., 12/6/18, 4.
128. IW, 6/28/19, 1; 7/14/19, 1.

pendence. "Our right to assert our Americanism and its resulting emolu-
ments," wrote one Polish editor, "was earned by the sacrifices of our
boys on the battlefields of France."[129] Backing up their words with
deeds, both socialist and nonsocialist factions within Chicago's Polish
community launched extensive new lobbying campaigns in 1918.[130]

Chicago's Irish and Polish communities, then, were integrated into
the national war campaign but on their own terms and under their own
conditions. Wartime service, far from inviting a deference to centralized
authority and to the corporatist power structures that had developed in
1917 and 1918, encouraged independence and assertiveness on foreign
policy issues. Chicago's Polish and Irish organizations not only vigorously championed the interests of their former homelands but also
defended a Madisonian vision of American democracy that entitled
them to an active role as agents in shaping U.S. foreign policy. This
vision of political power was clearly at odds with the corporatist blueprints of Samuel Gompers, but it shared some important points of convergence with the Chicago Labor party.

By war's close, a new battle for the loyalties of Chicago workers
loomed as a confusing array of groups and reform agendas competed
for their support and attentions. To date, most historians have emphasized the struggle among the AFL, the greatly weakened and divided
Socialist party, and the battered IWW for the allegiances of American
workers in 1918 and 1919. But the most important battle was fought
between AFL leaders and labor and ethnic organizations with far
stronger roots in local working-class subcultures. The struggle pivoted
as much on foreign policy as on domestic issues. Preoccupied with promoting his international programs in Paris during the first half of 1919,
Gompers returned home to find his corporatist schemes jeopardized by
a rebellion within the ranks.

129. *Chicago Society News*, 9/23, 4: WPA.
130. *Dziennik Zwiazkowy*, 4/27/17, 121: WPA. Gerson, *Woodrow Wilson*, 86–103.
On support within Chicago's Polish community for the Labor party, see Chapter 4.

CHAPTER THREE

Innocent Abroad: Gompers, the International Labor Organization, and AFL Foreign Policy, 1919–1922

ONE of the most famous visual images to emerge from the World War I era was captured in a photograph of a smiling Woodrow Wilson being greeted in Dover, England, during 1919 by throngs of well-wishers carrying American flags and tossing flowers in the president's path. On Wilson's shoulders, the photograph seemed to imply, rested the aspirations of millions for a world order free from war and tyranny. But a broad spectrum of liberal, labor, and socialist opinion banked their future hopes not on the president but on the growing power of the trade union movement. Thus, the *New Republic* commented toward the end of the war that "there is a wide consensus of opinion that . . . [the new world] will be particularly distinguished from the world that is passing by the heightened prestige and political power of labor." Its editors argued that "future democracy" within individual countries was "largely at the mercy of the recognized leaders of the labor movement" and also suggested that labor would be crucial to assuring the success of international institutions designed to guarantee peace. "The difference between a League of Nations in which each member is controlled by captains of industry and their satellites," they wrote, "and one in which each member is partly controlled by labor is the difference between a community of individuals naturally inclined toward peace and a community of turbulent feudists."[1]

Among those who shared this messianic vision of labor's postwar role in forging a new world order was Samuel Gompers. But Gompers dif-

---

1. NR, 6/29/18, 250; 5/24/19, 103.

fered radically with the editors of the *New Republic* about the methods that should be pursued to expand labor's power. The liberals who clustered around the *New Republic* argued that the AFL could best enhance its influence by establishing a labor party modeled on that in Britain and by developing a close relationship with European labor movements. They warned that "if the leadership of the [American] labor movement is caste-bound and untouched by the larger democratic idealism that is stirring in the world today, it will be a drag upon the forces of democracy and an elective ally of the forces of Tory reaction."[2] Yet Gompers, still convinced that American workers' best hope for advancement lay in strengthening the wartime partnership between business, labor, and the state, shunned labor party politics and directed his domestic efforts toward converting the war boards to peacetime use. He also tried to realize his longtime goal of extending corporatist power-sharing arrangements into the diplomatic realm by creating the International Labor Organization, an adjunct to the League that was to include business, labor, and government representatives. Gompers simultaneously repudiated the policies of the international labor movement at Berne, isolating himself from European trade union leaders. He continued to devote himself to revitalizing the wartime spirit of cooperation at home and to promoting a foreign policy that he believed served the "community of interest" shared by business, labor, and the state even after the Democratic defeat in 1920. Such policies further polarized the American working class and gave momentum to the Chicago-based labor party movement (see Chapter 4).

Gompers and several of his friends from the Civilian Advisory Commission secretly began working on plans to extend the mandates for war boards even before the armistice was signed. In March 1918, a commission member submitted a report to several colleagues suggesting that the Council of National Defense ought to be perpetuated in peacetime because it encouraged leaders of industry to work for a "common good," eliminated "profiteering," and served as an "official incubator" of new ideas.[3] The report inspired members of the council to collate positive information about its performance. Following the signing of the armistice, Gompers used this data as the basis for a letter to Woodrow Wilson outlining the major arguments in favor of extending the council's mandate. A peacetime defense board, he suggested, could

2. NR, 6/29/18, 250; 1/18/19, 324; 5/24/19, 103; 10/6/19, 68; 3/2/18, 127; 3/23/18, 226; 12/7/18, 155–56. See also *Nation*, 10/12/18, 400, for its support of a labor party.
3. Mr. Clarkson to Gompers, 3/28/18: CC-GMC.

serve as a crucial "central point" for examining important policies not specifically vested in any one government department. Gompers also argued that the council would provide an effective channel through which the "recognized voices of industry could be heard." Because so many different interests would have access to it, the council would become a useful "clearing house" of information on a wide variety of subjects. Finally, Gompers suggested that the council would be a good "distributing point" for federal measures; its members could work through the system of state, county, and municipal defense councils that had developed during the war to ensure that federal policies were enforced.[4]

Gompers and other AFL officials also continued to promote plans for creating new civilian advisory councils attached to executive departments and for expanding the system of industrial adjustment commissions. Gompers argued that departmentally based advisory councils would help to "democratize" policy-making by enabling cooperating elites to work closely and continuously with presidential advisers and appointees. He promoted a network of precinct, municipal, county, state, and national adjustment commissions on the grounds that it would systematize industrial arbitration and prevent needless strikes. Like the other constituent parts of the bureaucratic empire promoted by Gompers, both advisory councils and adjustment commissions were to be comprised of business, government, and labor representatives.[5] Few of Gompers's plans came to fruition, but they illustrate the extent to which he was swept up by the corporatist fervor that pervaded policy-making circles at war's end.[6]

British labor leaders, by contrast, showed no such enthusiasm for revitalizing corporatist infrastructures following the armistice. Harold Perkin suggests that like most victims of seduction, British labor leaders

4. Gompers to Wilson 11/37 [sic 27?]/18: CC-GMC. See also W. B. Wilson to Clarkson, 3/26/18; Gompers General Letter, 11/5/18: CC-GMC. *Proceedings of the AFL*, 1919, 70–80; 1920, 376.

5. Gompers, *American Labor and the War*, 75–82; Mr. Clarkson to Gompers, 3/28/18; Gompers General Letter, 11/5/18; Gompers to Frank Martin, 11/27/18; Gompers to Wilson, 11/37 [sic 27?]/18; W. B. Wilson to Clarkson, 3/26/18; Gompers to John Walker, 5/25/19; Gompers to Walker, 7/1/17: CC-GMC. See also *American Federationist* 26 (February 1919): 129–43. *Proceedings of the AFL*, 1919, 70–80; 1920, 376. Gompers to Fitzpatrick, 3/29/18, B6–F46: FP. Gompers, *Seventy Years*, 2: 513, 522–23.

6. For studies on corporatism after the war, see, especially, Hawley, *Great War*; Hogan, *Informal Entente*; McCormick, "Drift or Mastery?"; Rosenberg, *Spreading the American Dream*.

soon learned to "distrust the seducer." In particular, they grew wary of Prime Minister Lloyd George, believing that he had taken advantage of the wartime situation to sap labor's independence and militance. Extending the mandates on wartime institutions would only perpetuate an unhealthy dependence by British labor on shiftless politicians. But Perkin argues that Arthur Henderson and other key labor spokesmen did not entirely abandon a "corporate approach" after the war, for they continued to share a professional interest along with state and business leaders in preventing disastrous class conflict. In lieu of state-sponsored corporatist institutions, they sought a more flexible "bargained corporatism" in which labor's power within a business–state–trade union partnership might grow over time. Labor party politics and the threat of militant strike action both offered hope of enhancing labor's influence within this more informal framework.[7]

Different visions of the proper contours of business-state-labor relations in turn continued to propel British and American labor leaders along different international paths. During 1917 and 1918, British labor leaders had devoted themselves to rebuilding the international trade union movement. Just as labor party politics could gain trade union leaders more bargaining power at home, so also a unified international trade union movement could assure that labor exercised more influence over the terms of peace and over future diplomacy.[8] Gompers, on the other hand, shunned efforts to revitalize the spirit of labor internationalism and instead lobbied on behalf of a plan for labor participation, in equal numbers with business and state representatives, on the peace commissions and in any future international organizations. But by the winter of 1918, the AFL president had become skeptical that Wilson would grant his diplomatic demands. While on his tour of Europe, Gompers thus focused on organizing an international labor meeting for the same time and place as the peace conference. Gompers suggested that this meeting would be well situated to make recommendations to the conference about peace terms. He also indicated that it might frame a request for a separate labor adjunct to the proposed League of Nations.[9]

7. Perkin, *Rise of Professional Society*, 209, 151; Leventhal, *Arthur Henderson*, 77–82; Hinton, *Labour and Socialism*, 96–117.
8. See Chapter 2; MacDonald, *National Defence*; Arthur Henderson, *The League of Nations and Labour.*
9. *Proceedings of the AFL*, 1919, 257–63; Gompers, *Seventy Years*, 2: 322, 390–93, 476.

British labor leaders at first supported Gompers's initiatives, probably hoping that their endorsement of these plans might win his backing for the Stockholm meeting designed to promote a labor-negotiated peace. But after the armistice, Premier George Clemenceau made it clear that he would not permit belligerent labor leaders on French soil. Subsequently, British and European trade union officials changed the location of the proposed postwar labor meeting first to Lausanne and, then, to Berne, Switzerland. Gompers objected vigorously to these plans. The Germans, he argued, would come to a labor meeting in a neutral country on equal terms, would dominate proceedings, and would encourage the international trade union movement to pursue a disruptive and unproductive diplomatic course. The AFL president also suggested that trade union leaders could have a more direct impact on the peace conference if they were in Paris.[10]

Shortly after hearing of the European plans, Gompers and five other AFL delegates sailed for London. They arrived in the midst of an interallied labor conference and heatedly tried to convince delegates to cancel the Berne meeting. All trade union representatives except for two from Belgium refused to heed the AFL's advice and left for Berne during the coming week. AFL officials, disgruntled but still determined, traveled alone to Paris after the conference so that they could stay in "close touch with the Peace Commissioners."[11]

Upon arriving in the French capital, Gompers was appointed by Wilson to the Commission on International Labour Legislation. This body was charged with writing a constitution for a labor adjunct to the League and submitting a report on international labor standards to the future secretary general of the League of Nations. As mandated by the peace conference, the commission consisted of two representatives from each of the five contracting powers and Belgium. Cuba, Poland, and Czechoslovakia each sent one delegate. President Wilson appointed prominent businessman and shipping board member Edward Hurley as the other American representative. European nations, for their part, delegated positions to individuals from a variety of backgrounds. The

10. Arthur Henderson to Gompers, 12/30/18; Henderson to the American Secretary of State, 12/20/18; Secretary of State to Henderson, 12/24/18; Chester Wright to Gompers, 12/31/18; Oudegeest to Gompers, 1/16/19; Gompers Memoranda No. 1, 1/30/19: CC-GMC. *American Federationist* 26 (March 1919): 225–31; (April 1919): 305–8; *Proceedings of the AFL*, 1919, 18–19; Gompers, *Seventy Years*, 2: 475–80; Foner, *History of the Labor Movement*, 7: 354–56.

11. Gompers Memoranda No. 1, 1/30/19: CC-GMC. *American Federationist* 26 (March 1919): 227–29.

British, for example, appointed a member of the war cabinet and an undersecretary of state. French leaders chose two members from the ministry of reconstruction. When news of the developments in Paris reached Berne, trade union leaders there vehemently protested the appointments on the grounds that most of the European delegates were not bona fide trade union representatives. But Gompers refused to resign his position and was subsequently elected president of the commission.[12]

Under Gompers's direction, the commission created both the International Labor Office and the International Labor Organization (ILO). The commission designed the International Labor Office to collect information on global labor standards and to propose legislation to the ILO that would improve labor conditions and help prevent the "injustice, hardship and privation" that created "unrest so great that the peace and harmony of the world are imperilled."[13] The governing board of the office was to consist of twenty-four members: twelve government and twelve nongovernment officials. Important industrial nations would nominate eight of the twelve government officials, while state delegates to the ILO would directly elect the remaining four. Nongovernmental representatives would be chosen by the labor and business delegates to the ILO convention.[14]

Members of the Commission on International Labour Legislation feuded bitterly over the composition of the national delegations to the ILO convention itself. British representatives proposed that each participating nation be accorded one government representative who was to wield two votes within the convention. National delegations would also include one labor and one employer delegate who would each exercise one vote. Gompers objected to these plans, arguing that government delegates should be accorded only one vote. The commission compromised by opting in favor of a plan to allow two government representatives with one vote each on the national delegations. Members also agreed that the ILO would treat self-governing colonies

12. Gompers, *Seventy Years*, 2: 478–84; Frey, Memoir, 3: 438. J. C. Grew to Gompers, 1/29/19: CC-GMC. *Proceedings of the AFL*, 1919, 19. *American Federationist* 26 (March 1919): 226–31. Dictation of Gompers to Miss Lee Guard, 12/30/18; Gompers to Bowerman, 12/28/18: CC-GMC.

13. *Proceedings of the AFL*, 1919, 24; Minutes of the Commission on International Labour Legislation, February 1 to March 24, 1919, *ILO*, ed. Shotwell, 2: 149–322.

14. *Proceedings of the AFL*, 1919, 21. Labour Commission Report, *ILO*, ed. Shotwell, 2: 372–73.

as independent entities but that nonself-governing colonies would be represented by their mother country.[15]

Additional divisions arose over the issue of whether compliance with ILO legislation was mandatory. French and Italian representatives on the commission argued that all ILO legislation passed by the convention should automatically have the force of international law. Gompers objected that these proposals would make the ILO a "supergovernment" and destroy national autonomy. American and British opposition helped ensure that ILO legislation was binding on a country only if the proper governmental authorities within these states ratified it. ILO legislation could take the form of either recommendations or draft conventions. ILO recommendations were to be submitted directly to member countries of the League of Nations "with a view to their being given effect by national legislation." Draft conventions would be referred by the League to individual states for ratification so that they might be made a part of international law.[16]

Once the League secretary or ILO submitted legislation to a member state, that state had one year to bring the matter before competent authorities. If the authorities failed to pass legislation enforcing a recommendation or draft convention, then no further action was to be taken. But when a nation ratified a draft convention and failed to enforce it, a complaint could be lodged by another state. In such a case, the International Labor Office would communicate with the state and demand compliance. If the state still took no action, then the International Labor Office was entitled to publish the correspondence and set up a commission of inquiry that could recommend economic sanctions. League members would then vote on these sanctions. In the event that the membership could not reach a clear-cut decision, or if the state against which the complaint had been filed wished to appeal the decision, then the matter was to be referred to a Court of International Justice, which would be the final arbiter on all matters.[17]

15. Minutes of the Commission on International Labour Legislation, *ILO*, ed. Shotwell, 2: 157–78; *Proceedings of the AFL*, 1919, 20–31; *American Federationist* 26 (June 1919): 483–86; Gompers, *Seventy Years*, 2: 489–93; Foner, *History of the Labor Movement*, 7: 357.

16. Minutes of the Commission on International Labour Legislation, *ILO*, ed. Shotwell, 2: 185–93; Gompers, *Seventy Years*, 2: 489; *Proceedings of the AFL*, 1919, 22; *American Federationist* 26 (June 1919): 495.

17. *Proceedings of the AFL*, 1919, 24–31. Minutes of the Commission on International Labour Legislation, *ILO*, ed. Shotwell, 2: 185–93; Final Texts of the Labor Section of the Peace Treaty, *ILO*, ed. Shotwell, 1: 424–50.

Although Gompers spent a majority of his time in Paris helping to create the ILO, he probably devoted more emotional energy to ensuring that a labor bill of rights proposed by the American delegation was included in the peace treaty. Gompers seems to have believed that this document would establish the necessary base for cooperation among nations that Progressive reform had created among economic groups at home. The first and most important right demanded by the American delegation was modeled directly on the Clayton Antitrust Act. It declared that "in law and in practice it should be held that the labor of the human being is not a commodity or an article of commerce." AFL delegates also demanded an affirmation of the rights of seamen to leave their ships while in port; the banning of merchandise produced by children under sixteen or by convict labor; the recognition of the rights of workers to free speech, press, and association; a declaration that workers were entitled to an eight-hour day; and "wages commensurate with a standard of life conforming to the civilization of the time." In addition, the delegates opposed the sale of articles produced in the home and favored equal pay for women. If passed as a package, argued Gompers, this set of rights would undercut the positions of both reactionaries and revolutionaries and provide a strong foundation on which moderate workers, government officials, and businessmen could build a new world order.[18]

Unfortunately for the American delegation, their proposals were eviscerated by both the Commission on International Labour Legislation and the peace conference. Gompers's prized first right was changed to read that "labor should not be regarded *merely* as a commodity or article of commerce." As critic Andrew Furuseth of the Seamen's Union pointed out, inclusion of the new word "changed an absolute negative into an equally absolute positive." While speaking before the AFL convention, Furuseth drew a parallel. "Somebody says Andrew Furuseth is not a scab," he told the delegates, "somebody amends it to read he is not *merely* a scab . . . that is what you are asked to endorse."[19] The Commission on International Labour Legislation and conference delegates also made other significant alterations and deletions. They eliminated clauses demanding universal recognition of free speech and free press and detailing the rights of sailors. The pro-

18. Proposals Submitted by the Delegates of the United States of America, February 5, 1919, *ILO*, ed. Shotwell, 2: 328–29; *Proceedings of the AFL*, 1919, 29.
19. *Proceedings of the AFL*, 1919, 401.

posal that labor was entitled to wages "commensurate with a prevailing standard of life conforming to the civilization of the time" was
changed to read that labor ought to be provided with material compensation "adequate to maintain a standard of life as this is understood in
their time and country." Clauses on child labor and women's work
were likewise diluted.[20]

Although Gompers was unhappy with these changes, he did not
believe that they should be used to undermine labor support for the
Paris Peace Treaty, the League, or the ILO. In the wake of the deliberations in Paris, Gompers admitted that "we did not accomplish everything that we had hoped to accomplish." However, he argued that "we
feel that we have a right to say that the world will better understand the
needs of labor in the future as the result of our work abroad and that
the world will more readily find a way to satisfy those needs." He also
claimed that the League would be the "most powerful ally justice has
ever found in the history of man" and asserted that "secret diplomacy
dies by virtue of . . . [its] covenant."[21]

Gompers failed during the postwar era to explain fully why he
believed the League and its subsidiary bodies would help to destroy
secret diplomacy, but one may speculate on his reasoning. As President
Wilson often pointed out, the League mandated the registration of all
treaties and would ensure an open forum for discussing major international issues. The public would thus be more informed about foreign
affairs and could better wield their votes at home to influence the diplomacy of state leaders. The ILO, for its part, would provide a forum
through which the voice of labor could be heard on issues of economic
diplomacy. Gompers did not seek extensive legislative powers for the
ILO because he believed that its influence would derive primarily from
moral suasion and from the role it would serve as a "clearing house" of
information on labor issues. Like many participants on wartime defense
boards, Gompers tended to blame unenlightened policies on failures in
communication and information gathering; industrial experts in the ILO
could decisively shape world affairs by bringing the "true facts" of a situation before world opinion.

20. *Proceedings of the AFL*, 1919, 30; Gompers, *Seventy Years*, 2: 495–98.
Memorandum by James T. Shotwell to Colonel House, April 19, 1919, *ILO*, ed. Shotwell,
2: 410–11.
21. Gompers, *Seventy Years*, 2: 499; *American Federationist* 26 (August 1919):
718–21. See also Speech by Mr. Samuel Gompers Defending the League of Nations and
International Labor Organization, June, 1919, *ILO*, ed. Shotwell, 2: 430–38.

Upon returning from Europe, the AFL delegation devoted their efforts to winning the support of the AFL convention for the peace treaty. Debate in the convention centered on provisions for the ILO and on the issue of Ireland. Two different groups opposed the ILO. One, led by Andrew Furuseth, initially attacked the shortcomings of Labor's Bill of Rights. But misgivings about this document soon led to a more far-ranging critique of the ILO. Despite Gompers's success in limiting the legislative powers of the ILO, Furuseth argued that its mandate gave the organization "jurisdiction over the daily life of the working people of the entire world." He suggested that while recommendations would likely go through extensive legislative channels in the United States, draft conventions resembled treaties and would be subject only to the approval of the Senate and executive. Laws directly affecting standards of living might be imposed on the American people without the endorsement of the House of Representatives.[22]

Furuseth and his followers also criticized the proposed composition of the national committees to be sent to the ILO convention. These criticisms bore a striking similarity to the complaints that local leaders like Ed Nockels had lodged against the arbitration committees during the war. Trade union officials, Furuseth suggested, mistakenly assumed that the two government officials on each committee would work on labor's behalf. Furuseth contended that the current American administration might send prolabor delegates but that almost all other European government officials would probably support business over labor interests. In the future, even the United States might send probusiness delegates. To trust the power structure created by the Commission on International Labour Legislation, argued Furuseth, one would have to assume that "men all of a sudden have become saints." While admitting that the ILO would at first have little actual influence due to squabbles and questions about its legitimacy, Furuseth nonetheless claimed that it would eventually grow into a superlegislature. Furuseth cited as proof the relative weakness of the American executive during the earliest years of the U.S. republic and pointed to the ways in which it had subsequently accrued power. He argued that for American labor officials to

22. *Proceedings of the AFL*, 1919, 399–402; 24–31. Whether Furuseth was correct in his assumptions is problematic. At Gompers's behest, a clause was inserted into the ILO constitution that excluded federal states from the enforcement provisions established for ratified draft conventions. But if the Senate chose to ratify a draft convention anyway, then the scenario envisioned by Furuseth was theoretically possible. See also Gompers, *Seventy Years*, 2: 492–93.

forfeit trade union prerogatives to a centralized international body would be contrary to the wishes of average workers, who preferred to set standards for themselves.[23]

The other group opposing the ILO, while dismissing Furuseth's concern that the organization would develop into a superparliament, nonetheless worried that it could be used as a valuable public relations tool by leading capitalists. This group was comprised primarily of socialists. Delegate Heller from the International Ladies' Garment Workers' Union (ILGWU) championed their cause on the floor of the convention. Like Furuseth, she objected to the composition of the ILO, arguing that the "governments in existence" were "dominated by capitalists" and would send representatives who would promote business over labor interests. Heller doubted that the ILO would ever have the power to enforce its decisions, but argued that antilabor forces might use conservative pronouncements made by the ILO to label trade union demands unreasonable and to gain an edge on public opinion.[24]

The majority of League opponents, however, were not as concerned with the ILO as they were with the issue of Irish independence. These delegates were upset with Wilson for refusing to allow the Irish to plead their case for independence before the Paris Peace Conference. The treaty, they feared, would even further undercut the efforts of the Irish to obtain independence because it bound all contracting parties to respect the territorial integrity of the other signers. Gompers sensed that Irish nationalists had a strong foothold in the convention and wisely chose to accommodate them by attaching an amendment to the League bill proclaiming "that nothing in the League of Nations as endorsed by this convention shall be construed as denying the right of self-determination and freedom to Ireland as recommended by this convention."[25] The amendment effectively isolated the Furuseth and Heller factions and the bill endorsing the League subsequently passed by a vote of 29,909 to 420.[26]

Following the convention, Gompers and other AFL officials toured the country lobbying on behalf of the peace treaty. They also wrote articles and published pamphlets promoting the League and the ILO.[27] But because Gompers remained confident about the chances for securing

23. Proceedings of the AFL, 1919, 401, 399–402.
24. Ibid., 406.
25. Ibid., 403.
26. Ibid., 415.
27. Gompers, Seventy Years, 2: 499.

passage of the treaty at home during the summer of 1919, he soon diverted his attention to winning European trade union support for the ILO. The AFL president's plan was twofold: establish a foothold in the International Federation of Trade Unions (IFTU) in August, then use this organization to win over the dissident leaders from Berne. Initially, Gompers tried to secure a more influential position within the IFTU by attacking past German dominance of the organization. The Germans, he argued, had led the organization along a radical course that was incompatible with AFL aims and had also provoked the wartime split in the IFTU. AFL officials convinced allied labor leaders to demand a harsh confession of war crimes from German delegates. When the Germans officially acknowledged their war guilt, Gompers claimed the confession was insufficient. The other IFTU members accepted the German apology over his objections.[28]

Unsuccessful in his bid to humiliate German trade union leaders and strip them of their influence, Gompers instead tried to increase American power in the organization by altering the system of representation. Under the old rules, each country was entitled to one vote. The American delegation proposed replacing this scheme with a system of proportional representation. Each national delegation, they argued, ought to be given representation in proportion to the numbers of trade unionists it represented. The initial bill proposed by the AFL failed to win approval, but a modified version was subsequently passed. The new system of representation significantly increased the AFL's voting power.[29]

Armed with this victory, Gompers pressed for his main goal: an IFTU endorsement of the ILO and a pledge by trade union leaders from Allied countries to attend its first convention, scheduled for October in Washington. But when Gompers brought his proposals before the meeting, European delegates passed a resolution expressing dismay that the Charter of Labour [of the ILO] had been drawn up by those out of touch with the international trade union movement. Several European leaders, however, admitted that the ILO held promise. These delegates drew up a set of stipulations and agreed to attend the Washington conference if they were met. European labor leaders asked the AFL to invite delegates from both the Entente and Allied powers to the conference, to

28. *Proceedings of the AFL*, 1920, 131–41; *American Federationist* 26 (October 1919): 921–38.
29. *Proceedings of the AFL*, 1920, 131–41; *American Federationist* 26 (October 1919): 921–38.

work for the reduction of government delegates from two to one, and to seek support for a constitutional amendment ensuring that all resolutions could be passed by majority rather than two-thirds rule.[30] In response, Gompers proposed a substitute resolution proclaiming that

> The International Federation of Trade Union Conferences at Amsterdam declares that the Labor Charter as contained in the Peace Treaty does not give expression to the full demands of the working classes and urges all national centers to strive for the complete and early realization of the program of the newly formed international.[31]

But despite the increased voting power of the American delegation, the resolution was soundly defeated. The IFTU thus went on record as supporting the upcoming ILO conference provided Gompers worked to change the provisions of the ILO constitution to which they objected.[32]

Why European leaders chose belatedly to endorse, with qualification, the ILO is a complex question that cannot be fully answered here. However, one can get a sense of the dynamics operating within individual labor movements by looking at the attitudes toward the ILO of different groups within the British Labour party. Many radicals within the British Labour party denounced both the League and the ILO at war's end. They argued that the League would result in a "supreme concentration of capitalist power." The ILO, for its part, would be comprised of an "autocratic, bureaucratic set of officials" who would help the capitalists within the League to implement a form of "Benevolent Despotism."[33] But moderates like Henderson believed that the ILO held more potential. He agreed with Gompers that the organization could serve as an effective forum for bringing labor issues to the attention of ordinary people throughout the world. Like many other European representatives, however, he sought structural changes within the organization that would buoy the status of labor delegates. Even more fundamentally, he argued that working-class representatives would have true influence within the ILO and League only if world labor simultaneously built up a strong international trade union movement that was willing to pursue its own diplomatic course if state leaders ignored labor

30. *Proceedings of the AFL*, 1920, 148–50; *American Federationist* 26 (October 1919): 940. For more on the European position, see MacDonald, *National Defence*, 15, 80; Dawse, "The Independent Labour Party," 40; Leventhal, *Arthur Henderson*, 86–90; Henderson, *The League of Nations and Labour*.
31. *Proceedings of the AFL*, 1920, 148.
32. Ibid., 148–50; *American Federationist* 26 (October 1919): 940.
33. Dawse, "The Independent Labour Party," 40; MacDonald, *National Defence*.

demands. Within Britain, the Labour party and the threat of militant strike action had afforded British labor leaders more bargaining power in corporatist partnerships. Similarly, a strong international trade union movement could enhance the influence that labor delegates wielded within the ILO and on the League itself.[34]

Gompers abhorred the notion that the IFTU should pursue its own independent diplomacy. He also failed to share the sense of urgency felt by many European trade union leaders about structural changes within the ILO. But on returning from Amsterdam, Gompers nonetheless determined to act in good faith on IFTU stipulations in order to gain European trade union support for the Washington conference. Following their dictates, he first sent invitations for the conference to both German and Austrian trade unions. Whether by design or quirk of fate, however, the Germans and Austrians did not get their invitation until a few weeks before the conference and determined that they could not reach America in time. Gompers subsequently scored a public relations victory by claiming that the two countries planned to boycott the meeting. As requested by European trade union leaders, Gompers also wrote representatives from the Commission on International Labour Legislation and asked that the number of government delegates to the Washington conference be reduced. To no one's surprise, ILO representatives deferred this issue to the first session.[35]

Ironically, Gompers was not able to take advantage of his public relations victories because the United States had not signed the treaty by the time European labor representatives began arriving for the Washington conference. Since the AFL could not gain membership in the ILO until the United States officially became a member of the League, it was not entitled to send a delegation to the conference it had planned. European trade unionists invited the AFL to attend anyway, but it remained without actual voting power. Subsequently Gompers watched in frustration while European delegates elected a leader from the Berne conference, Albert Thomas, to be the new director of the organization. Thomas was a moderate and tried to encourage continued AFL participation in the conference. But Gompers, apparently upset by his disenfranchised status within the organization, increasingly isolated himself from the conference and dramatically cut back on the number of AFL representatives

34. Henderson, *The League of Nations and Labour*; Leventhal, *Arthur Henderson*, 76–92.
35. *Proceedings of the AFL*, 1920, 166–67. Oudegeest to AFL, 10/4/19; Gompers to Barnes, 9/2/19; Gompers Speech to International Labor Conference, 10/30/19: CC-GMC.

who attended the daily ILO meetings. Official AFL publications subsequently devoted very little attention to the conference.[36]

In the wake of the Washington meeting, Gompers continued to correspond with ILO leaders, but he rechanneled a majority of his efforts into stemming the tide of domestic chaos that was destroying the spirit of wartime cooperation, delaying ratification of the treaty, and preventing his effective participation in the ILO.[37] At war's end, Gompers had banked his hopes for future industrial peace on the perpetuation and expansion of the system of mobilization boards that had developed during 1917 and 1918. Yet, while Gompers was in Europe during the spring and summer, the Wilson administration allowed mandates on most of the war boards to run out. Much of the goodwill that propelled cooperative mobilization 'efforts also dissolved. Leading businessmen launched open shop offensives and attempted to roll back labor gains; workers responded with an unprecedented strike wave. Such industrial hostility polarized American society and further eroded support for corporatist principles.[38]

In an attempt to stem the tide of class conflict, Woodrow Wilson called an industrial conference to meet in Washington during October while the International Labor Organization Convention was being held. Wilson invited well-known business, government, and labor officials who had served on war boards in the hopes that they would rekindle the spirit of voluntary cooperation and create a new corporatist framework for resolving societal problems. Instead, the conference revealed the huge chasms that now separated these elites. All three groups endorsed the formation of cooperative agencies to resolve disputes. But business representatives argued that cooperative agencies should make

36. Gompers to Executive Council, 10/29/19: CC-GMC. Interestingly, almost no coverage of the conference was given in the *American Federationist* 26 (October–November, 1919), suggesting Gompers's increasing disillusionment with the ILO. See also *NR*, 11/12/19, 301; 12/10/19, 37.

37. See Albert Thomas to Gompers, 3/1/20 and 8/27/20; Greenwood to Gompers 11/18/20; *IFTU Newsletter*, 3/10/20: CC-GMC.

38. See, particularly, Thomas Ferguson, "From Normalcy to New Deal: Industrial Structure, Party Competition, and American Public Policy in the Great Depression," *International Organization* 38 (winter 1984): 64–69; Fite and Peterson, *Opponents of War*; Brody, *Steelworkers in America*, 214–78; Maurer, *It Can Be Done*, 222; Montgomery, *Fall of the House of Labor*, 406–7, "New Tendencies," "Immigrants, Industrial Unions, and Social Reconstruction," 103; Foner, *History of the Labor Movement*, 8: 1; Conner, *National War Labor Board*, 172–82; *NR*, 11/2/21, 275. Stuart Chase to Walsh, 11/4/18; Employers Association to Members, 11/28/18; Basil Manley Memo n.d. (circa 12/1/1918); Walsh to Wright, 11/9/18; Nockels to Walsh, 11/25/18; Walsh to Olander, 12/4/18: B7, WP.

strikes unnecessary and announced their approval of a bill outlawing strikes. In addition, they voted against an AFL proposal demanding recognition of the principle of collective bargaining. AFL officials believed that the business vote against collective bargaining signaled a fundamental refusal by business to recognize the right of workers to choose their own representatives and establish unions. When government officials failed to take steps to ensure the sanctity of unions, AFL representatives walked out of the conference. Subsequently, Wilson scheduled another conference with businessmen for the winter; he did not invite labor representatives.[39]

Many radicals in the labor movement hoped that the Washington trade union conference marked the end of Gompers's experiment in collaboration. In their eyes, the conference revealed that business had cooperated with labor on executive boards or adjustment commissions only because they hoped to destroy the union movement after the war. Moreover, the conference seemed to confirm that even a liberal administration like Woodrow Wilson's would favor business in a crisis. When AFL representatives walked out of the conference, Illinois State Federation of Labor president and Chicago Labor party member Duncan McDonald sent a resolution to Gompers asking him to call a special AFL convention for the purpose of "developing an effective union plan of action to meet the onslaught of capitalists."[40] Gompers and AFL executive officials quickly seized upon the idea but not for the reasons McDonald envisioned. They sought to use the conference to convince the Wilson administration that "responsible elements" of the labor movement could still be trusted. To achieve this effect, Gompers modeled the new conference on the March 1917 meeting at which the AFL had endorsed the war. Once again, he refused to invite state and local federateds despite substantial protests by these bodies (especially the Illinois State Federation of Labor).[41] Gompers also drafted a statement of labor aims before the convention rather than allowing the convention itself to construct a document.

The new proclamation, "Labor, Its Grievances, Protests and Demands," was largely a restatement of long-standing AFL policies. It also,

39. *Proceedings of the AFL*, 1920, 81–85; Conner, *National War Labor Board*, 177–78; Gompers, *Seventy Years*, 2: 519. Walsh to Josephine Casey, B28: WP. Green, *National Civic Federation*, 429; NR, 11/19/19, 336.
40. Duncan McDonald to Gompers, 10/23/19: CC-GMC.
41. Gompers to Martin Joyce, 10/29/19; Lawrence Grace to Gompers, 10/31/19; J. W. Adams to Gompers, 12/1/19: CC-GMC. NR, 12/24/19, 95.

however, affirmed the AFL's support for corporatist structures, calling for new institutions that would promote "cooperation between scientists of industry and representatives of organized labor." In addition, it voiced vigorous support for the Paris Peace Treaty and declared that U.S. participation in the League of Nations and ILO was crucial to the future welfare of mankind.[42] Much to the dismay of AFL officials, the statement failed to have the same impact as their wartime declaration. In late December, Wilson allowed the mandate on the final war board then in existence—the Council of National Defense—to expire despite labor objections. The administration also rebuffed trade union suggestions that cooperative federal agencies be constructed to deal with questions of labor's civil liberties. Most importantly, government officials failed to invite AFL officials to the industrial conference planned for January 12. When delegates at the industrial conference agreed on a new arbitration system, the AFL denounced it, proclaiming that it was "constructed in the seclusion of the secret chamber entirely out of the contact with the life for which it was designed and entirely unfitted for the needs of that life." In particular, AFL leaders complained that the system proposed by the conference would give "encouragement and permanency to company unions."[43]

Despite the increasingly antilabor policies of the Wilson administration, Gompers continued to promote Wilsonian principles of voluntarism and class harmony. To assure that these principles would triumph in the upcoming presidential election, Gompers launched the AFL Non-partisan Political Campaign in 1919. As the name implies, the campaign was ostensibly designed to create worker support for candidates in any party who supported labor causes or programs that labor deemed to be for the public good. Among many trade unionists, however, the campaign was jokingly referred to as the "AFL Non-partisan Democratic Campaign" because the overwhelming majority of candidates supported by AFL leaders were Wilsonian Democrats.[44] Moreover, Gompers used the campaign to attack the general philosophies of both the Republican and Labor parties. Gompers claimed that the Republican party deserved labor's scorn because its position on issues demonstrated that it was "an unqualified defender of the enemies of labor." He hinted that the Republicans sought to destroy cooperative frameworks for solving

42. *Proceedings of the AFL*, 1920, 64–69.
43. Ibid., 85; Conner, *National War Labor Board*, 179.
44. *Proceedings of the AFL*, 1920, 74–77; Harry B. Sell, "The A.F. of L. and the Labor Party Movement of 1918–1920" (Master's thesis, University of Chicago, 1922), 123.

domestic and international problems. "Harding," argued Gompers, "says I am for going backward, Cox says I am for going forward."[45]

Gompers opposed labor party politics on the grounds that labor candidates had no chance of winning either local or national elections and would only divert votes from mainstream politicians who were sympathetic to workers' causes.[46] The AFL Executive Council adopted a number of different plans to undercut support for the Labor party. Initially, it conducted a publicity campaign against party leaders comparable to that it was conducting against the Republicans. In monthly editions of the *American Federationist*, Gompers frequently printed the letters of Labor party members and then criticized their naivete. AFL leaders also publicly denounced the dire effects of splitting the labor vote and sent out reams of nonpartisan political propaganda to those local unions known to be supporters of the Labor party.[47] They additionally revitalized the wartime AALD and used it to undermine Labor party activities at central federated bodies.[48]

In the wake of the November election, Gompers and other AFL leaders lamented their failure to stifle Labor party sentiment. AFL official John Frey, for example, wrote Gompers shortly after the election and noted that "What we both regret, is that labor's position was not more unanimous and that some of our most prominent leaders through their activities indicated their lack of confidence in the non-partisan program." He contended that many "fair weather friends" had jumped on the bandwagon of trade unionism during the war and had brought with them "strange, fantastic and revolutionary ideas." These ideas, in his view, had partly caused the backlash that resulted in the Republican victory.[49] Such reasoning seems farfetched unless one understands the importance that AFL leaders attached to a spirit of cooperation. They believed that this spirit had fostered corporatist institutions during the war. Its breakdown among workers caused other segments of society to doubt the validity of corporatist institutions on both a national and

45. *American Federationist* 27 (June 1920): 656; (October 1920): 913. On the history of the AFL's nonpartisan politics, see Greene, "The Strike at the Ballot Box."

46. *American Federationist* (March 1920): 257; and *Proceedings of the AFL, 1919*, 107.

47. See *Proceedings of the AFL, 1919*, 102–7. *American Federationist* 26 (January 1919): 37; 27 (March 1920): 257; 27 (December 1920): 332–35. NR, 5/26/20, 399; 2/25/20, 375.

48. *Proceedings of the AFL, 1919*, 314, 447. See also Mr. Hendrick to Gompers, 12/6/19; William Hutcheson to Gompers, 12/4/19; J. M. Cline to Gompers, n.d.; Robert Maisel to Gompers, 2/26/19: CC-GMC. Gompers to Walsh, 12/31/18, B7: WP.

49. Frey to Gompers, 11/4/20: CC-GMC. Frey, Memoir, 2: 211; 3: 439–40.

international scale. As a result, the public rejected the party of the AFL's hero, Woodrow Wilson.

Although AFL executive officials realized that a period of retrenchment would follow in the aftermath of the election, they nonetheless decided it was best to pursue cooperationist tactics so as to regain that "invaluable assistant, public support."[50] To that end, Gompers and other AFL leaders participated in several economic conferences held by the Warren Harding administration. The AFL president argued that the government could "supply counsel and information on industrial problems" and also provide a format where "industries and all elements concerned . . . finally work out the solution."[51] AFL leaders also pursued a foreign policy designed more to revitalize a partnership between American business, government, and the state than to foster international labor solidarity. Evidence of the AFL's continued corporatist orientation in the international arena became most apparent in its attacks on the IFTU and the ILO, in its response to revolutionary nationalism, and in its activities on behalf of the Pan-American Federation of Labor.

In the aftermath of the Washington Trade Union Conference, Gompers had been moderately hopeful that relations between the American trade union movement and its European counterparts would improve. Gompers was interested in fostering better relations with European movements in order to establish harmony in the ILO once the United States joined. In late 1919, Gompers therefore conveyed AFL interest in obtaining a permanent membership in the IFTU to officials of European trade union movements. But during 1920, a wave of socialism swept through the organization. Subsequently, the IFTU executive committed it to supporting a massive food import to Russia in defiance of the Allied blockade, a boycott of certain types of goods produced by those nations intervening in Russia, and an embargo of munitions to Poland.[52] Gompers, much perturbed by these activities, recommended that the AFL convention delay accepting membership in the organization. When the IFTU conducted similar campaigns in 1921, he suggested that the AFL should vote definitively against affiliation. In part, Gompers's rationale was pragmatic. The system of dues, he suggested, was excessive and would put a heavy financial burden on the AFL. But he also argued that the IFTU constitution "abrogated the principle of complete autonomy for each national trade union federation." Most

50. Frey to Gompers, 11/4/20: CC-GMC.
51. Gompers, *Seventy Years*, 2: 353, 521.
52. Lorwin, *Labor and Internationalism*, 205–9.

important, Gompers opposed American trade union participation in the
IFTU because the organization had committed its constituent members
to "revolutionary ideals" that the AFL "uncompromisingly opposed and
to which no labor movement guided by democratic ideals should give its
approval." The AFL convention followed Gompers's advice and voted
against affiliation.[53]

Gompers also wrote ILO president Albert Thomas asking him to
repudiate the IFTU. Only by dissociating itself from radicals, Gompers
argued, could ILO leaders hope to maintain the support of League officials and wield influence in the organization. Thomas, although sympathetic toward the AFL, argued that he would not promote one trade
union philosophy over the other. Instead, he sought to use the ILO office
for collecting and disseminating information about a variety of trade
union movements and philosophies. Gompers responded by publicly
and privately chastising Thomas for lending credibility to radical movements. The AFL president subsequently refused to participate in ILO
activities despite persistent invitations by Thomas.[54]

In some respects, Gompers's decision to boycott ILO activities
seemed a strategic error, for Thomas's tolerance cut both ways. Although he failed to repudiate the IFTU, Thomas would have allowed the
AFL to use the organization's publications and meetings to promote
conservative trade union values and to win European supporters. But
Gompers, preoccupied with rehabilitating labor's image at home, wished
to avoid associating the AFL with an organization that refused to denounce radical labor diplomatic tactics. Gompers also believed Thomas
was destroying the credibility and potential influence of the ILO itself.
Just as Gompers thought that labor's power at home rested in part on
the AFL's ability to win respect from important elites, so, too, he perceived that the ILO's influence depended to a significant extent on the
kind of reputation it built among world leaders.[55]

Essentially cut off from European trade union movements, the AFL
developed its policies toward the revolutions that menaced Ireland,
Russia, and Mexico in isolation. Two considerations, in particular,
shaped the thinking of the AFL hierarchy. On the one hand, AFL leaders
were influenced by the kinds of methods that supporters of these revolutions asked the AFL to adopt in order to help their cause. On the other

53. *Proceedings of the AFL*, 1921, 80.
54. See Thomas to Gompers, 3/1/20, 8/27/20; and Greenwood to Gompers, 11/18/20:
CC-GMC.
55. Ibid.

hand, they considered whether revolutionary governments in these countries would promote policies that would close off markets to industrial-creditor nations and disrupt the world capitalist economy. Both of these considerations were in turn linked directly to their preoccupation with revitalizing the collaborationist partnership between business, labor, and the state in the arena of foreign affairs.

Generally neglected by American labor historians, the Irish revolution won more support within the AFL than its Russian or Mexican counterparts and threatened to disrupt fundamentally Gompers's postwar international agenda. Irish nationalists and AFL leaders had first scuffled over the issue of Irish independence at the annual convention in 1918. These battles continued during conventions in each of the following two years. But the real showdown did not come until 1921. Determined to force the AFL to take meaningful action, leading Irish nationalists like Frank Walsh tried to forge an alliance prior to the convention between traditional union leaders with strong Irish sympathies and progressive unionists like John Fitzpatrick, then head of the Labor Bureau of the Commission on Irish Independence. In particular, Walsh sought the help of these two factions in winning support for a resolution calling on the AFL to institute a boycott of British goods. He unofficially appointed Peter Brady, a union leader with close ties to the "official machine," to champion the boycott cause within the AFL.[56]

But even before Irish advocates began to lobby on behalf of the boycott, Gompers got wind of their plans and moved quickly to sabotage their efforts. As John Frey later reminisced, the boycott resolution "involved so many issues to which Sam was opposed that Sam did what he could to prevent the Walsh idea from gaining ground in the Federation of Labor." Because Irish revolutionaries were untainted by the stain of socialism, Gompers had previously acquiesced in AFL resolutions expressing support for Irish self-determination. But the AFL president vigorously opposed direct economic action by labor to achieve foreign policy goals. He believed that labor should instead be working with business and state leaders to promote a foreign policy that served the public interest. Gompers also likely feared that a U.S. labor boycott of British goods might sour the Anglo-American cooperation that he, like Wilson, believed so necessary to a stable postwar order. By contrast, supporters of the boycott resolution argued that it was the necessary

56. Harry Boland to Frank Walsh, 5/18/21: WP. *Proceedings of the AFL*, 1921, 202–3, 239, 387–89, 447–48; 1919, 324–27.

"enacting clause" without which all other resolutions expressing support for the Irish revolution would be meaningless.[57]

Gompers's first step in trying to thwart the drive for a boycott amendment was to encourage Frey to bring the major Irish factions together in a hotel room during the AFL convention and serve ample amounts of whiskey. Frey gladly complied and later argued that participants in the hotel conference hammered out a compromise resolution that excluded the boycott provision.[58] Progressive unionists like Ed Nockels, John Fitzpatrick, and Sam Evans, on the other hand, told a different story. They argued that AFL officials bribed Irish spokesman Peter Brady by offering him a trip to Britain as a fraternal delegate if he successfully suppressed the boycott movement. So seriously did Brady take his job that he had detectives follow those who continued to support the boycott resolution—apparently in an effort to find evidence that would discredit them. Sam Evans claimed that one such detective even tried to encourage him to go into a "house of ill repute." Progressive unionists persisted in the boycott campaign despite harassment by the AFL hierarchy, eventually gaining enough signatures to submit the boycott resolution for official consideration by the AFL. But the resolutions committee proposed a substitute resolution that officially endorsed Irish independence but excluded the boycott proposal.[59]

Progressive unionists responded by proposing, on the floor of the convention, an amendment to the substitute resolution that called for inclusion of a boycott clause. The amendment, however, was denied on the grounds that the committee had essentially voted nonconcurrence on the boycott issue by proposing a substitute resolution. The next day, delegate Christian Madsen of the CFL appealed the committee's decision. By substituting one resolution for another without allowing amendments, he argued, AFL leaders were burying important issues without a popular vote. Gompers, enraged by the suggestion of impropriety, declared Madsen's attacks on the committee unwarranted. Subsequently, progressives unsuccessfully tried several more parliamentary tactics to bring the boycott resolution before the convention, further irritating its opponents. Gompers finally stymied boycott promoters by ruling that under parliamentary law the only way the issue could be reconsidered

---

57. Frey, Memoir, 3: 427. Sam Evans, Supplemental Report to Frank Walsh on the Trip to the Forty First Annual Convention of the American Federation of Labor, 1, B26: WP.

58. Frey, Memoir, 3: 426–30.

59. Evans, Supplemental Report, 23, 1–24; Nockels to Walsh, 6/26/21, 1–7; Fitzpatrick to Walsh, 6/18/21: B26, WP. *Proceedings of the AFL*, 1921, 202–3, 239, 447–48.

was if the substitute legislation was defeated. Not wanting to vote against Irish independence, progressive unionists finally succumbed and accepted the substitute resolution. It subsequently passed overwhelmingly.[60]

While AFL leaders opposed substantial aid to Irish revolutionaries, they officially endorsed Ireland's right to independence. By contrast, AFL officials wished to avoid even the appearance of supporting the new Bolshevik regime in Russia. Once again, they used substitute resolutions to blunt the initiatives of revolutionary supporters. Conflict over Russia first surfaced in 1919. At the annual convention that year, a trade unionist proposed a series of resolutions calling for the withdrawal of American troops from Russia and demanding an end to the Allied economic blockade. The Committee on Resolutions proposed a substitute resolution that changed the demand that troops be withdrawn immediately to a request that the United States withdraw its troops at the "earliest possible moment." The issue of the economic blockade was eliminated entirely. In addition, the committee attached a statement to the end of the resolution that declared that "this convention refuse its endorsement of the Soviet government . . . until the people of Russia . . . through popular elections shall have reestablished a truly democratic form of government."[61] The new substitute resolution not only watered down the original resolutions but changed their symbolic meaning from one of support for the new Bolshevik regime to one of criticism. Despite protests from supporters of the Russian revolution, however, the new substitute resolution passed easily.[62]

After 1919, debate in the AFL over Russia focused primarily on the issues of resuming trade and diplomatic recognition. Gompers opposed both and successfully stifled attempts by radicals to gain AFL support for either of these causes in 1920 and 1921.[63] Opponents of the AFL's Russian policies made slightly more headway in 1922. At the convention, the Committee on International Relations spoke as usual against the resumption of trade with Russia or recognition of the Bolshevik regime. Afterwards, however, it gave a long report on the adverse conditions that existed in Russia and asked that it be recognized as the official

60. *Proceedings of the AFL*, 1921, 202–3, 239, 387–89, 447–48. Evans, Supplemental Report, 16–24; Nockels to Walsh, 6/26/21, 1–7: B26, WP. NM, 9/10/21, 7.
61. *Proceedings of the AFL*, 1919, 333.
62. Ibid.
63. See *American Federationist* 27 (February 1920): 159; (October 1920): 920. *Proceedings of the AFL*, 1921, 90, 442–43.

AFL position on the situation there. The report spurred considerable debate, with many questioning whether any outside power could actually know what was going on in a country during a state of revolution.[64] Dissenters subsequently drew up a minority report that gave their interpretations of conditions in Russia. The report admitted that there was some repression and bloodshed in Russia. However, in discussions on the subject, dissenters argued that bloodshed was inevitable in any revolution and noted the violence that had characterized America's conflict with Britain in 1776.[65]

Gompers, disgusted by the comparison of the American and Russian revolutions, argued that the American struggle for independence was "no pink tea party" but, rather, a "big, self sacrificing revolution."[66] The Americans, he argued, had fought for freedom. The Soviets, on the other hand, were interested only in stirring up unrest both at home and abroad. Gompers also opposed the minority report on the grounds that if it were passed, no government would "take the AFL seriously."[67] Gompers then wrote Commerce Secretary Herbert Hoover and Secretary of State Charles Evans Hughes asking for the government's official position on trade with Russia and diplomatic recognition. Hughes's reply was subsequently read to the convention. According to Hughes, the conditions for resuming normal trade with Russia included the safety of life, the recognition of private property, the sanctity of contract, and the rights of free labor. Gompers claimed that none of these conditions existed in Russia. To endorse the Soviet regime in any way, he suggested, would make the AFL appear both disloyal and ignorant.[68]

Gompers's arguments were significant, for they demonstrated that he opposed AFL support for the Soviet regime not just because he disagreed with communist principles but because he believed that such support would damage the AFL's reputation with government leaders both at home and abroad. AFL power, he perceived, ultimately depended on the goodwill of these leaders. Also implicit in Gompers's arguments was a sense that the Soviets were not entitled to membership in the world family of nations because they threatened international stability. Just as socialist and communist groups undermined the attempts of government leaders to encourage cooperation between different classes at home, so

64. *Proceedings of the AFL*, 1922, 422–28.
65. Ibid., 1922, 426.
66. Ibid., 433.
67. Ibid., 434–35, 465.
68. Ibid.

also the Soviet regime hindered the efforts of world leaders to create an integrated international capitalist order that would encourage cooperation among different classes of nations (that is, between developed and underdeveloped countries). Like Wilson, he suggested that the Soviet regime must be shunned for the good of the world community. The AFL convention endorsed Gompers's policies by overwhelmingly voting in favor of the majority report on Russia. Subsequently, Gompers was able to prevent either substantive or symbolic AFL support for the Russian revolution.[69]

The AFL's policies toward the Mexican revolution, by contrast, were quite supportive. Intimately involved with the revolution from its beginning, Gompers had applauded the overthrow of Porfirio Díaz because he believed that Díaz's free-for-all open investment policy had created economic instability in Mexico. He was concerned, however, about finding a replacement for Díaz who would shun socialism and direct Mexico along a moderate course. At first, Gompers oscillated in his views of whom to support; none of the hopeful candidates between 1912 and 1914 offered the kind of qualities he desired in a Mexican president. By 1915, however, Gompers had decided that General Venustiano Carranza was the best of the alternatives and advocated U.S. recognition of his regime. Subsequently, Gompers claimed credit both for gaining recognition of the Carranza regime and for preventing American intervention during the early years of his presidency.[70] Gompers continued to have qualms about Carranza, however, because the Mexican president was extremely nationalistic. The AFL president's misgivings were confirmed when Carranza gave his support to an article in the Mexican Constitution of 1917 that vested in the state ownership of all the subsoil of Mexico and gave foreign capitalists only indefinite leases on the property held there. In addition, Carranza's antilabor policies upset AFL leaders.[71]

In 1920, General Álvaro Obregón overthrew Carranza. Gompers supported Obregón for several reasons. First, the Mexican president chose to placate foreign capital and restimulate investment. Second,

69. Ibid. *NR*, 7/5/22, 150; Samuel Gompers and William English Walling, *Out of Their Own Mouths: A Revelation and an Indictment of Sovietism* (New York: E. P. Dutton, 1921); Foner, *History of the Labor Movement*, 8: 44–62. On Wilson and the USSR, see Levin, *Wilson*, 183–251.

70. *Proceedings of the AFL*, 1916, 57; AFL, *Labor and the War*, 136–37. See also Chapter 2.

71. Levenstein, *Labor Organizations in the United States and Mexico*, 100–110. Andrews, *Shoulder to Shoulder*, 70–98.

Obregón had a close relationship with the conservative trade union movement in Mexico and brought top officials from the Confederación Regional Obrera Mexicana (CROM) into his administration. Obregón worked through CROM to discourage radicalism in Mexico. Of greatest importance, Obregón used the AFL as one of Mexico's prime diplomatic voices in America. Unlike supporters of the Irish or Russian revolutions, however, Obregón did not ask the AFL to obstruct administration policy. Rather, he requested only that the AFL serve as a channel of communication between himself and the Harding administration. Gompers relished this role because he believed that it was one of the most positive ways for labor to influence foreign policy. Both he and the AFL Executive Council worked wholeheartedly to prevent American intervention in Mexico in 1920 and 1921. Likewise, they persuaded the AFL convention to endorse and work for recognition of Mexico.[72]

Taken together, AFL policies toward Ireland, Russia, and Mexico suggest that by 1922 the AFL had defined a role for American labor in shaping U.S. policy toward revolutionary regimes that was premised in part on corporatist principles. AFL leaders perceived that labor's primary duty was to facilitate communication between new regimes and the American government. They did not believe that labor should use its economic power to obstruct the policies of legitimately elected U.S. administrations. AFL officials instead tried to use informal networks to dissuade government officials from adopting policies that they believed would be harmful to workers either at home or abroad. The AFL also tried to influence diplomacy by using its contacts in revolutionary countries to gain support for American policy. When revolutionary leaders tried to force the American labor movement to adopt more militant tactics, AFL leaders denied them aid; labor's diplomatic power depended on proving to the American government and to key business elites that the trade union movement was a valuable ally.

But whether revolutionary regimes agreed to play according to corporatist rules was only one factor in shaping AFL policy toward revolutions after the 1920 election. AFL leaders also developed an informal set of assumptions about the kinds of revolutionary regimes that threatened world stability. These assumptions seemed heavily influenced by the productionist thinking of many state and business leaders. As a result of its work for the National Civic Federation and

72. Gompers, *Seventy Years*, 2: 319, 541; Frey, *Reminiscences*, 3: 431, 514. Andrews, *Shoulder to Shoulder*, 99–139; Levenstein, *Labor Organizations in the United States and Mexico*, 100–110.

on war boards, the AFL had begun to link gains for workers at home to increased industrial efficiency. Greater efficiency would ensure that the size of the national economic pie increased and that everyone's slices grew larger. Similarly, the AFL attacked socialist and other revolutionary governments abroad that propounded theories of economic nationalism because trade and financial barriers would allegedly undermine the efficiency of the free international marketplace and hinder world economic growth. AFL leaders believed that working people in newly formed nation-states should protect themselves through conservative unionism like that practiced in the United States rather than through artificial political constructs. Such attitudes reflected little understanding of the special needs of underdeveloped countries but were consistent with the AFL's voluntarist orientation at home.[73]

In addition to creating a set of precepts to guide American labor's response to revolution, AFL leaders also devoted their efforts to developing regional replicas of the ILO after the 1920 election. These organizations, they hoped, could assist the ILO in preventing the privation and social unrest that fostered revolution in underdeveloped areas. Concerned in particular with Latin America, AFL leaders channeled their energies into developing the Pan-American Federation of Labor (PAFL). Gompers had first sought to form a hemispheric labor organization during the war in order to combat pacifism among Central American workers.[74] But these plans were postponed when he became preoccupied with events in Europe during 1917. After much delay, PAFL was finally launched in November 1918. Its postwar goals were to raise labor standards in Latin America, foster the growth of responsible unionism, and curb the abuses of capitalists throughout the Americas.[75]

To promote the organization, AFL leaders established contacts with conservative trade unionists throughout Latin America and invited them to attend PAFL meetings. After accepting membership, Latin American trade union leaders were encouraged to monitor the activities of American businessmen in their countries and to report these activities to the AFL so it could inform proper authorities of any misconduct by U.S.

73. For discussions of the concept of productionism, see McCormick, "Drift or Mastery?" 318–30; Hogan, "Revival and Reform," 301–2. For an excellent explanation of the concept of international comparative advantage, see Godfried, *Bridging the Gap*, 1–18. See also Rosenberg's discussion of liberal developmentalism in *Spreading the American Dream*, 7–13.

74. Lorwin, *Labor and Internationalism*, 286; Gompers, *Seventy Years*, 2: 318–21.

75. Lorwin, *Labor and Internationalism*, 286; Gompers, *Seventy Years*, 2: 318–32; AFL, *Labor and the War*, 171–72.

industrialists.[76] AFL leaders also took advantage of PAFL contacts to send its own investigating teams to Puerto Rico, Santo Domingo, the Dominican Republic, and Nicaragua. These teams subsequently submitted extensive reports to the Harding administration outlining labor conditions and business practices in those countries.[77]

While Gompers believed the primary purpose of PAFL was to improve labor standards, he also hoped that it would serve regional defense purposes. Shortly after PAFL's founding, the AFL president asserted that he still hoped for American participation in the League of Nations and that he had faith that it would help to prevent future wars. But he argued that if the League should fail in its attempts to eliminate international conflict, then PAFL would help to protect the Western hemisphere. The Pan-American labor organization, he argued, was founded in the spirit of the Monroe Doctrine. If European nations should develop evil designs on the Americas, then PAFL would take a solid "stand against aggression."[78]

The AFL's foreign policy programs between 1920 and 1922 won it tentative support from the Harding administration, and some cabinet officials appointed AFL representatives to newly constructed civilian boards. Secretary of State Charles Hughes, for example, invited Gompers to serve on commissions on disarmament and on councils dealing with U.S. policy toward China and the Near East. Similarly, Commerce Secretary Herbert Hoover appointed the AFL president to a number of economic commissions that dealt peripherally with foreign policy. Gompers never viewed these boards as a sufficient replacement for the extensive corporatist system that had developed during the war.[79] Labor participation on these boards nonetheless marked a victory for the AFL president; through vigilant attention to public image, the AFL had won the renewed loyalty of government officials.

The years from 1919 to 1922 witnessed a sustained and partially successful attempt by the AFL to create a corporatist diplomatic role for itself. Initially unsuccessful in its efforts to promote Wilsonian domestic and international institutions, AFL leaders constructed a foreign policy

76. AFL, *Labor and the War*, 171–72; Gompers, *Seventy Years*, 2: 318–21; Lorwin, *Labor and Internationalism*, 286.
77. *Proceedings of the AFL*, 1920, 240; and in general, 240–57. See also AFL, *Labor and the War*, 171–72; *Proceedings of the AFL*, 1919, 88. Conference, Gompers with Morris, Iglesias, and Wright, 1/25/23: Con C-GMC. See also NR, 6/29/21, 128; 7/23/21, 184.
78. Gompers, *Seventy Years*, 2: 512, 323–32.
79. *Proceedings of the AFL*, 1922, 87–88; Gompers, *Seventy Years*, 2: 511.

program in the aftermath of the 1920 election that was partly premised on corporatist and productionist principles. The AFL's foreign policy programs won it a position in emerging corporatist institutions within the Harding administration. But the AFL's policies further damaged its reputation among local labor movements and labor party proponents. Hurt by AFL offensives in the wake of the armistice, municipal labor activists would continue to seek very different kinds of power for workers and to spar with Gompers over his foreign policy agenda.

CHAPTER FOUR

The Labor Party Offensive and the Evolution of an Alternative Labor Foreign Policy

W HILE European and American labor leaders clashed with each other over diplomatic issues at international labor conferences in the postwar era, their initiatives were often threatened from below by the eruption of grass-roots workers' movements promoting alternative international agendas. Spurred by a sense that labor leadership had betrayed the rank and file through their collaborationist wartime foreign policies, local militants from Berlin to San Francisco experimented after the armistice with direct forms of action by workers to achieve diplomatic goals. In Britain, 350 "councils of action" drawn from the old shop stewards' movement, local trade councils, labor constituency parties, and socialist groups initiated a "Hands off Russia" campaign, threatening a general strike if the government failed to heed their demands. The councils helped persuade the British Labour party and the Trades Union Congress to pass a resolution decrying the Allied intervention in Russia as a "crime against humanity" and threatening strike action if troops were not withdrawn. The councils also unsuccessfully promoted plans for a general strike to end British intervention in Ireland. Similar institutions proliferated throughout Europe in the immediate postwar period and helped propel trade union, socialist, and Labour party leaders toward more militant international actions.[1]

1. On Britain, see Perkin, *Rise of Professional Society*, 211; Hinton, *Labour and Socialism*, 24–29, 76, 99; Pelling, *Labour Party*, 47; Leventhal, *Arthur Henderson*, 82. On continental Europe, see Nolan, *Social Democracy*; Steenson, *Not One Man, Not One Penny*; Stansky, *The Left and the War*; and James Cronin, "Labor Insurgency and Class Formation: Comparative Perspectives on the Crisis of 1917–1920 in Europe," in *Work, Community, and Power*, ed. Cronin and Sirianni, 32.

Within the United States, the new spirit of rank-and-file assertiveness in foreign affairs was best embodied in the local labor parties that spread throughout the country following the armistice. Such parties were often led by local dissidents who, like those promoting direct-action movements in Britain, had vigorously criticized the collaborationist foreign policies of labor officials during the war. The agendas of the new parties organically connected struggles for industrial, political, and diplomatic democracy. Surprisingly, given their local character, many labor parties developed comprehensive foreign policy platforms on every conceivable international issue. While drawing inspiration from revolutionary movements abroad, labor party leaders portrayed their efforts to gain more power for workers in the workplace, in Washington, and in international politics as the logical culmination of a democratic revolution dating back to the founding fathers. Such an approach proved ideologically attractive to American workers, who elected Labor party mayors in numerous mid-sized cities during the municipal elections in spring 1919. Equally significant, Labor party candidates made impressive showings in several large urban centers such as Chicago and Kansas City with complex political alignments and histories of ethnic and racial tensions.[2]

Yet when Chicago and Illinois labor leaders tried to rally support for a national Farmer-Labor party, their uncompromising emphasis on rank-and-file assertiveness and direct forms of democracy in industry and politics alienated moderate supporters who could provide the party with crucial funding, publicity, and prominent candidates. Simultaneously undercut by AFL opposition, the red scare, and disillusioning strike defeats, the Farmer-Labor party performed poorly in the elections of 1920. Local militants remained committed to labor party politics after the election but, buoyed by the militant spirit of labor internationalism sweeping through Europe, many became increasingly enmeshed in campaigns designed to utilize labor's economic power to achieve foreign policy goals. In Britain, the shockwaves of the new rank-and-file foreign policy movements would be largely absorbed by the British Labour party and Trades Union Congress; in the United States, they would polarize the labor movement and the working class and inhibit the further growth of labor party politics.[3]

Although the CFL-sponsored Chicago Labor party was not the most successful of the municipal labor parties, its vital role in the creation of

2. Shapiro, "'Hand and Brain,'" 412–13.
3. On Britain, see, Hinton, *Labour and Socialism, First Shop Stewards' Movement.*

the Farmer-Labor party makes it key to understanding the movement for independent labor political action. As the war drew to a close, the Chicago Federation of Labor was abuzz with activity. Following on the heels of the successful stockyards campaigns, CFL leaders in the summer of 1918 received AFL permission to lead an organizing drive in the steel industry. They began their activities in the Chicago-Gary area and then spread into other important steel regions such as Ohio, Colorado, West Virginia, and Pennsylvania. The campaign was a pivotal one, for it involved organizing thousands of skilled and unskilled workers and coordinating the efforts of twenty-four different unions operating in the industry. The basic strategy of steel organizers, according to William Z. Foster, was to "make a hurricane drive simultaneously in all steel centers that would catch the workers' imagination and sweep them into the union en masse."[4]

So preoccupied with organizing efforts were CFL leaders in the winter of 1919 that one wonders how they even had time to proceed with labor party campaigns. But John Fitzpatrick argued that political action, rather than being a distraction from industrial campaigns, was a vital complement to it. Speaking before the National Labor Party Conference later that year, Fitzpatrick drew a stark portrait of a society in which workers were flagrantly murdered for exercising their first amendment rights to picket. Industrial campaigns, he seemed to imply, could never be successful until the state took seriously its responsibility to protect the civil rights of workers. And in contrast to Gompers, Fitzpatrick argued that trade unionists could not obtain sufficient protections by working within the framework of the current political system because the two major parties were dominated by big businessmen and financial interests "drunk with power and influence as a result of their profiteering during the war."[5]

As the new year dawned, CFL leaders forged ahead with plans for the Chicago Labor party. One of their first steps was to create a labor party platform based on the declaration of political principles adopted during the last few weeks of the war. Once again, CFL leaders demanded democratic control of industry. They also continued to insist that workers be given representation on government councils and in the League according to their proportion "in the armies, navies and workshops of the world."[6]

4. Foster, *Great Steel Strike*, 21; Brody, *Steelworkers in America*, 180–262; Foner, *History of the Labor Movement*, 8: 154.
5. *Proceedings of the First National Convention of the Labor Party of the U.S.*, November 22, 1919, 2–5.
6. "Declaration of Labor Party Principles," *CFL Minutes*, 11/3/18, 13–21.

But apart from these demands, the stated goals of the new Labor party were quite modest. CFL leaders asked for recognition of the rights of workers to organize and reiterated demands for legislation regulating labor standards. One plank called for the establishment of an eight-hour day and minimum wage; another demanded the abolition of unemployment. Still others addressed issues of old age insurance and workmen's compensation. The most important plank outlined plans for extending the insurance of soldiers and sailors to all men and women and establishing a governmental subsidy program to protect workers against accident and illness. CFL leaders also called for a graduated income tax and public ownership of utilities. They further asked that "Kaiserism" in education be abolished and demanded the restoration of free speech. So in line with longstanding AFL policies were these demands that Gompers included most of them in his own reconstruction program.[7]

Labor party advocates adopted a deliberately moderate tone because they wished, in the words of Illinois State Federation of Labor president John Walker, to avoid the kind of program that would "disorganize our people and organize our enemies."[8] Comparing themselves repeatedly to the British Labour party, local organizers avoided revolutionary language that might alienate mainstream trade unionists or disillusioned progressives. Even the demand for democratic control of industry, while sounding a militant note, failed to conjure up socialist images because it neatly avoided defining the parameters of private enterprise in a labor-dominated social order. Similarly, demands for proportional representation on government councils and in the League implied a logical extension of American democratic ideals rather than a proletarian revolution.

After the platform was adopted, Fitzpatrick sent it and the official proposal to create a labor party to the entire local union membership for a referendum vote. The response was overwhelming. Local unions voted 158 to 12 in favor of a labor party. Even more striking, combined union vote totals showed that rank-and-file union members favored the formation of a labor party by a margin of ten to one.[9] Such statistics, of course, present a skewed picture of rank-and-file support for the party

7. Ibid.; Sell, "The A.F. of L. and the Labor Party Movement," 97; Shapiro, "'Hand and Brain,'" 412.
8. *Proceedings of the First National Convention of the Labor Party*, 1919, 14. See also *ISFL Proceedings*, 1920, 139.
9. *CFL Minutes*, 12/1/18, 17–21; 12/15/18, 17. Staley, *ISFL*, 363–64; Roger Horowitz, "The Failure of Independent Political Action: The Labor Party of Cook County, 1919–20" (Bachelor's essay, University of Chicago, 1982), 25. Nockels to Walsh, 11/25/18, B7: WP.

since only the most active and militant members were likely to vote. Nonetheless, the margins impressed Illinois State Federation of Labor officials so much that they put the issue to a test of their constituent membership. Affiliates of this body endorsed plans for a labor party by a margin of 333 to 37.[10]

Armed with these favorable statistics, CFL officials scheduled an organizational convention for January. Seven hundred fifty delegates attended; they represented 165 unions from the Chicago area. These delegates officially established the Cook County Labor party and endorsed the Labor party platform written by the CFL. They created a constitution and organizational structure for the party similar to that of the British Labour party. Unions were given special membership privileges and allowed to join for the small fee of twelve and one-half cents per capita per year. By contrast, persons who joined independently were charged one dollar per quarter. Both union and independent members were required to work for their ward or township branches. These bodies elected a delegate committee, which in turn appointed a citywide executive board of fifteen members. Like its British counterpart, the Cook County Labor party also instituted referendum, initiative, and recall procedures. In other words, rank-and-file members were legally entitled to suggest new policies to the board and could also demand that votes of the entire membership be taken on controversial policy issues or to determine whether board members should be retained for their full terms.[11]

Delegates to the convention chose two tactics to promote the new party. They created a Labor party newspaper entitled the *New Majority* to carry information about political campaigns "to every precinct and every party member." In a typically optimistic fashion, CFL secretary Ed Nockels predicted that if the party could get the new paper "out to the people, we will win."[12] The second strategy adopted by the convention was to run a candidate for the Chicago mayoral election in April. Labor party advocates never expected to win an election only a few months away but argued that if they could garner a hundred thousand votes, the new party would be born. Not surprisingly, a nominating convention chose John Fitzpatrick as the Labor party mayoral candi-

10. *ISFL Proceedings*, 1919, 55–56; NM, 1/3/20, 8; Green, "Labor Party," 38; Staley, *ISFL*, 363–64.

11. NM, 1/4/19, 2; 1/11/19, 15; 1/3/20, 8; and Horowitz, "Failure of Independent Political Action," 1–2.

12. NM, 1/4/19, 2. Nockels to Walsh, 3/21/19, B8: WP.

date.[13] The plans for developing a labor newspaper and launching a mayoral campaign were modest in scale, but they soon revolutionized the party.

Robert Buck, a prominent local journalist and former Chicago alderman, assumed management of the New Majority. Buck and his staff proposed to operate their paper like the "jack screw—slow but sure. Not too slow but slow enough to prevent disorganization and fast enough to wreck the old system of graft and cheating within a few months or years."[14] The analogy symbolized their commitment to the far-reaching but evolutionary policies of the Labor party. New Majority editors perceived a dual role for the paper. On the one hand, they sought to chisel away at the public image of the Democratic and Republican parties until both had been discredited. On the other hand, they tried to sketch a favorable portrait of the Labor party that would win it an increasing number of votes every year. Like CFL officials, staff members believed that this latter goal could best be achieved by emphasizing that the Labor party, far from being a radical new departure, was a natural outgrowth of the trade union movement. Ironically, the logic of applying class analysis to the programs of the Democratic and Republican parties soon led New Majority staffers to burn the ideological bridges that still linked them to the AFL.

Initially, the New Majority staff concentrated on local issues. In a series of stunning exposés, the staff uncovered corruption within both the Chicago Republican and Democratic parties. The paper also reported on several public utility scandals in which area politicians were involved.[15] Despite the fact that the paper was the organ of a county labor party, its editors soon devoted most of their attention to national and international affairs. Workers, they believed, were unduly influenced by the high-minded rhetoric of the Wilson administration. If the Labor party was to be a success, it needed to demonstrate how badly the Democrats had deceived workers during the war. "A Bargain was made," wrote one editor, "between the United States and each Soldier sent to Europe. The soldier agreed to risk life and limb in battle, the United States in turn agreed to make the world safe for democracy. By

13. Walsh to Fagin, 12/31/18, B7; Walsh to Nockels, B8: WP. Stanley Shapiro, "Hand and Brain: The Farmer-Labor Party of 1920" (Ph.D. diss., University of California at Berkeley, 1967), 117 (hereafter designated with a "d" to distinguish it from his article by the same title). NM, 1/3/20, 8.

14. NM, 1/4/19, 6.

15. Ibid., 1/4/19, 12; 2/22/19, 5.

democracy, we meant, above all, a fair and square deal for the common man in America as well as in Europe."[16] But Buck and his staffers argued that the Wilson administration had impeded rather than quickened the growth of democracy.

At home, they suggested, the Wilson administration severely curtailed workers' civil rights during the war. Abuses of workers' constitutional guarantees to free speech continued even after the signing of the armistice. *New Majority* staffers claimed that many laborers remained as political prisoners in American jails. In one exposé, a reporter suggested sarcastically that the Wilson administration should not allow crippled veterans from the Letterman hospital in San Francisco to visit San Quentin and see dissident Tom Mooney because "any disabled soldier capable of clear thinking" would then realize that the government had made a mockery of its wartime pledges.[17] Staffers also argued that economic democracy had decreased since Wilson took office. During the European conflict, big businessmen made massive profits at consumers' expense. Meanwhile, workers' wages failed even to keep pace with inflation. Reporters suggested that the administration was now in collusion with the nation's leading magnates to prevent soldiers from receiving adequate benefits for their services. This evil cabal of business and government leaders also sought to institute a peacetime draft.[18]

The *New Majority* devoted equal space to recounting the ways in which Wilson had violated his pledges to improve democracy abroad. In particular, Buck focused on the revolutions in Ireland and Russia. Buck argued that the *New Majority* had a responsibility to cover activities in these countries because "we may be sure that all we hear from Europe is as unreliable as the stuff the *Tribune* and other loop daily newspapers dish up for us about our own hometown and country."[19] Staffers carefully documented the failed attempts of Irish revolutionaries to obtain a hearing at the Paris Peace Conference and argued that Wilson deliberately ignored the Irish delegation. Rebutting Wilson's claims that the British sought a fair peace settlement in Ireland, staff members instead reported on British atrocities in the Anglo-Irish war and argued that Britain's real "program" was "Irish bloodshed."[20]

16. Ibid., 4/26/19, 15.
17. Ibid., 4/26/19, 15; 5/3/19, 4; 2/22/19, 5.
18. Ibid., 1/4/19, 12; 4/5/19, 16; 2/22/19, 4–5.
19. Ibid., 2/1/19, 4.
20. Ibid., 4/5/19, 6; 4/12/19, 7–9.

Even more print was devoted to the Russian revolution. During January, the paper published important Soviet documents it claimed the major papers had suppressed. Among them were the Soviet constitution and an eloquent letter from V. I. Lenin to English troops asking them to cease hostilities. As American military involvement in the Russian civil war increased, the staff carefully explained troop movements and detailed atrocities committed by White Russian forces.[21] Reporters also began investigating American financial interests in Russia. Their disclosures provided the evidence necessary for editors to discredit the claim that America became involved in the internecine conflict to preserve democracy there. "We have been told," they wrote, "that we fought Russia because the Bolshevik was blood thirsty and cruel. Now the cat is out of the bag—the Allies and America, dominated by bond holding statesmen, are having American, British and French troops killed in Russia simply to compel the Bolsheviks to pay bonds incurred by the Czar. Can you beat it?"[22] After many American businessmen shifted in favor of recognition for the new Russian regime, the paper praised their pragmatism and chastised the Wilson administration for playing "the imperialist game of the allied imperialist states of Europe."[23]

New Majority editors also attacked the continuing peace negotiations in Paris. "Pledged to abolish secret treaties, secretly arrived at," they wrote, "the 'Big Four' sit in secret cooking up a secretly arrived at covenant based not at all on creating a world family of free contented peaceful peoples but on dividing up the swag between the national groups of money hogs."[24] They prophesied that such a treaty would bring only a very fleeting cessation of hostilities. Staffers additionally complained about the League. Far from preventing the oppression of small nationality groups, they argued, the organization would hinder their attempts to win freedom. Buck and other reporters wisely avoided criticizing the ILO directly, but they nonetheless printed in full Andrew Furuseth's extensive critique under the banner headline, "Furuseth Reports Inside Peace Dope—May God Save the Working People."[25]

By spring 1919, Buck's attempts to discredit the Democrats and build a working-class agenda for the Cook County Labor party had led him and the *New Majority* staff to reject the collaborationist and Wilsonian

21. Ibid., 1/4/19, 12; 4/5/19, 16; 2/22/19, 4–5.
22. Ibid., 2/15/19, 4.
23. Ibid., 5/24/19, 4.
24. Ibid., 4/26/19, 1.
25. Ibid., 5/17/19, 11, 14–15.

principles that lay at the heart of AFL diplomacy. The wartime alliance between labor and the state, Buck hinted, had failed to advance the position of labor at home or to ensure democracy for workers abroad. If labor were to gain ground in the postwar era, then it must break its bonds with the Wilson administration and engage in independent political action. Party organizers, defying advice to stick with local issues, subsequently used the national and foreign policy analyses of the *New Majority* to help promote Fitzpatrick's mayoral campaign.

Winning support for a labor party among the multiethnic working-class population of Chicago was not easy. Chicago's ethnic groups not only contended with each other for local power but had conflicting national and international interests. War intensified rather than diminished workers' nationalist loyalties. The Labor party tried to overcome ethnic divisions within the working class partly through traditional means. Like the major parties, the Labor party tried to draw votes by slating candidates of different ethnic backgrounds. Fitzpatrick was chosen to head the ticket partly to draw the Irish vote. Polish labor leader and National Alliance member John Kikulski was slated for city clerk in the hopes that he would garner support from Chicago's Slavic communities. Meanwhile, the party hoped to attract northern Europeans by nominating Swedish house painter Knute Torkelson for city treasurer. The Labor party also tried to win ethnic support by engaging speakers at ethnic events and pledging Labor party support for a wide variety of nationalist causes. Fitzpatrick, for example, spoke often at Friends of Irish Freedom events and donated periodically to other Irish groups. He also wrote articles in support of Polish freedom for the socialist paper, *Dziennik Ludowy*, and worked for the Negro Worker's Advisory Committee, Friends of Freedom for India, and an Italian labor group.[26]

Yet, officials realized they needed to transcend the particularistic demands of ethnic groups if they were to secure the loyalties of the local working class; the Labor party, as a newcomer in Chicago politics, was unlikely to beat Democratic and Republican masters at the game of ethnic patronage. While engaging in a limited way in the traditional Chicago art of coalition building, the party also tried to forge an independent working-class identity. The local issues around which the party centered its campaign were home rule, municipal ownership and operation of all public utilities, and a city-built system of cooperative housing

26. Receipt from Commission on Irish Independence, B9–F63; Letter from *Dziennik Ludowy* to Fitzpatrick, n.d., B12–F84; Forrester B. Washington to Fitzpatrick, 2/16/19, B8–F56; Agnes Smedly to Fitzpatrick, 5/25/19, B8–F60: FP. NM, 1/4/19, 5.

and warehouse storage. The party also sought passage of ordinances recognizing the right of workers to bargain collectively and instituting an eight-hour day and forty-four hour week for all workers.[27]

The safest policy for Labor party officials would probably have been to focus on this local program. Yet, like Buck, they also tried to realign the national political loyalties of Chicago workers. In particular, they sought to discredit Wilsonian internationalism and create support for a class-based diplomacy. Foreign policy was a potential quagmire for the Labor party because of the conflicting international loyalties of Chicago's ethnic groups. But by spring 1919, many of these groups shared a common disillusionment with the Wilson administration: Few believed that Wilson had sufficiently fulfilled his pledges to their homelands. Labor party leaders gave timely voice to this disillusionment by citing *New Majority* editorials. Wilson, they suggested at mass meetings throughout the city, had failed to fulfill his pledges not just to their own homelands but to numerous countries. In failing to make good on his overworn promise to make the world safe for democracy, Wilson had betrayed the American worker who so gallantly fought under the stars and stripes. Labor party leaders suggested that the honor of American soldiers and workingmen could be restored only if laborers united politically and fulfilled Wilson's promises for themselves.[28]

CFL officials also followed Buck's lead in trying to rally workers behind the causes of the Russian and Irish revolutions. Evidence suggests that workers were surprisingly receptive to their pleas. In the fifteenth ward, Labor party officials convinced a large meeting of workers from a variety of ethnic backgrounds to pass a resolution viva voce on Russia asking that the United States withdraw all troops from Russia, raise the trade blockade, and speed domestic production so as to provide the "suffering people in Russia with food" and "American unemployed with work." The group then composed its own addendum. "We ask these things," they proclaimed, "for the starving people of Russia, but even more, we ask these things that the United States may share in righting a terrible wrong, that no man in this war shall have died for empty words and worthless phrases and that from this time forward the world may be made forever safe for experiments and new adventures in democracy."[29]

A group of eight thousand workers at the stockyards rallied and voted unanimously to demand the recognition of the Irish republic. The

27. Shapiro, "Hand and Brain," d, 115; NM, 3/15/19, 1.
28. NM, 3/15/19, 1; 2/1/19, 6.
29. Ibid., 2/1/19, 6.

crowd also condemned with "loud acclaim" any nation that "wars upon other nations for democracy and the right of self-determination and then proceeds to hypocritically ignore the principles which it so loudly proclaimed." The rally may have been organized by Irish workers, but a majority of the crowd was probably Polish.[30] At yet another meeting, a Black local of the Amalgamated Meat Cutters and Butchers Workmen extended its sympathy to the cause of Ireland despite a long history of racial conflict between Irish and Blacks in Chicago.[31]

The enthusiastic multiethnic support the Labor party received for its foreign programs at local rallies seemed to bode well for the future of the party. Unfortunately, just as the Labor party movement was gaining momentum on the streets of Chicago, the AFL launched its Non-Partisan Political Campaign. The campaign almost certainly lost the Cook County Labor party the support of many local unions. It probably also cost the party votes among nonunion workers who reasoned that the party was doomed without AFL backing. During the April election, Fitzpatrick made a respectable but not outstanding showing. In a bitterly fought five-way race, Fitzpatrick garnered fifty-five thousand votes, or 8 percent of the final tally.[32]

Although Labor party leaders fell short of their goal of one hundred thousand votes, they decided to proceed with plans to form a state labor party. Several factors likely influenced their decision. Despite the fact that the party had not done as well as expected in Chicago, it had finished significantly ahead of the more well-established Socialist party and had elicited support from a broad spectrum of the city's neighborhoods. Perhaps most significant, the party won impressive vote tallies in the heavily Polish and Lithuanian twenty-ninth ward next to the stockyards: 13 percent of the electorate there supported Fitzpatrick, while aldermanic candidate and Stockyards Labor Council president Martin Murphy garnered a striking 20 percent of the ward's vote. The favorable showing in stockyards districts illustrated the close link between union-organizing campaigns and interest in Labor politics and seemed to suggest that the two would advance hand-in-hand in the postwar era.[33]

30. Ibid., 3/15/19, 1.
31. Ibid., 3/8/19, 3; 4/26/19, 5. See also William M. Tuttle, Jr., Race Riot: Chicago in the Red Summer of 1919 (New York: Atheneum, 1970), 102–3.
32. NM, 4/5/19, 1; 3/6/20, 8. Shapiro, "Hand and Brain," d, 18; Horowitz, "Failure of Independent Political Action," 32; Sell, "The A.F. of L. and the Labor Party Movement," 142; Kantowicz, Polish-American Politics, 143.
33. Barrett, Work and Community in the Jungle, 207.

The optimism of Chicago Labor party leaders was probably also kindled by the election of eight Labor party mayors in medium-sized cities in Illinois in the spring elections, including the important industrial centers of Aurora, Elgin, and Rock Island. In nearby Joliet, the Labor party candidate for mayor lost by only 247 votes. Labor parties also ran well in the more socioeconomically and ethnically diverse municipalities of Kansas City and Topeka, Kansas. News that labor parties had spread to a number of other states, including Pennsylvania, Indiana, Michigan, Ohio, Kentucky, Iowa, and California, probably also buoyed the spirits of Chicago activists.[34]

Further contributing to the mood of optimism was the support given to the Labor party movement by prominent liberals such as Frank Walsh, who proclaimed unabashedly prior to the mayoral election that if Fitzpatrick won, it "would be the most beneficial thing to mankind since the signing of the American Declaration of Independence." Not a rich man, Walsh contributed $500 to Fitzpatrick's campaign. Less moving, but equally crucial, were the general endorsements of Labor party politics by leading liberal journals such as the New Republic, Nation, Dial, and Survey. Finally, one negative consideration influenced Labor party activists: Many were convinced that a local labor party could not survive without some affiliation with a state or national labor party. They feared that independent local labor parties would be particularly vulnerable to attack by the AFL and to red-baiting by local opponents.[35]

Only a month after the municipal elections, leading Labor party advocates held a convention at which they framed a platform for a state labor party. The new document bore the strong imprint of militant Chicago activists like Robert Buck and John Fitzpatrick, who were devoted to the concepts of democratic management and direct democracy in politics. Its preamble suggested that the new party had been "organized to assemble into a new majority the men and women who work but have been scattered as helpless minorities in the old parties under the confidence men of big business." The entire platform of the Cook County Labor party was incorporated into the state program, but several new planks were added. One called on the state to provide free houses for workers. Another demanded that "cooperative trade and industrial legislation be instituted so as to give laborers more control

34. Shapiro, "Hand and Brain," 412–13.
35. Walsh to Nockels, 3/26/19; Walsh to Nockels, 3/25/19: B8, WP. Shapiro, "Hand and Brain," 412–13; Green, "Labor Party," 48; NR, 4/26/19, 398–400; Nation, 10/12/18, 400.

over the work place." Still others called for abolishing the state senate and asked for amendments that would make it illegal for the Supreme Court to rule a law unconstitutional without the support of three-quarters of the judges.[36]

The new state document also differed from the old party platform in that it included a set of resolutions to "guide" policy. Many of these were drawn directly from articles and editorials in the *New Majority* or were reworked versions of motions passed at ward meetings in Chicago. At least one-third of the policy statements dealt with foreign policy. One resolution incorporated all previous demands regarding Russia that had been made by the Cook County Labor party. Others voiced support for a free India and a free Ireland. The authors proclaimed that the Indian people had suffered intensely under the "rule of an autocratic alien power which claims to have fought in the recent war for liberty and justice" and called on Congress to endorse resolutions supporting Indian self-determination. They also condemned England for its policies in Ireland and demanded that the U.S. Senate refuse to ratify any peace treaty that did not fully and completely recognize the Irish republic. Perhaps most important, the platform denounced the "secrecy that surrounds the negotiations [in Paris]" and demanded either that "this veil of secrecy be lifted or that U.S. representatives boycott the conference and withdraw American forces from Europe."[37]

Confident that the new state party would give their movement the appearance of viability, CFL leaders officially traveled to the AFL convention in June to try to win AFL endorsement for a national labor party. Chicago officials probably realized that they would not gain the approval of a majority at the convention. But support for a labor party among national and international trade unions was growing. By the end of 1919, the memberships of the machinists, brewery workers, cigarmakers, bakers, carpenters, quarry workers, painters and molders, bricklayers, and glassworkers had all endorsed proposals for a labor party. Also rallying behind independent labor politics were the powerful International Ladies' Garment Workers' Union, the United Mine Workers, and the sixteen unions in the Railroad Brotherhood.[38] Illinois Labor party leaders doubtless hoped to use the AFL convention to rally leaders of some of these unions around the Illinois party and to convince them to work with them in forming a national labor party.

36. *NM*, 4/19/19, 6–7.
37. Ibid., 4/19/19, 8–9.
38. Shapiro, "Hand and Brain," 412.

But much to the dismay of Illinois leaders, Gompers effectively routed their labor party campaign at the convention's opening session by asking for a reaffirmation from the delegates of the AFL's nonpartisan policies. When delegates overwhelmingly endorsed the AFL's political programs, Gompers felt free to deny the floor to Chicago officials who sought to introduce a resolution calling on the AFL to form a Labor party. The AFL's political strategies, he argued, had already been voted upon. Illinois Labor party advocates struggled in vain to convince prominent dissident officials within the AFL to protest Gompers's ruling against them. In the aftermath of the convention CFL leaders complained most bitterly about the failure of so-called progressive trade union leaders to support them in their fight with Gompers, bemoaning the lack of "effective, radical leadership in the AFL."[39]

On one level, the lack of support for labor party politics at the AFL convention seems surprising, since the rank and file of so many national and international trade unions had officially voted in favor of proposals to create a labor party. Indeed, Stanley Shapiro estimates that endorsements by individual unions should have "ranged" some one-third to one-half of the AFL's voting power behind independent labor political action.[40] But it must be kept in mind that many trade union officials likely did not support their union's endorsement of labor party politics and felt no special compulsion to work on its behalf. Even those officials who did favor a labor party may have shunned an alliance with the Illinois group, fearing its militant tendencies and seeking an alternative led by more prominent national labor leaders. Such considerations must have been particularly important in the context of the "red scare." Although Illinois Labor party leaders tried to avoid revolutionary language, their emphasis on workers' control and restoring trade relations with Russia spelled Bolshevism to many conservative observers. Whatever the individual motives of prominent union leaders, their failure to support the labor party proposals of Illinois delegates at the convention signaled a growing breach between local and national labor leadership.

To the surprise of many, Illinois Labor party officials decided to proceed with plans to form a national labor party despite the lack of support from AFL national and international union leaders. Only a few days after the AFL convention, CFL leaders scheduled a convention for

39. NM, 6/28/19, 2; 7/5/19, 4; 11/1/19, 10. Shapiro, "Hand and Brain," d, 124; Fine, *Labor and Farmer Parties*, 389.
40. Shapiro, "Hand and Brain," 412.

November to consider the formation of a national labor party. In the meantime, Chicago labor leaders immersed themselves in strike activities and campaigns among meat-packing and steel workers; events in both industries would have repercussions for the labor party campaign.

In the stockyards, CFL leaders tried to build on their successful war campaigns, seeking new federally mediated agreements that would ensure that workers' wages kept up with inflation. But new problems vexed union leaders at war's end. Returning veterans flooded the job market, further increasing the vulnerability of workers and depressing wage rates. Disillusioned by the new state of affairs, Chicago's packing-house workers staged a rash of unsanctioned strikes during the spring and summer of 1919. Amidst this chaos, a brutal race riot broke out on a sweltering Chicago beach in July and quickly spread to the stockyards floors. The race riot helped destroy the multiracial, multiethnic union movement that flourished in the stockyards during the war and signifi-cantly dampened the spirit of labor solidarity that made the stockyards a Labor party stronghold in the 1919 mayoral elections.[41] The riot had national implications for labor party politics, signaling the difficulties that labor leaders would face in welding into a single party a diverse working class often divided against itself.

Events came to a climax in the steel industry in September, when over 365,000 workers supported a strike launched by the national commit-tee. The steel corporations mounted a fierce counterattack, importing strikebreakers and encouraging local police to break up picketing activi-ties and arrest strike leaders on often spurious charges. Business propa-ganda and press coverage portraying the strikers as alien radicals undercut public support for the strike and also promoted interethnic hostilities among union members. Poor cooperation among AFL unions further impeded the strike. By December, the number of strikers had dipped to one hundred thousand, and on January 8, 1920, the strike was officially called off. Steel organizers vowed a new campaign in the industry, but the strike marked a severe defeat for labor.[42]

Adding to the problems in the packing-house and steel industries was a conservative backlash within the Chicago labor movement. A local group clustering around a new paper called *The Unionist* charged that CFL leaders were trying to "tear down the industrial institutions" that

41. Barrett, *Work and Community in the Jungle*, 202–24. Brody, *Butcher Workmen*, 85–91; Tuttle, *Race Riot*. Walsh to J. W. Johnstone, B8: WP.
42. Brody, *Steelworkers in America*, 231–62; Foner, *History of the Labor Movement*, 8: 148–69.

guaranteed the economic health of the United States. Echoing the corporatist mentality of the AFL leadership, they argued that "industrial development and prosperity can only come about through proper cooperation between employers and employee."[43] The group was not above red-baiting, denouncing one CFL-sponsored group advocating renewed trade with Russia as a "rot infested boil on the black body of Bolshevism in America."[44] They urged conservative rank-and-file workers to start attending CFL meetings and to "throw the radicals out." They also suggested that the "rational elements" within the organized labor movement must prevent CFL leaders from undermining Wilsonian foreign policy. "It is up to you," they wrote, "to do what you can to save the world from ruin by giving all assistance and moral support to President Wilson in his struggle to save the world from impending disaster." Whether the group had much support within the Chicago area is unclear, but *Unionist* editors followed their own advice, regularly attending CFL meetings and heckling Fitzpatrick and supporters at every opportunity.[45]

Rather than encouraging caution among Chicago labor leaders, strike defeats and conservative attacks steeled their determination to proceed with independent labor political action. Only a labor party, they reasoned, would provide sufficient protections for their organizing and strike campaigns and unify the working class. Reinforcing this view was the loathing they now felt for the Wilson administration. Despite the president's collapse in September 1919, the *New Majority* repeatedly reported on the antilabor actions of Wilson's advisors at the autumn industrial conference and editorialized about the futility of trying to deal with such an administration. Commenting on the Wilson administration's actions during the steel strike, it suggested that

> The Mask is off.
> The Cat is out of the bag.
> It is no longer possible to evade the conclusion that our government
> is consciously serving Wall-Street.[46]

The *New Majority* also lambasted the final results of the Peace Treaty, declaring that it was "dictated by the imperialists of the great world powers, in behalf of international capital, the United States assisting." In

43. *Unionist*, 12/25/19, 1; 11/3/19, 1.
44. Ibid., 2/19/21, 1.
45. Ibid., 12/18/19, 1; 9/11/19, 4; 10/23/19, 1.
46. NM, 11/15/19, 4.

addition, the staff intensified its coverage of the Irish and Russian revolutions and published news from the Berne Conference Committee that was harmful to both the Wilson administration and the AFL hierarchy.[47] Most important, the paper attacked Wilson personally. A hard-headed, pragmatic thinker, Robert Buck particularly criticized Wilson's use of lofty, eloquent rhetoric to rationalize his postwar plans. Immediately prior to the president's stroke, one editorial proclaimed that "President Wilson has turned demagogue. Heretofore there has seemed to be something in his beautiful phrases. But since he has been out on the swing-around-the-circle defending his British League of Nations he has said things that forfeit his right to the respect of his fellow citizens."[48] *New Majority* editors continued to attack the president even after his collapse, publishing a poem in November asserting,

> He kept us out of war,
> He kept us out of peace,
> He kept us out of flour,
> He kept us out of grease,
> He kept us out of sweets,
> He kept us out of booze,
> He kept us out of meats,
> He kept us out of fuel,
> He kept us out of Kale,
> He kept us out of wool,
> He kept us out of clothes,
> He kept us out of pie,
> He didn't keep us out of Russia—will someone tell us why?[49]

Despite all the setbacks they had encountered during the past year, Labor party officials went ahead with preparations for the November Labor party convention. Invitations were sent to over twenty-five thousand international, national, and local unions; state and city federated bodies; and local and state labor parties. Approximately twelve hundred delegates from thirty-three states attended the convention. Most disappointing was the turnout among national union officials: Not a single major national or international union officially sent delegates. Yet, local and state organizations within these unions responded enthusiastically to the labor party call, ensuring a diverse mix of craft and industrial interests. Leading the pack were the United Mine Workers with 179 del-

47. Ibid., 9/6/19, 1, 3; 7/26/19, 5.
48. Ibid., 9/3/19, 4.
49. Ibid., 11/29/19, 16.

egates, the Railway Brotherhoods with 65, and the Machinists with 40. In all, some fifty-five different craft and international unions sent delegates. Over fifty central labor unions were also represented, ranging from the large and powerful municipal councils of New York City, Boston, and Baltimore to the more modest councils of medium and small-sized cities like Kalamazoo, Michigan; Pocatello, Idaho; Coffeyville, Iowa; and Independence, Kansas. Also sending delegates were the state federations of Illinois, Indiana, Wisconsin, and Washington. Representatives from some twenty local labor party organizations, including those from Chicago, New York, Cleveland, Hartford (Connecticut), and many of the successful downstate Illinois labor parties, comprised most of the remainder of the delegates at the convention. Also in attendance were a few observers from sympathetic organizations like the Non-Partisan League, Committee of 48, and the Socialist party.[50]

Because so many of the delegates were local union representatives who had little national political experience, they were excited by the hubbub surrounding the convention and they were in high spirits upon arriving in Chicago. Many saw themselves as participants, for the first time during their lives, in the making of history and proudly posed for *New Majority* photographs along with other delegates from their states. Chicago party officials appeared buoyed by the crowd's exuberance and affirmed their commitment to creating a viable national party.[51]

At the opening session, delegates nominated John Fitzpatrick and John Walker as chairmen of the convention, but they declined in favor of Max Hayes, a former AFL official and socialist who was more well known nationally. In his opening address, Hayes signaled the party's dual concerns with domestic and international issues, suggesting that it would not "distinguish between the imperialism of a Hollenzollern and a Gary," but would support a policy of "America for the Americans, . . . Russia for the Russians, . . . Mexico for the Mexicans and freedom for all peoples."[52] Warning delegates that revolutionary or class rhetoric would only hurt the party, Hayes and others stressed that their political efforts aimed not at a dictatorship of the proletariat but at an extension

50. *NR*, 12/10/19, 53; *Proceedings of the First National Convention of the Labor Party*, 1919, 126–31; *Chicago Tribune*, 11/27/19, 14. Nockels to Walsh, 11/27/19, B8: WP. Green, "Labor Party," 61; Shapiro, "Hand and Brain," d, 160; Sell, "The A.F. of L. and the Labor Party Movement," 102–3. Max Hayes to Mrs. Hayes, 11/23/19: Hayes Papers (HP), Ohio State Historical Society, Columbus.
51. *NM*, 12/19/19.
52. Ibid., 1–2. Hayes to Mrs. Hayes, 11/22/19: HP.

of American democratic ideals. Such a goal, they emphasized, would be attractive to all except big business and financial interests. They welcomed support from farmers, salaried "brain" workers such as schoolteachers and technicians, new women voters, reformers, trade unionists, and all other wage earners.[53]

Recognizing that winning and maintaining the support of such groups would depend in part on the structure of the new party, the convention devoted much time to complex organizational problems. Two issues particularly vexed the delegates: how to attract women voters to the party and what relationship should exist between the party and the trade union movement. Significantly, the Chicago Labor party had created a special section led by Lillian Herstein to recruit women and the Chicago party delegation at the convention included more women than men. These Chicago women played an instrumental role in encouraging New Majority editor Robert Buck to sponsor a farsighted motion that each state be accorded one male and one female representative on the national committee. Other delegates objected to the motion on the grounds that representatives should be chosen irrespective of sex. But defenders of the resolution argued that women had a "tremendous handicap" to overcome and temporarily needed special assistance from the party. Echoing the sentiments of many feminists of the era, they further implied that women could help redeem the world from war and senseless destruction. One promoter of the resolution thus argued that "the mother life must come in now if this world and its civilization is to be saved." Some also supported the resolution for pragmatic reasons, suggesting that the success of the Labor party ultimately "hung on its ability to capture the women's vote" and that it would be important to "have women put to the fore of our work." The convention subsequently passed the motion to include one male and one female representative from every state on the national committee.[54]

53. Proceedings of the First National Convention of the Labor Party, 1919, 7–15, 26–27.

54. Ibid., 67–84, 126–31. NR, 12/10/19, 53; United Labor News Reports, 4/18/25, B1–F1: Hr P. On women's internationalist thought, see, especially, Edward P. Crapol, ed., Women and American Foreign Policy: Lobbyists, Critics, and Insiders (Westport, Conn.: Greenwood Press, 1987); Cynthia Enloe, Bananas, Beaches, and Bases: Making Feminist Sense of International Politics (Berkeley: University of California Press, 1990); Rosemary Foot, "Where Are the Women? The Gender Dimension in the Study of International Relations," Diplomatic History (fall 1990): 615–22; Judith Papachristou, "American Women and Foreign Policy, 1898–1905: Exploring Gender in Diplomatic History," Diplomatic History (fall 1990): 493–509; Beth McKillen, "Irish Feminism and Nationalist Separatism, 1914–23," Eire-Ireland (fall 1982, winter 1982): 52–67, 72–90.

The issue of the trade union movement and its role in the Labor party proved more problematic. Illinois State Federation of Labor president John Walker spoke for many when he emphasized the need to get "the whole labor movement into the Labor Party, working together to provide means of education." Another delegate, concerned with attracting prominent union leaders into the movement, suggested that national and international unions should be given proportional representation on the national committee of the new party. Representatives from the unions would in turn share power with the two Labor party delegates who would be chosen in state elections. But many objected to this plan, fearing both that it would create an unwieldy executive committee and that it would give national and international union leaders excessive power within the party. The issue caused so much controversy that it was deferred to the next convention, leaving the official relationship between the trade union movement and the Labor party in a state of flux.[55]

Less controversial was the set of Labor party principles adopted by the convention. These incorporated most of the demands enunciated by the Cook County and Illinois Labor parties but applied them on a national scale. The only principle that differed significantly from those of the Illinois and Cook County Labor parties was the first, which officially condemned the League of Nations. Illinois groups had previously criticized the peace negotiations and the proposed composition of the League but had not attacked the organization itself. Voicing their ultimate rejection of Wilsonian internationalism, Labor party delegates proclaimed that they would "not be satisfied with a League of imperialist governments dominated by an international League of money bosses to cement an international control of industry by a small group of men who manipulate the bulk of the world's wealth."[56] The platform of the new party was thus fundamentally at odds with the postwar diplomatic agenda of the AFL.

The other major action taken by the convention was to create a visionary labor press service. The proposed service was the brainchild of Robert Buck and about forty other editors who attended the convention. These men, always concerned about the bias of the major papers,

55. *Proceedings of the First National Convention of the Labor Party,* 1919, 57–58, 80–84.
56. *NM,* 12/19/19, 8. *Proceedings of the First National Convention of the Labor Party,* 120–25. *NR,* 12/3/19, 3–4; 12/10/19, 53–56; 12/31/19, 133. *Nation,* 12/6/19, 707; 11/29/19, 672.

had become convinced during the course of the Labor party crusade that even the press services unfairly reported on labor issues. If socialist and labor editors were to get accurate information about the conditions of workers throughout the world, then a labor corollary to the Associated Press must be constructed.[57]

After approval from the convention, Buck and other editors met in special session and officially constituted the Federated Press Service. They also created a governing board of nine members and appointed Robert Buck chairman. E. J. Costello of the socialist *Milwaukee Leader* was elected managing editor of the news service itself. The group then made plans to establish offices in Washington, Chicago, and Seattle and to lease transatlantic cables so as to obtain news from major British and European labor papers. Eventually, they hoped to establish offices in London and other European cities.[58] The new service took several months to organize fully, but it proved a vital source of information for the *New Majority* and the Labor party, profoundly influencing their positions on national and international issues.

In the immediate aftermath of the convention, party strategists devoted themselves to building coalitions with sympathetic groups. Now painfully aware that they could not expect much help in the near future from national and international trade union leaders, party officials likely reasoned that such coalitions provided the only means of gaining the necessary credibility and money to run a presidential candidate in 1920. Party leaders first solicited the aid of various socialist fragments; almost all refused to consider seriously the offers of Labor party officials because they believed themselves to be the true representatives of the workers. They also accused the Labor party of lacking sufficiently far-reaching programs. When attempts to court socialists faltered, party leaders tried to develop alliances with progressive farm groups. These initiatives bore some fruit, with a number of farm groups accepting invitations to the Labor party convention in July.[59]

But the tentative support of agricultural organizations was insufficient: Labor party leaders still needed campaign funds and more prominent candidates for their national slate. In an effort to resolve these problems,

57. NM, 12/13/19, 9; 2/21/20, 6; Stephen J. Haessler, "Carl J. Haessler and the Federated Press: Essays on the History of American Labor Journalism" (Master's thesis, University of Wisconsin-Madison, 1977).

58. NM, 12/13/19, 9; 2/ 21/ 20, 6.

59. NM, 5/22/20, 10; Shapiro, "Hand and Brain," d, 161–208; NR, 12/31/19, 133; Weinstein, *Decline*, 223–24.

party officials sought an alliance with the Committee of 48. This organization, comprised of old-time Progressives and disillusioned Wilsonians, hoped to build a new reform coalition. The group had two primary merits from the perspective of Labor party leaders: They possessed an ample supply of money, and they had close contacts with Robert LaFollette.[60] A LaFollette presidential candidacy had much to recommend it, for, in Stanley Shapiro's words, "no other politician was so closely and broadly identified with the 'little man's' interests." LaFollette could attract a wide range of support from reform, labor, socialist, and agricultural interests. His previous opposition to the war would also likely win him votes among German- and Irish-Americans, as well as among pacifists and isolationists. Equally significant, LaFollette could lure money to the campaign and gain it coverage and editorial support from the Hearst newspaper chain.[61]

During December, the leadership of the Labor party entered into preliminary negotiations with the 48ers. Disputes arose almost immediately. Both groups favored programs for restoring civil liberties, public ownership of utilities, and nationalization of transportation facilities. The 48ers, however, disliked the Labor party demand for democratic control of industry. Firm proponents of a strong central government, they suggested that centralization of decision making in industry was necessary to assure the efficient use of economic resources. They also argued that to democratize management would infringe on the rights of property owners and incite class hostility. Labor party members were equally adamant about maintaining their plank on democratic control. The 48ers, they suggested, seemed less interested in creating a genuinely new political coalition than in developing a "harmless liberal party like the Old Bull Moose Outfit." Similar disagreements arose over the name of the new party. Representatives of the Committee of 48 objected to calling it the Labor party on the grounds that it would provoke class division. Buck and labor officials, however, insisted that the new party must spring from a "recognized economic group," or, in other words, from the laboring population.[62]

60. Shapiro, "Hand and Brain," d, 127–89. NR, 12/31/19, 133. Walsh to Fred Gardner, 12/9/19, B8: WP.
61. Shapiro, "Hand and Brain," 415.
62. Shapiro, "Hand and Brain," d, 189. Fagin to Walsh, 5/5/20; Walsh to J. A. Hopkins, 6/15/20; John Hopkins to Walsh, 6/5/20; Manley to Walsh, 6/24/20; Fagin to Walsh, 8/6/20: B9, WP.

Given their differing attitudes about centralized power and class, a compromise between the two groups was unlikely. The fate of the alliance was sealed, however, when leaders from the two groups decided to postpone further negotiations until the summer when both organizations were scheduled to hold their conventions in Chicago.[63] During the intervening months, Buck used the pages of the *New Majority* to construct an even more militant working-class agenda for the National Labor party.

One reason, as Buck saw it, that the party had not attracted more rank-and-file support was because most workers had a confused image of it. During 1919, the Labor party had been attacked simultaneously by both right- and left-wing elements in the labor movement. The AFL criticized party leaders for alleged Bolshevist tendencies. At the same time, socialist and leftist groups characterized the party as a liberal reform organization and attacked it for its lack of militancy. In spring 1920, Buck tried to discredit both images and to portray the party as the champion of the hardheaded, pragmatic American worker. Again and again, Buck and his staff argued that the charges of Bolshevism hurled at the Labor party were false. More importantly, they suggested that the red scare itself was a fraud: Wall Street was not really worried about communists in the United States but instead feared the newfound independence of workers. "If long haired men and short haired women," suggested one editorial, "wish to dream about a rosy hued millenium, either on earth while alive, or in the skies when dead, the forces smile in amused tolerance." But it claimed that "when hard muscled, practical men who dream no dreams and see no vision, except the shrinking purchasing power of their weekly wages, set their jaws and say, 'We will not permit our wages to come down,' it is then that the forces are hit and the 'red' alarm is sounded."[64] In their attacks on the red scare's perpetrators, *New Majority* editors thus killed two birds with one stone; they discredited both the perpetrators and the "misty eyed" radicals attacking the party from the left. Center stage was thereby left for the rank-and-file workers who they believed must be the core of the movement.

New Majority editors further honed the image of the party by defending it against charges of unAmericanism. They identified three different definitions of Americanism currently in vogue. One, espoused

63. Shapiro, "Hand and Brain," d, 192.
64. *NM*, 1/10/20, 4.

by big businessmen, made the duties of American citizenship synonymous with slavery. Proponents of this view defined a loyal American as
one who unquestioningly accepted whatever bones the capitalist system
threw out to him or her. Many educators, on the other hand, argued
that an American citizen was one who had destroyed all vestiges of an
old-world identity. The Labor party, by contrast, defined an American
as an individual who fulfilled his or her duties as an American citizen
while at the same time contributing to the cultural enrichment of
America through ethnic institutions. The obligations of citizenship,
according to the New Majority, included supporting strikes that would
benefit large numbers of Americans and organizing politically to assure
that the majority ruled in the United States. According to this definition,
immigrant packing-house and steelworkers who belonged to the national Labor party were the truest Americans.[65]

In addition to honing the image of the new national party, editors
continued to publicize its policy agenda. Domestically, the New Majority hammered away on the themes of democratizing industry and
restoring civil liberty. Little about the paper's analysis of these two issues
changed, for they meshed well with the working-class image it was trying to promote. But editors refined many of their international positions. Previously, they had denounced American military intervention in
the Soviet Union and called for renewed trade and diplomatic recognition of the new Soviet regime. Many assumed this signaled support for
the Bolsheviks. During the early months of 1920, editors fleshed out the
position of the New Majority on the Soviet regime. "The American people," they wrote, should not be "concerned with the Soviet form of government."

The question of its advantages or disadvantages for the Russian people is
no business of ours. We have troubles enough of our own. If the Russians
want to establish Sovietism, anarchy, democracy or monarchy let them go
to it. We do not want to interfere with their institutions any more than we
would welcome interference in ours. What we want is freedom to work
out our destiny unhampered by designing tricksters of any class. The
Russians are entitled to the same right: Labor should not protest that
right.[66]

This new policy statement seemed designed to enhance the pragmatic
working-class image Buck was trying to build for the national Labor

65. Ibid., 11/1/19, 8.
66. Ibid., 2/7/20, 4.

party. By insisting on Russia's right to determine its own fate, Buck successfully dissociated the Labor party both from the socialists and communists who favored intervention on behalf of the new regime and from the Wilsonian idealists who sought to create an American-styled democratic system in Russia.[67]

The paper's coverage of British imperialism also changed. Previously, staffers had concentrated almost exclusively on British atrocities in Ireland and India. But with the help of the new Federated Press Service, the paper began running stories on British oppression in New Zealand, New Guinea, the Samoas, Egypt, and Germany.[68] The *New Majority* also delved more deeply into the economic roots of British foreign policy. One reporter concluded that Britain had assisted in overthrowing the democratic Ebert regime in Germany because the newly installed candidate offered greater profits and economic security for British investors.[69] Other articles documented the activities of British capitalists in the newly acquired Samoan Islands and determined that Britain was abandoning its pledge of self-determination for these islands in order to obtain a cheap labor force for hard-pressed British industrialists.[70] Staffers also reported on ties between British capitalists and big businessmen from other countries. In an article entitled "Why England Wants to Borrow Our Money," one reporter painted ominous pictures of an international capitalist network that conspired to deprive workers worldwide of their rights. British capitalists, the author suggested, were trying to borrow money from American financiers "to help French capitalists tighten the screws on Germany, to continue warfare with Soviet Russia, to form an alliance with France which will insure Clemenceau's autocratic and militaristic dominion over all Europe." The lesson, according to the article, was that "capitalism is joining hands against the people the world over."[71]

These conclusions about international conspiracies inspired *New Majority* staffers to take a closer look at the relationship between American financiers and Wilsonian foreign policy. Previously, the paper had portrayed Wilson primarily as a dupe of European imperialists. Now, however, the paper looked more systematically into U.S. foreign

67. For more on the editors' changing attitudes toward Russia, see *NM*, 7/15/19, 4; 5/1/20, 6; 4/17/20, 6; 5/22/22, 8.
68. *NM*, 1/17/20, 3; 4/24/20, 7; 5/8/20, 4–8; 7/10/20, 2.
69. Ibid., 3/3/20, 8.
70. Ibid., 4/4/20, 7.
71. Ibid., 1/17/20, 3.

policies in Latin America and concluded that the United States constituted an imperial power in its own right. Staffers wrote lengthy series on
the oil industry's role in Mexico and on the sugar industry in Puerto
Rico. In Mexico, the paper argued, "American capitalism intends to
establish once and for all, that foreign governments are of no consequence whatever when they stand in the way of . . . capitalists." Editors
claimed that the "State Department, acting in obedience to the wishes of
Wall Street, is prepared to back up this infamous doctrine with the
might of its authority."[72] Reporters characterized Puerto Rico as a slave
pen of the United States and documented the intense exploitation of
workers by businessmen. In other articles, reporters argued that U.S.
imperialism also hurt workers at home: Lower wages in the colonies
encouraged businessmen to invest their money in these areas rather than
in the mainland. U.S. businessmen also used lower wages in Latin
America as a rationale for lowering wages in the United States. Labor
party politics thus forced Irish nationalists within the CFL to move
beyond their obsession with British imperialism and to focus more systematically on the deleterious effects of U.S. interventionism in the
Western hemisphere.[73]

    According to *New Majority* editors, Americans knew very little
about U.S. or English imperialism because the old parties perennially
fooled the voters into "sham battles over fake issues." One such issue
was the League. As Buck saw it, imperialism would continue with or
without the League because it did not change the balance of world
power in any fundamental way. Democrats nonetheless rallied around
the League because it provided a useful disguise for its foreign ventures. Republicans opposed it because they wished to create the illusion
that they favored isolationism. But *New Majority* staffers argued that
the Republicans would continue the imperialist policies of the Democrats if their candidate won the election. By contrast, the Labor party
had no vested interest in perpetuating imperialism because American
workers were as badly hurt by exploitative relations with underdeveloped nations as were laborers in these countries. As a consequence, the
Labor party would eschew political and military intervention in Latin
America to support the investments of U.S. profit mongers. Instead, it
would work out mutually beneficial trade relations with sister
nations.[74]

72. Ibid., 1/3/20, 5.
73. Ibid., 4/24/20, 10; 5/1/20, 10.
74. Ibid., 5/29/20, 4.

Unfortunately for the Labor party, Buck was a better writer than financial planner. In line with his antagónism toward the business class, he at first refused to take advertisements. As a consequence, editors lacked the funds to promote the paper. The financial situation worsened when some local unions canceled their subscriptions in the wake of Gompers's nonpartisan campaigns. By November 1919, the paper was reported to be losing one thousand dollars a month.[75] Subsequently, Buck began selectively accepting advertisements from area businessmen sympathetic to labor. But the number of suitable sponsors was small and the paper remained in the red. Subscriptions stagnated at around five thousand throughout 1920, enough to ensure that the *New Majority* made the rounds of local union halls but not to enable the editors to pay its debts and to expand operations.[76]

Although the *New Majority* remained a financially troubled and a small-scale publishing venture, its incisive editorials and exposés probably played an important role in preventing compromise between Labor party activists and the 48ers. As the July conventions of the two groups approached, Labor party leaders resolved not to sacrifice the content of their demands—many of which had first been formulated in the *New Majority*—for a few votes or dollars from the 48ers. The conventions of the two groups were held in close proximity in Chicago during mid-July, yet they could not have been more different. The 48ers met in the plush Morrison hotel while the laborites crowded into a neighborhood union hall. The two groups immediately established a conference committee to negotiate an alliance, but it made little headway. Buck and other Labor party leaders insisted even more vehemently than before that democratic management was crucial to their platform. The 48ers, on the other hand, objected to democratic management on the grounds that it would result in labor union domination of the economy. Moreover, they told Labor party members that their potential presidential candidate—LaFollette—would never agree to it. Disputes also continued over the name of the party. After the 48ers once again rejected the simple Labor party title, Buck instead proposed the nomer Farmer-Labor party. The 48ers, however, objected even more strenuously to this title. After continued angry debate, the Labor party members declared that they would not sacrifice their principles for the sake of the

75. Ibid., 1/11/19, 12; *CFL Minutes*, 6/1/19, 15, and 11/2/19, 10; Shapiro, "Hand and Brain," d, 116–28; Keiser, "John Fitzpatrick," 171.
76. Keiser, "John Fitzpatrick," 170–72.

LaFollette "vote-catching machine" but would if necessary "wait until 1940" for the success "they knew must come."[77]

Abandoning the deliberations with the 48ers, labor representatives returned to the Labor party convention and insisted on proceeding with the adoption of a platform. Capturing the uncompromising spirit of his colleagues, Robert Buck argued that "the 48ers can stay here a year because they're plutes . . . but this convention cannot. We are working-men, losing money by staying away from our jobs." CFL secretary Ed Nockels, tossing his suit jacket to the side and emerging in shirtsleeves, concurred with Buck, suggesting that "unless the third party has for its backbone labor there isn't going to be a third party." In the meantime, a handful of 48ers who had grown discontented with their conservative leaders suddenly bolted their own convention and marched over to the Labor party gathering, where they were greeted with a chorus of "Hail, Hail the Gang's All Here." A delegation from the Nonpartisan League then joined the jubilant group, insisting that "we farmers have found that your interests and ours are identical."[78]

The combined convention passed without alteration the entire plat-form proposed by the Labor party leadership.[79] Several of the planks for the new party were old hat. One reiterated Labor's Bill of Rights; others called for the restoration of civil liberties, readjustment of tax rates, and reduction in the cost of living. New demands, however, were made with respect to democratic control. The new party not only requested increas-ing representation in the management of industry but in addition asked for democratic control of all public utilities and natural resources. Building on Buck's disclosures in the *New Majority*, party leaders also drew even stronger links between domestic and foreign exploitation than they had previously. "Having robbed the people first of their power and then of their wealth," they wrote, "the wielders of financial power . . . seek to extend these enterprises to such lengths that our nation today stands in danger of becoming an empire instead of a republic."[80]

One plank in the platform outlined the policies of the Labor party toward every major foreign policy issue of the day. Its most important

77. Shapiro, "Hand and Brain," d, 196. *Chicago Tribune*, 7/12/20, 2; 7/13/20, 1–2. *NR*, 7/28/20, 256. Fagin to Walsh, 8/6/20, B9: WP.
78. *Chicago Tribune*, 7/13/20, 2; 7/14/20, 2–3. *NM*, 7/24/20, 5.
79. Shapiro, "Hand and Brain," d, 192–200.
80. *NM*, 7/24/20, 5. *Chicago Tribune*, 7/15/20, 1–2; Shapiro, "Hand and Brain," 192–200; Green, "Labor Party," 74–76.

demand was for the "withdrawal of the United States from further participation (under the Treaty of Versailles) in the reduction of Conquered
peoples to economic or political subjection to the small group of men
who manipulate the bulk of the world's wealth." The plank also called
on the United States to recognize the legitimate governments of Mexico,
Ireland, and Russia and to refrain from further intervention in these
countries. It asked additionally that economic and military assistance be
denied to other countries that might try to subvert the legitimately
elected governments in these nations. Much influenced by Buck's recent
coverage of Latin America, Labor party leaders also called on the United
States to withdraw from "imperialistic enterprises upon which we have
already embarked in the Phillipines [*sic*], Hawaii, Cuba, Samoa and
Guam." The platform finally warned the people of the United States to
reject any form of conscription and reaffirmed the commitment of the
Labor party to a "league of free peoples, organized and pledged to the
destruction of autocracy, militarism and economic imperialism throughout the world."[81]

Not surprisingly, the leaders of the 48ers were outraged by the Labor
party platform. LaFollette proclaimed that the document was "full of
revolutionary language" that would have a "psychologically bad"
impact on the American people. In a news conference after it was
adopted by the convention, the aging senator repudiated the Labor
party leadership and announced that he would not run on their ticket.
The hierarchy of the 48ers, meanwhile, officially dissociated themselves
from their colleagues who had endorsed the platform.[82] With LaFollette
gone, the new party elected former 48er Parley Christensen, "a pleasant
and almost unknown Utah attorney," for its presidential candidate, and
Max Hayes as his running mate.[83]

The defection of LaFollette and the 48er leadership cost the Labor
party key support. Even Frank Walsh, previously a warm advocate of
the party, was disillusioned by the July convention. During the spring,
Labor party leaders had courted Walsh for a possible vice-presidential
slot. But with LaFollette's defection, Walsh lost any interest he had in
the position. Writing to CFL secretary Ed Nockels after the convention,
Walsh commented that "Yourself, good old john [Fitzpatrick], and Buck

81. *NM*, 7/4/20, 5.
82. Shapiro, "Hand and Brain," d, 202. *Chicago Tribune,* 7/15/20, 1–2. Robert
LaFollette, Jr., to Walsh, 8/17/20, B9: WP.
83. Shapiro, "Hand and Brain," d, 205. *Chicago Tribune,* 7/15/20, 1–2. Nockels to
Walsh, 7/15/20, B9: WP. Christensen to Hayes, 7/18/20: HP.

seem to have got what you have been driving for all these months . . . a real third party movement inside of labor going on, and the rest of us have no particular responsibility." To Robert LaFollette, Jr., Walsh confessed that he was "bitterly disappointed" in the results of the convention and unclear as to his future political actions. Subsequently, Walsh continued to give money to the Farmer-Labor party but confided to friends that he was not at all impressed with Christensen, who was a "well meaning man" but had no "fundamental basis of appeal." By October, Walsh was leaning toward Eugene Debs in the presidential race.[84]

Party officials made valiant attempts to promote the presidential ticket after the convention. Buck and the *New Majority* staff continued to produce incisive reports on domestic and foreign issues important to the election. Meanwhile, party officials and organizers struggled to bring their campaign to the masses. Aware that few voters had ever heard of Parley Christensen, they tried to develop compelling state and local tickets that would draw rank-and-file workers to the party. In Illinois, for example, party officials ran Fitzpatrick for senator and Walker for governor, and compiled an impressive list of candidates for the state legislature. Since party leaders were too short of manpower and money to conduct extensive door-to-door canvasses, they staged mass meetings and picnics in important industrial cities comparable to those that had been used successfully in labor party mayoral campaigns. Party leaders also attended a wide variety of ethnic functions and in return received favorable publicity in some ethnic papers. In addition, they successfully lobbied to have the party officially put on the ballot alongside the Democratic and Republican candidates in twenty-one states. These victories were crucial, for voters were far less likely to vote for Farmer-Labor candidates if they had to write in their choices.[85]

Also important was the endorsement the Farmer-Labor party won from the *Nation* and the *New Republic*. Like much of the progressive community, the editors at these papers deplored the revolutionary rhetoric of the party. But they argued that American democratic institutions were being threatened by the "preponderence and the dominion"

---

84. Walsh to Nockels, 7/20/20; Walsh to Robert LaFollette, Jr., 8/13/20; Walsh to Treasurer of Farmer-Labor Party, 9/6/20; Walsh to Fagin, 10/11/20: B9, WP.

85. NM, 3/20/20, 6; 8/7/20, 4; 8/21/20, 3–7; 8/28/20, 6; 10/9/20, 4. Agnes Smedley, Friends of Freedom for India, to Fitzpatrick, 10/25/20; Bazaar for Relief of Jewish War Sufferers to Fitzpatrick, 10/23/20; Letter from General Fields Branch, Friends of Irish Freedom to Fitzpatrick, 10/30/20, 2: B9–F66, FP. Shapiro, "Hand and Brain," d, 124, 212–13.

of one class over another. According to Herbert Croly at the *New Republic*, progressives needed to recognize "the temporary need of strengthening the wage earners to resist capitalist domination" so that a "wholesome balance of economic and social power" would be restored in the "American commonwealth." Croly argued that organized labor could not make the readjustment alone, for without progressive guidance it would likely "become blindly and destructively pugnacious" and would "tend more and more to depend exclusively on direct action." Unlike many progressives, Croly supported the Labor party demand for industrial democracy because he believed it was essential to the health of political democracy. In summing up his arguments, he suggested that progressives should support the Labor party because it was "born of a sound application of the traditional American ideal of a homogeneous equalitarian democracy to the existing facts of American economic and social life. It looks like the best way in 1920 of vindicating American nationality as an expression of an essentially ethical and human ideal."[86]

The expectations of the party on the eve of the election were modest: *New Majority* staff members predicted that the party would elect three senators and that Christensen would carry Washington, South Dakota, Wyoming, Montana, Nevada, Illinois, and New Mexico.[87] Yet even by these standards, the election was disappointing. Christensen failed to carry a single state and won only about 250,000 votes, or about 1 percent of those who cast ballots. By contrast, Socialist Eugene Debs, who campaigned from jail, won over 915,000 votes, or about 3.5 percent of the tally. Even in Washington and Illinois, where Christensen fared best, his vote totals were discouragingly low. Christensen received fewer total votes for all of Illinois (49,630) than Fitzpatrick received from Chicago alone in 1919 (55,000). The party also failed to win any national senatorial races.[88] If there was one bright spot in the electoral picture, it was that local Farmer-Labor party candidates did significantly better than their national counterparts in the states of Washington, New York, Minnesota, and Illinois. The most glaring example was that of Lillie J. Anderson, Farmer-Labor candidate for secretary of state for Minnesota: she polled 193,000 votes to Christensen's 5,800. Within Illinois, Christensen trailed Walker by a vote of 49,630 to 56,480. Commenting

86. *NR*, 10/27/20, 210–16. *Nation*, 7/24/20, 88; 9/25/20, 344.
87. *NM*, 10/30/20, 1.
88. *NR*, 1/5/21, 152; Fine, *Labor and Farmer Parties*, 423; Staley, *History of the ISFL*, 377; Sell, "The A.F. of L. and the Labor Party Movement," 139–41; Shannon, *Socialist Party of America*, 156–57; Green, "Labor Party," 91–92.

on these results, the *New Republic* suggested that the Farmer-Labor party represented "a series of sporadic but widespread local movements rather than a coherent national one."[89]

If the presidential election proved a disaster for the Farmer-Labor party, the history of the broader labor party movement in 1919 and 1920 nonetheless seems crucial to understanding postwar labor alignments. In the narrowest sense, the movement is important because it suggests a major political rebellion among a layer of labor leadership neglected by historians. Older schools in labor history tended to focus on national and international union leaders; "new" labor historians have devoted primary attention to workplace struggles. Neglected by both groups are municipal labor leaders and local union officials who were active in their state and city federateds. Catalyzed by their wartime experiences, many local activists formulated political and diplomatic agendas after the armistice that were fundamentally at odds with that of the AFL. Rejecting the AFL's nonpartisan politics, they argued that labor's right to organize could be protected only by a Labor party. More than national and international leaders, local activists were also committed to the goal of industrial democracy and believed that political power was essential to achieving this aim. Exhibiting much political creativity, they grounded local labor party movements in American democratic traditions and ideals rather than in prevailing radical orthodoxies.

The foreign policy agendas of local activists also proved strikingly original. Chicago labor leaders differed from AFL officials both in the kind of diplomatic power they sought for workers and in the type of international role they promoted for the United States. Like grass-roots activists in Britain and Europe, CFL officials viewed the collaborationist arrangements that developed between trade union leaders, the state, and business during the war with a good deal of suspicion. Through their political activities, policy platforms, and speeches after the armistice, Fitzpatrick and his colleagues signaled that they objected both to institutionalizing corporatist forms of power sharing at home and to using them as a model for international organizations. At best, corporatist wartime structures had accorded labor and business equal representation; since workers constituted the overwhelming majority of the population, democratic traditions mandated that they deserved far greater influence. Thus, the CFL rhetorically demanded that workers be

89. *NR*, 1/5/21, 152; Green, "Labor Party," 92.

represented in government councils in proportion to their "voting strength" and in the League in proportion to "their numbers in the armies, navies, and workshops of the world."

But local officials never really looked to such institutions to solve international problems because, in contrast to national trade union leaders, they had a profound distrust of centralized power. Instead, their plans for ensuring future peace and for eliminating imperialism focused on educating and mobilizing the masses around foreign policy issues. In emphasizing international events like the Irish and Russian revolutions during the mayoral campaign of 1919, Chicago activists hoped not only to win votes but also to lay the groundwork for more direct participation by the masses in diplomacy. They believed that the first prerequisite to a more democratic diplomacy in the United States was an informed electorate. Beyond that, the two-party system had to be destroyed because it essentially disenfranchised voters on international issues by offering them only "sham battles over fake issues." CFL officials argued that whichever of the two parties voters chose, they ended up supporting an imperialist and expansionist agenda. A third party pledged to an alternative foreign policy would a priori guarantee workers more international influence because it would afford them a chance to cast a vote on the basis of real issues. Once a Labor party was in power, it would further increase workers' diplomatic influence by holding periodic referenda and by supporting or creating international labor organizations that were far more democratic than those promoted by Gompers. The attempts of local activists to gain more international power for workers expanded even further in the wake of the disastrous 1920 election to include economic campaigns on behalf of foreign causes. Such activities mirrored those of direct-action proponents in Europe.

Local officials like those in Chicago also differed from the AFL hierarchy in their view of the relationship between the domestic and international realms, and in their attitudes about America's proper international role. Influenced by their participation in National Civic Federation activities, AFL leaders increasingly tied gains for American workers to greater industrial efficiency and to foreign economic expansion in the early twentieth century. A desire to increase the U.S. share of world markets led AFL officials to support various forms of economic and political imperialism and to oppose revolutionary nationalist movements that imposed too many restrictions on trade. AFL leaders rationalized American foreign interventionism in underdeveloped countries by arguing that the United States often played an important role in encouraging political stability and economic growth in such areas. CFL leaders, in contrast to the AFL hierarchy, emphasized that the welfare of American workers depended more on a democratization of industry at home than on either increasing industrial efficiency or promoting trade expansion. Dismissing notions that businessmen channeled profits from foreign trade back into wages, they suggested that workers would benefit from international financial exchanges only when labor controlled a majority of national governments in the world. As CFL leaders grounded their domestic political thought in American democratic ideals, so, too, they rooted their foreign policy platforms in longstanding U.S. diplomatic traditions. Echoing the strains of early American presidents like George Washington and John Quincy Adams, local activists argued that the United States must avoid political and military intervention in the affairs of other countries. Such interventionism, even when initiated for ostensibly laudable reasons, corrupted American democratic ideals at home and often resulted in the destruction of democracy abroad. Thus World War I, far from promoting democracy as Wilson claimed, had corrupted American democratic institutions and actually hindered the independence campaigns of many oppressed nationalities. Carrying the diplomatic thinking of early American presidents one step further, local leaders argued that excessive U.S. economic influence in foreign countries was also at odds with American democratic ideals; U.S. businessmen used their economic power to subvert democratic workers' movements in such countries and to consolidate their control over workers at home.

Some will be tempted by the dismal showing of the Farmer-Labor party in 1920 to dismiss local labor activists as insightful but powerless critics of American foreign policy. But by so doing they risk misunderstanding the complex ways in which changing local subcultures reshaped working-class political alignments in the postwar era. Local institutions, newspapers, and prominent municipal leaders played critical roles in politicizing workers during an age before radio and television. Because workers lived in communities that tended to be segregated along lines of race and national origin, immigrant leaders and local ethnic presses were usually more important than labor organizations in shaping working-class political orientations. But through their strike and organizing activities during the World War I era, municipal labor leaders penetrated the "insular" communities created by immigrant workers and their leaders in significant ways.[90] In the process, they won a tentative audience for their class-based critiques of Wilsonianism.

That their political agendas had appeal was evidenced in the spontaneous and massive labor political rallies that became commonplace on American streets, in the municipal Labor party successes during spring 1919, and in the growing momentum for labor party politics within AFL trade unions. Although ethnic organizations and immigrant leaders were clearly most crucial in stimulating an interest among workers in foreign policy issues, local Labor party activists were important in linking immediate ethnic concerns to a broader critique of Wilsonian internationalism that stressed its inherently undemocratic and imperialist tendencies. They also educated workers on the interconnections between local economic hardship and the Wilson administration's failed diplomacy. Local Labor party advocates thus likely added critical momentum to the swelling wave of revulsion against the Wilson administration in 1920.

That the ultimate heir to the widespread disillusionment with Wilsonianism was the Republican party rather than the Farmer-Labor party requires an understanding both of broad trends hindering independent labor party politics and of the goals and tactics of specific local labor party movements like the one in Chicago. Perhaps the most important factor inhibiting the growth of the national Farmer-Labor party movement in 1920 was the opposition of the AFL. Without its support, local revolutionaries lacked what David Montgomery has termed a "coordinating center" for launching their national political efforts and for winning the allegiances of trade unionists—one-third to one-half of whom had endorsed proposals for independent labor political action. Thus, as the *New Republic* commented, the Farmer-Labor party represented "a series of sporadic but widespread local movements rather than a coherent national one."[91]

The opposition of the AFL had another consequence as well: It left local labor leaders open to charges of Bolshevism and helped encourage a conservative backlash against labor politics within local movements. Equally important in inhibiting labor party politics in 1920 were the devastating strike defeats of the postwar era and the breakdown of

90. For a study emphasizing ethnic and racial residential segregation and the "insular" quality of working-class life in Chicago before 1919, see Cohen, *Making a New Deal*, 1–52. On the ways in which the local labor movement encroached on the lives of Chicago workers, see, especially, Barrett, *Work and Community in the Jungle*.

91. Montgomery, "New Tendencies," 110. *NR*, 1/5/21, 152; Shapiro, "Hand and Brain," 412.

national organizing campaigns in the packing-house and steel industries. These trade union setbacks in turn fanned the flames of already growing interethnic and interracial rivalries.[92]

But the failures of labor party politics in 1919 and 1920 cannot be blamed exclusively on factors external to the movement. Chicago activists themselves may have undermined support for the Farmer-Labor party in 1920 by their insistence on direct forms of democracy in industry, politics, and diplomacy. Such demands were a logical outgrowth of their disillusionment with AFL wartime collaborationism, but they alienated progressive national and international trade union leaders and liberal supporters who could have provided financial support and enhanced the party's reputation.

The unwillingness of Chicago and Farmer-Labor party leaders to compromise in order to gain liberal and national union support raises a critical question. Why, in the absence of substantial endorsements and aid from either national trade union leaders or liberal groups like the 48ers, did local officials attempt national organization rather than focusing on building strong municipal and regional parties? Invariably, voters in 1919 and 1920 proved more willing to experiment with labor party candidates in local elections than in national ones. Here again, the wartime experiences of local labor officials seem crucial. Like AFL leaders, many municipal officials became increasingly convinced during the war that the problems facing workers required national and international solutions. But they disagreed with the trade union hierarchy over the forms of power it was pursuing. To waste time on local political victories in the face of the global offensive against labor and the flawed corporatist strategies of the AFL was to enable the forces of capital to consolidate their strength. From the perspective of many local labor leaders, it was therefore more important to launch a doomed national campaign that would highlight the broad scope of problems that labor was facing, and would discredit the labor coalition with the Democrats, than it was to achieve immediate electoral victories.

Not surprisingly, then, Chicago Labor party officials claimed partial victory in the wake of Christensen's devastating defeat. In an article written immediately after the election, Robert Buck argued that workers had "stampeded" to Warren G. Harding in an act of revenge against the Wilson administration. By this action, they demonstrated that they

92. For a summary and analysis of the abundant literature emphasizing the national factors at work in hindering labor political development, see Mink, *Old Labor*. See also Weinstein, *Decline*, 272–339; and Fine, *Labor and Farmer Parties*.

knew the Democrats were only a shade less reactionary than the Republicans. Buck optimistically suggested that "the first part of . . . [the] gigantic task of weaning voters away from their old parties has been accomplished." He argued that Labor party leaders must now commence with the second part of the campaign: convincing workers "in large masses of the necessity of having and financing a party of their own."[93]

While CFL leaders continued valiantly to promote the *idea* of a Farmer-Labor party in the aftermath of the election, new coalition building would come only with the congressional elections of 1922. In the interim, the "big three"—Ed Nockels, Robert Buck, and John Fitzpatrick—rechanneled most of their political energies into foreign policy campaigns, which suggested that they were increasingly influenced by the direct-action movements then convulsing Europe. Although only tangentially related to the immediate activities of the Chicago Labor party, the campaigns had important ramifications for the future of the Labor party movement.

Frustrated by the reactionary resolutions that Gompers had helped force through the AFL convention on Russia, CFL secretary Ed Nockels tried to rally support for a special AFL session to discuss the Soviet revolution in the wake of the election. Such a conference, he argued, would give U.S. labor leaders a chance to discuss European plans for calling a general strike in the event that the Allies again tried to intervene militarily in Russia. It would also enable them to develop an American trade union strategy for dealing with the Russian civil war.[94]

Predictably, Nockels's plan backfired. Gompers, infuriated by the proposal, accused Nockels and the CFL of endorsing Bolshevism and trying to incite an economically disastrous strike. Nockels countered that Gompers had misread the letter; the CFL, he argued, was not calling for a general strike but was asking that a conference be called to consider what position the U.S. labor movement should take on Russia. Provoked even further by this reply, Gompers subsequently published the correspondence on the issue, along with a new reply, in the *American Federationist*. After another exchange of letters, Nockels invited Gompers to attend a meeting in Chicago and defend his position, but Gompers declined. A bitter correspondence continued between

93. *NM*, 11/6/20, 1; 11/13/20, 1–2.
94. Ibid., 8/1/20, 1.

the two until the end of 1920, heightening tensions between the Chicago council and the AFL and enabling Gompers further to smear the local Labor party movement as communist-inspired.[95] Robert Buck, for his part, became increasingly enmeshed in the international activities of the Federated Press Service. Functioning press offices had been established in Washington and New York by late spring 1920. Correspondents for the offices initially obtained most of their foreign information from major European labor papers and from diplomatic and news sources in Washington.[96] Editors on the executive board of the press service appreciated this coverage, but they believed that unbiased reporting could be obtained only when the press service had its own correspondents in Europe. During summer 1920, the service sent a reporter to London to set up an office. To their great dismay, he was deported in October. When the director of the Federated Press Service traveled to England to investigate, he was also barred from the country.[97]

Buck and other Federated Press Service officials were outraged by the events in London, suggesting that Britain had ordered the deportation of the Federated Press correspondent at the behest of the American secretary of state. Following the election, Buck and other press service leaders organized a mass meeting protesting the event.[98] They also went ahead with plans to form a European press network, setting up their own office in Germany and organizing the Federated Press of Europe. Forming the key contingent within the European press service were labor organizations from Holland, Belgium, Germany, Russia and Scandinavia, which agreed to communicate information to the main office in Germany in return for releases from the press service. Labor organizations in Canada and Australia also eventually subscribed to the press service.[99]

95. Ibid., 8/1/20, 1; 10/23/20, 12–13; 10/20/20, 13; 12/11/20, 12; 12/25/20, 13.
96. See Letter from Editor of Federated Press to Fitzpatrick, n.d., n.s., B10–F71: FP. See also Keiser, "John Fitzpatrick," 161–69; press articles of Paul Hanna and Lawrence Todd, NM, 11/27/20, 7, and 11/13/20, 8.
97. NM, 10/30/20, 1; 11/27/20, 6.
98. Ibid., 10/30/20, 1; 11/20/20, 5. Whether Buck was correct in his assertions about U.S. State Department involvement in the deportations is unclear. But American military intelligence did keep tabs on the New Majority and viewed it as subversive. See Robert A. Bowen, "Report on the Radical Press in the U.S., November 1918 to January 1921," December 22, 1920, U.S. Military Intelligence Reports: Surveillance of Radicals in the United States, 1917–1941, Reel 20, Frames 584–85.
99. Federated Press to Fitzpatrick, n.d., n.s., B10–F71: FP. Keiser, "John Fitzpatrick," 161–69; NM, 1/15/21, 9; 4/9/21, 8.

Buck used the new information obtained from the Federated Press Service to improve the quality of foreign reporting in the *New Majority*. The paper provided more detailed coverage of events in both Europe and Latin America.[100] It also began examining such far-flung issues as politics in Asia, oil in Persia, and U.S. economic interests in Lithuania.[101] Meanwhile, press correspondents in Washington and New York disclosed new information on the immense profits made by big business during the war and detailed the renewed efforts of some business groups to create a peacetime military.[102] The additional foreign coverage spurred complaints from conservative unionists who argued that the *New Majority* concentrated too much on international affairs and ignored local social events. But Buck refused to change the format of the paper. "Workers," he wrote, "do not legitimately belong to the labor movement unless they are conscious that their interests are identical with those of the workers, yellow, black and white, in every part of the world, who are fighting to free themselves and the world from the slavery which greed and the desire for power have created." The exchange suggested that while local labor leaders were becoming increasingly radicalized by international events in 1920 and 1921, important segments of the local labor movement were moving in the opposite direction. This increasing polarization would have dire consequences when CFL leaders sought to revive the Labor party movement.[103]

Fitzpatrick also proved preoccupied with foreign policy in the wake of the election. Like Buck, Fitzpatrick viewed the Farmer-Labor party defeat as a setback but not a permanent defeat for Labor party politics. During 1922, he would play an important role in building new coalitions among groups sympathetic to labor. But in the meantime, Fitzpatrick became increasingly involved in Irish nationalist campaigns. When the AFL refused to support the Irish-American campaign for a labor boycott of British goods, he used city and state federated bodies to implement an independent boycott. His Irish campaigns were subsequently used as a model by other CFL activists to launch movements on behalf of Indian independence and Russian famine relief. As I discuss in Chapter 5, these campaigns illustrated both the possibilities and the difficulties of direct-action campaigns on behalf of diplomatic ends in the

100. See *NM*, 11/27/20, 6–13; 11/6/20, 9; 11/27/20, 7; 4/21/21, 9.
101. Ibid., 1/15/21, 1–2; 7/9/21, 5; 11/6/21, 3.
102. Ibid., 6/18/21, 4; 8/13/21, 1.
103. Ibid., 12/4/20, 10.

United States. They also illuminated the problems that Labor party advocates would continue to face in channeling the forces of ethnic nationalism in ways that redounded to the benefit of independent labor political action.

By the end of 1920, the Chicago insurgency was at a crossroads. Its forays into labor politics had yielded encouraging results at the local level but the national Farmer-Labor party had performed abysmally. The trade union movement had also suffered several severe strike defeats during the year. Faced with these unfavorable circumstances, local leaders might have pursued a policy of retrenchment and focused on strengthening the local movement. But because they were convinced that the AFL's corporatist approach would continue to yield dire results, they vowed to pursue their national labor party crusade. Meanwhile, many of the prime movers in the CFL were caught up in the international fervor of the era and devoted even more of their attentions to foreign policy campaigns. The involvement of Fitzpatrick and others in the nationalist crusades of area immigrant communities would prove the most critical in shaping the future of the insurgency and in influencing the foreign policy attitudes of Chicago workers.

CHAPTER FIVE

John Fitzpatrick and Ethnic Resurgence in Chicago

W HEN Woodrow Wilson first coined the term self-determination to explain his wartime goals for small nations, Secretary of State Robert Lansing warned that it was "loaded with dynamite" and "would raise hopes that can never be realized."[1] Lansing's remarks proved prophetic: During 1918 and 1919, Irish, Poles, Magyars, Lithuanians, South Slavs, and Czechs in the United States all mobilized to win freedom for their homelands. Italians also lobbied to assure that fellow countrymen in the disputed areas of South Tyrole, Trieste, Dalmatia, and the Dodecanese islands were accorded rights to self-determination. When Wilson failed to accommodate some nationality groups at the peace conference, they rallied against the peace treaty and League.

Such groups are often portrayed as part of a vanguard movement promoting renewed isolationism in the postwar era. Disillusioned by the failures of Wilsonian diplomacy, they allegedly sought to return America to a simpler past in which the United States was unencumbered by entangling alliances with foreign powers.[2] But many immigrant leaders, far from being isolationists, envisioned a more far-

---

1. Gerson, *Hyphenate*, 76. See also Ambrosius, *Woodrow Wilson*; and Montgomery, "Nationalism, American Patriotism, and Class Consciousness."

2. See, especially, Adler, *The Isolationist Impulse*, 80–92; Thomas Bailey, *A Diplomatic History of the American People*, 9th ed. (Englewood Cliffs, N.J.: Prentice-Hall, 1974), 614–16; Smith, *Great Departure*, 180, 187. For views emphasizing the internationalist and economic aspects of ethnic critiques of the League, see Cuddy, *Irish America and National Isolationism*; and Jeffreys-Jones, "Massachusetts Labour and the League of Nations Controversy, 1919."

ranging international role for the United States than the Wilson administration. Rejecting the League because it would reinforce the international status quo, they sought to expand U.S. support for a broad range
of oppressed nationalities struggling for freedom and to force governmental leaders to develop policies that would encourage a redistribution of world power and wealth. Equally important, they objected to
the Wilson administration's suppression of dissent during the war and
defended interest-group lobbying as vital to ensuring a democratic
diplomacy that served the interest of all Americans. The international
agendas of anti-League immigrant groups were clearly at odds with
those of the AFL, but they often meshed well with the foreign policy
programs of local labor groups and stimulated municipal labor party
campaigns in 1919. Although CFL officials failed to convince most
immigrant leaders of the viability of the Farmer-Labor party during
1920, Chicago labor officials like John Fitzpatrick remained convinced
that ethnic nationalism could be guided to benefit labor politics. They
also believed that the labor movement could be used successfully to
promote nationalist causes.[3]

In the wake of the 1920 election, the CFL launched creative direct
action-movements on behalf of Ireland, India, and Russia that elicited
the support of a broad range of other city labor councils. These
campaigns suggest that local labor activists played a significant, but
hitherto neglected, role in the nationalist campaigns of immigrant
communities during 1920 and 1921. They also help to shed light on
popular opposition to some of the foreign policies promoted by the
Harding and Coolidge administrations. Diplomatic historians have
long noted that the Republican presidential administrations of the
1920s, although uninterested in joining the League, remained committed to promoting certain Wilsonian internationalist policies. In
particular, they sought to develop private international financial
structures that would encourage many of the same kinds of cooperation between major industrial-creditor powers that the League was
designed to promote. Also like the Wilson administration, Republican
presidents of the 1920s tried to encourage a corporatist partnership
between business, labor, and the state in fostering American economic
expansion and in undermining revolutionary nationalist movements
that threatened American economic penetration of underdeveloped

3. See, especially, Fitzpatrick speech, n.d., n.s., B11–F78: FP; *NM*, 11/1/19, 8;
1/15/21, 4. Harry Boland to Walsh, 5/18/21; Walsh to Malone, 4/21/20: B9, WP.

areas.[4] Diplomatic historians acknowledge, however, that policymakers were unable to implement a fully consistent foreign policy after 1920 because of sporadic popular opposition to corporatist forms of power sharing and to cooperationist international principles. The role of xenophobic ethnic fraternals in hindering American internationalist policies has often been documented, but historians have ignored the more sophisticated appeals and influence of jointly sponsored labor and ethnic foreign policy campaigns.[5] The Chicago example suggests that such campaigns were crucial in shaping working-class international alignments in the early 1920s.

The CFL's postelection diplomatic activities, while only tangentially related to Farmer-Labor party programs, also had immense repercussions for labor party politics. Historians suggest that in Britain, working-class consciousness and political solidarity "grew directly out of the fragmented community experience of the working class." They argue that it was neighborhood institutions like the Oddfellows, the Ancient Foresters, and local branches of friendly societies that enabled the working class to remake itself during the early twentieth century in ways that promoted labor party politics.[6] Because ethnic organizations were such a vital part of the American social infrastructure, their support was crucial to the future success of independent labor party politics. Fitzpatrick and other municipal labor leaders correctly sensed an affinity between their own internationalist goals and those of immigrant leaders and developed alliances with ethnic groups in the wake of the 1920 election that helped further to discredit Wilsonian internationalism. But whether international affairs provided enough common ground

4. See Hogan, *Informal Entente*, "Revival and Reform," 287–310, "Corporatism," 153–60; McCormick, "Drift or Mastery," 318–30; Rosenberg, *Spreading the American Dream*, 138–60; Joan Hoff Wilson, *American Business and Foreign Policy, 1920–1933* (Boston: Beacon Press, 1971); Leffler, *The Elusive Quest*; Burton Kaufman, *Efficiency and Expansion: Foreign Trade Organization in the Wilson Administration, 1913–1921* (Westport, Conn.: Greenwood Press, 1974); Frank Costigliola, *Awkward Dominion: American Political, Economic, and Cultural Relations with Europe, 1919–1933* (Ithaca, N.Y.: Cornell University Press, 1984).

5. On opposition to corporatist forms of power sharing, see, especially, McCormick, "Drift or Mastery," Rosenberg, *Spreading the American Dream*, 157–60; Thomas Ferguson, "From Normalcy to New Deal: Industrial Structure, Party Competition, and American Public Policy in the Great Depression," *International Organization* (winter 1984): 64–88. On xenophobic ethnic fraternals, see, especially, Adler, *Isolationist Impulse*, 91–92.

6. Perkin, *Rise of Professional Society*, 109. See also Hinton, *Labour and Socialism*. On the relationship of the CFL's Irish activities to Labor party politics, see Walsh to Fitzpatrick, 3/12/19, B8; Walsh to Malone, 4/21/20, B9: WP.

to enable Labor party leaders to forge a lasting political coalition with ethnic activists remained less certain.

Among those most profoundly influenced by Wilson's proclamations about self-determination were Irish-Americans. After the outbreak of war, almost all Irish organizations in Chicago had counseled against American involvement. Yet, when Wilson proclaimed self-determination for oppressed nationalities to be a wartime goal, even militant groups like the FOIF abandoned their opposition and threw their energies into the Liberty Loan Campaign. Wilsonian rhetoric about self-determination served another role as well: It put an end to bickering between officials of local Irish groups. Previously, leaders within the Chicago Irish community had split over the issue of Ireland's independence. Some favored home rule for Ireland while others advocated complete independence. Still others argued that some form of British-American protectorate ought to be established. Self-determination, however, neatly resolved these issues; representatives of all major Irish groups and socioeconomic strata within the Irish-American community in Chicago claimed to favor giving the Irish people a chance to decide their own form of government after 1918.[7]

The banner of self-determination also proved attractive to Irish-American activists because it provided legitimacy for their views of America's role in international affairs. In response to pressure for a British-American alliance in the late nineteenth century, Irish-Americans had promoted a vision of America as a defender of revolution. They argued that the United States, as a revolutionary nation itself, should refuse to assist the British or any other imperial power in extending their empires. Rather, America ought to help small nations win their independence. Irish-American meddling in foreign affairs provoked hostility both from successive presidential administrations and from nativist groups who championed other forms of internationalism. President Wilson became a particularly vocal critic of Irish-American and other forms of nationalist lobbying, suggesting that diplomacy was properly the preserve of the president and his advisers; only they possessed enough knowledge and detachment to construct a sound foreign policy for the United States. But Irish-American leaders argued that by proclaiming his support for self-determination, the president had sanctified continued efforts by ethnic groups to win freedom for Britain's colonies.[8]

7. IW, 10/5/18, 4; 11/16/18, 1. CC, 11/8/18, 1; 1/3/19, 4; 3/28/19, 1. GA, 12/21/18, 1.
8. See, especially, CC, 8/30/18, 7.

Equipped with these kinds of rationales, Irish-American leaders mobilized to ensure that the Irish case was brought before the peace conference. In November 1918, Chicago branches of the Ancient Order of Hibernians, United Irish League, Irish Fellowship Club, FOIF, and Clan na Gael all joined together and staged a self-determination week in concert with other groups throughout the country. In addition to holding mass parades and rallies throughout the city, Irish-American groups conducted a mailing campaign designed to force the Illinois state legislature and U.S. Congress to frame resolutions in support of Irish freedom. By February, both the Illinois house and the U.S. House of Representatives had passed legislation requesting a hearing for Ireland. Irish groups in several other states quickly followed suit and forced their legislatures to pass similar resolutions.[9]

Despite the favorable publicity, Wilson ignored the Irish issue throughout the winter of 1919. Concerned New York politicians staged the Third Irish Race Convention in March to map new strategies. Delegates from Irish groups throughout the country, including Chicago, attended. The convention drafted a policy statement warning Wilson that the "great task of establishing a permanent peace" would not be completed until the "Irish question was settled on the principle of self-determination."[10] A commission of three was then sent to speak personally with Wilson. When members arrived at the White House, Wilson refused to meet with one member of the commission who had worked against him in the 1912 Democratic convention, thereby rekindling old animosities between himself and an important Irish contingent within the New York Democratic party. At the conference upstairs, Bishop Peter Muldoon reminded the president that the Slavic peoples had been recognized by the peace conference. Wilson responded tersely, "These nations, Bishop, fell into our lap."[11]

Wilson's remarks confirmed Irish leaders' worst fears. The American delegation, they now realized, planned only to work for the rights of those nationality groups oppressed by the Central Powers; England was to be allowed to retain her colonies. During the next several months, Irish groups worked feverishly to bring Wilson's hypocrisy to light. In April, they sent a commission to Paris to confront Wilson yet again.

9. CC, 11/21/18, 1; 12/6/18, 4; 12/20/18, 1; 1/24/19, 1; 2/7/19, 1. IW, 12/14/18, 1; 12/21/18, 12; 12/30/18, 3; 1/11/19, 3; 3/15/19, 1. GA, 11/30/18, 2; 12/14/18, 1; 12/21/18, 1. See also Walsh to Reedy, 7/29/19, B8: WP.
10. IW, 3/1/19, 1.
11. Cuddy, *Irish America and National Isolationism*, 171.

Wilson dined with the Irish-American delegates, but he refused to grant either the U.S. commission or envoys from Ireland an official audience before the peace conference. Even normally conservative elements within the Irish-American community were outraged by the incident. The taciturn editors of the *Chicago Citizen*, for example, bannered a headline across their front page proclaiming, "U.S. Delegation, Headed by Woodrow Wilson, Snubs the American-Irish Envoys to Paris: Won't Ask Hearing for Just Claims of Ireland." The article noted that Wilson had snubbed not just the delegates but thirty million Irish-Americans. The *Irish World* endorsed the opinions of the *Citizen*, arguing that Wilson had defamed his title as "champion of oppressed nationalities."[12]

Following the debacle in Paris, Irish-American groups bitterly attacked the peace negotiations. "The longer the conference sits at Versailles," wrote the editors of the *Chicago Citizen*, "the more convinced the world grows that . . . the project to prevent wars is like a Junior debate in an American college." The editors argued that while Wilson pontificated about noble ideals, "French hatred and English greed backed up . . . by American subserviency are pursuing a policy that cannot but arouse racial animosities which will not subside in two generations."[13] A draft of the treaty released in May reinforced Irish-American opinions. "The Peace at Versailles," wrote the *Chicago Citizen* staff, "appears to thinking men as the inauguration of an intermission between a great war and one that may prove more cataclysmic."[14] Specifically, Irish-American leaders complained that the treaty was harsh toward the Germans but left the British empire intact. The resulting power imbalance, they argued, was bound to create tension in the future. They also predicted that blood would flow over the failure of the peace negotiators to deliver on their promise of self-determination for small countries like Ireland.[15]

The most biting attacks, however, were reserved for the League of Nations. Wilson argued that the League would be Ireland's ticket to freedom because one article in the League covenant allowed small

12. CC, 5/30/19, 1. *IW*, 6/7/19, 4. See also CC, 4/4/19, 1; 3/4/19, 1. *GA*, 6/7/19, 4. Nockels to Walsh, 11/22/21, B10; Walsh to Robert Lansing, 5/27/19; B28; Diary of Frank Walsh at the Peace Conference, 66–78, B29: WP. Cuddy, *Irish America and National Isolationism*, 165.
13. CC, 6/3/19, 1. *IW*, 5/24/19, 4. See also H. L. Fagin to Walsh, 2/17/19, B7; Walsh Peace Diary 66–73: WP.
14. CC, 6/27/19, 4. *IW*, 5/24/19, 4.
15. *GA*, 7/26/19, 4. CC, 6/3/19, 1; 6/11/19, 1; 2/21/19, 1.

nations to present their claims for self-determination to the League for international arbitration. Irish-American representatives denounced Wilson's claims as "ridiculous tommyrot."[16] They pointed out that the article to which Wilson referred required that a member nation first demand a hearing for the country requesting its freedom. This article, argued Irish-Americans, would effectively prevent adjudication on the rights of most small nations because if one colonial power were to work for the "destruction of another's colonies, then that power would vote for the destruction of the other's colonies."[17] Just as the United States had been afraid to offend Britain at the peace conference by supporting Irish freedom, so, too, would it be reluctant to champion the cause of oppressed nationalities in the League. Irish-American representatives further suggested that Britain would block the League from taking action on the Irish issue even if a member nation agreed to serve as Ireland's representative. Britain, they argued, could object to hearing the case of Ireland or other colonies on the grounds that it was a domestic issue and that the League constitution prohibited it from meddling in domestic affairs. If this tactic failed, British officials could vote down any measure for Irish freedom because they were guaranteed a majority in the Executive Council due to the six colonial votes they controlled.[18]

But Irish-American leaders did more than disprove Wilson's argument that Ireland would benefit from the League; they also demonstrated that the League might positively damage the causes of both Irish and American freedom. Article ten of the League covenant required member nations to respect and help protect each other's territorial integrity. Irish-Americans suggested that this clause committed the United States to preserving the status quo in Europe. Although most officials doubted the administration would actually send troops to Ireland on Britain's behalf, they nonetheless argued that the League would prevent Americans from rendering financial aid to Ireland in her struggle. Such funds were as crucial to Irish independence as French aid had been in the case of the American revolution. "Were a League of Nations," wrote one editor, ". . . in existence in the days when George Washington fought and won, we would be still an English colony." As a revolutionary nation itself, the United States had an obligation to support twentieth-century nationalist struggles. Moreover, the United States

16. CC, 10/10/19, 4.
17. Ibid., 9/19/19, 1.
18. Ibid., 10/2/19, 4; 10/17/19, 1; and Cuddy, *Irish America and National Isolationism*, 194–95, 200.

would be compromising its own sovereignty if it allowed a League of Nations dominated by Britain to determine its foreign policy.[19] In order to ensure that the Paris Peace Treaty, and the League, were defeated by Congress, Irish-Americans joined forces with Republican William Borah. A long-time isolationist, Borah was one of a handful of irreconcilables in the Senate who opposed the treaty even if reservations were added to dilute the power of the League. Borah early realized that the Irish were potentially valuable allies and cultivated their loyalty by sponsoring resolutions in support of Irish freedom. In addition, he gained a hearing for Irish-American groups in front of the Senate Foreign Relations Committee. After a draft of the treaty was released, Borah asked for a repayment on his debts. A mass campaign against the League was necessary, he argued, in order to convince undecided senators to reject the treaty. Eastern Irish-American leaders concurred and ordered groups throughout the country to begin an assault.[20]

Over sixty-seven Irish organizations in Chicago responded to the call and conducted anti-League activities.[21] The focal point of the new campaign became the Friends of Irish Freedom (FOIF). Deliberately created to encourage greater mass interest in the Irish cause, the group's weekly neighborhood meetings served a role comparable to that of Labor party rallies; they provided a cathartic release for the average worker who believed he had been duped by the Wilson administration into fighting the war. Yet, where Labor party officials could offer only the hope of retribution in the distant future, the anti-League campaign gave workers a chance to seek immediate revenge. Perhaps as a result, membership in the organization soared to 275,749 in 1920.[22]

The activities planned by FOIF groups were varied. All, however, participated in fund-raising and assisted in the distribution of over 1.3 million pamphlets denouncing the League in 1919. FOIF groups also staged rallies similar to those conducted during self-determination week. One such rally held at Wrigley Field attracted over forty thousand partici-

19. Quote from CC, 10/29/20, 4. See also GA, 7/26/19, 4. IW, 3/22/19, 4; 3/29/19, 18. CC, 3/21/19, 8, 12; 9/19/19, 1, 4; 10/29/20, 4. Walsh Peace Diary, 32–33; Walsh to Patrick Lyden, 10/20/21, B26: WP.
20. CC, 6/3/19, 1. IW, 6/21/19, 2. Fiscal Agent to Walsh, 10/29/21, B26; Telegram to Walsh, 6/11/19, B28: FP. Buckley, *New York Irish*, 260–62. Ambrosius, *Woodrow Wilson*, 143, 227. William Widenor, *Henry Cabot Lodge and the Search for an American Foreign Policy* (Berkeley: University of California Press, 1980).
21. CC, 6/20/19, 1.
22. Funchion, *Irish-American Voluntary Organizations*, 120. CC, 5/23/19, 1; 1/2/10, 1; 1/9/20, 6; 1/16/20, 6; 1/30/20, 1; 2/30/20, 6; 3/26/20, 6.

pants (an overflow crowd, since current seating capacity is about thirty-six thousand). Another, in Boston, drew seventy thousand people.[23] FOIF members also directly lobbied senators. Judge Daniel Cohalan, an avid New York patriot, kept lists of those legislators who expressed uncertainty about the League and then counseled FOIF branches throughout the country to bombard them with mail. When Senator Joseph Frelinghuysen of New Jersey confided privately to Cohalan that he was undecided on whether to support the treaty if reservations were attached, seventy thousand postcards arrived within a period of two days warning him about the dangers of the League.[24]

Despite the defeat of the treaty in the Senate in November 1919 and March 1920, leaders of Irish-American groups remained obsessed with Wilson and the League. Pro-British elites, they argued, wielded important power in America and might at any time convince the Senate to rescind its verdict. To ward off any new attempts to win passage of the treaty, Irish-American groups renewed their propaganda war against the administration. They also attacked the Anglophile press and exhorted Irish-American editors to extend their efforts to gain more subscribers. Most important, they searched out Wilsonians in every branch of government and launched smear campaigns against them. So intense did the battle against the League become that ethnic editors often urged Irish-Americans to vote against candidates for state and local offices primarily on the basis of their stance toward the treaty.[25]

Historians have typically attributed the myopia of Irish-Americans to two factors. They suggest that Irish-Americans worked against the League in part because they genuinely believed it would impede Ireland's fight for freedom. Equally important, they argue that Irish-Americans sought revenge on the Wilson administration for its failure to deliver on wartime promises.[26] But these explanations, while correct as far as they go, do not fully account for the tenacity of Irish-American campaigns against the treaty. Ethnic leaders also sought to

23. IW, 6/28/19, 1; 7/14/19, 1. CC, 1/9/20, 6; 3/26/20, 6; 1/16/20, 6; 5/8/20, 6; 1/7/19, 8; 12/3/20, 16; 8/15/19, 1.

24. O'Grady, The Immigrants' Influence on Wilson's Peace Policies, 78. CC, 2/13/20, 6; 2/20/20, 1; 3/26/20, 6.

25. CC, 3/26/20, 1; 11/28/19, 1; 7/1/21, 4; 10/29/20, 3; 11/5/20, 1; 12/31/20, 8. GA, 11/1/19, 4; 10/9/20, 1. IW, 10/26/18, 4. Walsh to Lyden, 10/20/21; Walsh to New York Times, 10/20/21: B26, WP.

26. See, especially, Adler, Isolationist Impulse, 73–76, 80–92; Bailey, A Diplomatic History, 614–16; Smith, Great Departure, 180, 187.

defeat the League in order to assert their right to a voice in future foreign policy decisions and to defend their vision of American internationalism.

Irish-American leaders believed that by courting their support during the war and then failing to live up to the promises he had made to them, Wilson had shown a flagrant disregard for the American pluralist system. Special interest groups, they believed, had a right to voice their opinions on diplomatic issues and to use their voting power to persuade candidates to support their causes. If candidates then violated their pledges, special interest groups had a duty to defeat them. Only by continuously asserting their political powers could special interest groups prevent foreign policy powers from falling into the hands of a few exclusive pro-British elites, as it had during the war. Irish-Americans must mobilize, they argued, because the same "empire that with brazenly hellish force attempts to suffocate the in-born spirit of freedom in the Irish people is burning up the oxygen in the atmosphere of freedom in America with fiendish ingenuity."[27]

Irish-Americans also worked against the League because they were convinced that Wilsonian internationalism was fundamentally flawed. World peace, they believed, would be achieved only when the major European empires, in particular the British empire, had been destroyed. They argued that the League, by reinforcing British hegemony, only enhanced the chances for war in the future. In accord with their view of America's world role, they suggested that the United States ought to shun the British and instead help to construct a future world order in which power and markets would be more equitably distributed. One of the ways to achieve this balanced world order was to aid oppressed nationalities throughout the world in gaining their independence. This goal, they claimed, had been at the heart of American foreign policy since 1776. To demonstrate their cosmopolitan worldview, Irish-American activists participated extensively in the campaigns of the Friends of Freedom for India, an organization modeled on the FOIF. They also proceeded with plans to form a League of Oppressed Nationalities, courting support among such diverse groups as Lithuanians, Estonians, Liberians, Koreans, Chinese, Egyptians, Guatemalans, Filipinos, and Puerto Ricans.[28]

27. CC, 2/11/21, 4.
28. Walsh Peace Diary, 32–33, B29; Walsh to Reedy, 7/29/19, B8; Sean T. O'Caillaigh to Walsh, 5/30/21, B29; Arthur Upham Pope to Walsh, n.d., B8; S. N. Glase to Walsh, 4/17/20, B9: WP. Agnes Smedley to Fitzpatrick, 5/25/19: FP.

That Irish-American leaders were concerned as much with asserting their own vision of internationalism as with helping Ireland to win her freedom became apparent in autumn 1919, when Irish president Eamon De Valera arrived in the United States. Initially, De Valera supported antitreaty campaigns for he, too, resented Wilson's hypocrisy and believed that the League constitution might prevent the United States from aiding Ireland. After De Valera witnessed the bitter Senate debates in March, however, he expressed doubt that America would ever enter the League. The Sinn Fein leader also argued that, in the remote event the United States did become a member nation, the Senate would attach so many reservations to the League constitution that the organization would be rendered powerless. Irish-American leaders, he believed, were squandering precious funds on the League battle. More important from an Irish perspective were arms to fight the escalating war against Britain.[29]

In spring 1920, De Valera initiated two new campaigns in an attempt to divert the attention of Irish-Americans from the League. The first was a bond certificate drive. In return for donations to the Irish cause, Americans were given certificates that were redeemable with interest ten years after British troops left Ireland. The FOIF executive council proved wary of De Valera's interference in Irish-American affairs and refused to give its wholehearted assistance. De Valera instead asked the newly formed American Commission on Irish Independence to oversee the campaign. The commission capitalized on techniques learned from the FOIF to mobilize the Irish-American public. Executive members of the commission wrote church pastors throughout the country asking that they form bond units in their churches. In Chicago alone, over eighty parishes complied. Members of bond units then sold certificates after mass and at other church functions. The campaign proved a tremendous success, raising over $5 million for Ireland. In a stroke, De Valera thus effectively diverted the pocket money of Irish-American workers from the hands of anti-League advocates to his own.[30]

29. IW, 7/14/19, 1; 10/25/19, 1. CC, 7/18/19, 1; 10/24/19, 1. Cuddy, Irish America and National Isolationism, 186; Buckley, New York Irish, 304. Elected Government of Irish Republic to Wilson, 1/16/20: WP.

30. Funchion, Irish-American Voluntary Organizations, 124; Cuddy, Irish America and National Isolationism, 217. CC, 1/16/20, 1, 7; 1/16/20, 18; 1/9/20, 1, 7; 3/20/20, 1. Irish Republican Bond issued to Joseph McKillen: now in the hands of the author. See Walsh to New York Times 10/21/21; 6/2/22: B26, WP, for analyses emphasizing the large contribution made by the working class to such campaigns. Walsh argued that contributions from the few wealthy men "have always been a mere drop in the bucket compared with the immensely larger sums which have been given freely by millions of men and women of small means."

Less successful, however, were De Valera's attempts to rechannel the political energies of Irish-Americans. Shortly after launching the bond certificate drive, De Valera also initiated a new campaign to win American recognition of the Irish Republic. Previous attempts to promote diplomatic recognition had foundered due to the lack of support from major Irish-American groups. During June and July of 1920, however, De Valera personally requested the help of FOIF executives. At his urging, Irish-American leaders encouraged both the Democratic and Republican conventions to accept planks on the recognition of the Irish Republic. A severe dispute arose, however, when the Republican party agreed to express sympathy for the Irish Republic in its platform but failed to demand recognition. Irish-American leaders, anxious to form a coalition with the Republicans, urged De Valera to accept the plank. But the Irish president pronounced the expression of sympathy meaningless and continued to demand a clause calling for diplomatic recognition. Subsequently, the Republicans refused to include any statement whatsoever on Ireland in their platform. A few weeks later, a recognition plank was also rejected by the Democratic party.[31]

The dispute over diplomatic recognition created a rift between De Valera and the leaders of major Irish-American organizations that prevented any concerted political action in the months preceding the election. During the late summer, De Valera announced that as a foreigner he would not interfere in the American elections but then added that he was "perfectly satisfied with the third party [Labor party] plank for the recognition of the Irish Republic."[32] Following his announcement, a few independent Irish-American editors called for a protest vote in the November elections. Patrick Ford of the *Irish World and American Industrial Liberator*, for example, argued that "two of the presidential candidates stand for England, two others, Christensen and Debs, are for American independence." Ford thus urged his readers to vote for either the Socialist or Farmer-Labor party.[33] The editors of the *Chicago Citizen* also proclaimed that "neither Senator Harding nor Governor Cox is fit to be president of the United States" and asked their readers to give consideration to "that most admirable execration, 'A plague on both your houses.' "[34]

31. CC, 6/18/20, 4; 7/2/20, 4. See also Cuddy, *Irish America and National Isolationism*; Buckley, *New York Irish*.
32. CC, 8/6/20, 8.
33. Buckley, *New York Irish*, 349.
34. CC, 10/1/20, 1.

Other Irish-American organizations, however, supported the viewpoints of *Gaelic American* editor John Devoy. Devoy argued that Irish-Americans should "stand solidly behind the men who will beat the League of Nations and will help down Wilsonism for all time." Harding, argued Devoy, was the only candidate strong enough to defeat Cox and assure America's sovereignty; a vote for the Socialist or Labor party candidate would be a wasted one. Devoy also asked his readers to elect local, state, and congressional representatives who would work against the League. "Vote even for [Tom] Watson of Georgia," Devoy counseled; "he is anti-Catholic but he will vote against the League of Nations every time it comes up."[35] In order to assure that voters knew who would work against the League, leading Irish-American organizations conducted a survey that asked congressional representatives to give their views on the League. These groups then sent their findings to papers throughout the country. Irish-Americans were undoubtedly influenced by a variety of factors on election day, but their voting patterns were heavily Republican and anti-League.[36]

Although De Valera failed to rally Irish-Americans behind the Labor party, many CFL officials were encouraged by the resurgence of political activity in the Chicago Irish community. If Irish-Americans voted Republican, immigrant leaders from all factions of the community nonetheless adopted positions on many issues that closely resembled those of the Labor party. Irish-American leaders, like Labor party officials, attacked Wilson for creating elitist institutions and destroying democracy. Likewise, both protested Wilson's failure to fulfill his promises of self-determination and denounced the League as an instrument that would perpetuate the current balance of power. The Irish-American vision of America as a defender of revolution seemed likewise compatible with Labor party goals. Labor party leaders argued that Irish-Americans would quickly become discontent with the Republicans because they would also pursue a foreign policy that denied the rights of small nations and served the interests of the British. Once Irish-Americans recognized, as Buck put it, that "the two old parties are alike, that there is no difference between them," then the preconditions

35. *GA*, 10/30/20, 4. See also *GA*, 10/16/20, 14; and Cuddy, *Irish America and National Isolationism*, 230–31.

36. *CC*, 10/29/20, 4. See also *CC*, 9/10/20; 9/25/20; 8/27/20; 10/29/20; and Buckley, *New York Irish*, 350.

would be established for transferring Irish-American political loyalties to the Labor party.[37]

To secure the political allegiances of Irish-Americans and other ethnic minorities, Labor party leaders needed not only to discredit the two major parties but also to demonstrate that labor political action could be effective in promoting nationalist campaigns and ethnic agendas. Since the 1920 election had illustrated that the Labor party would not win a major election for many years to come, CFL leaders needed to show that they had effective means for promoting short-term ethnic goals in the interim. They also needed to prove that the Labor party had long-term political viability.

During autumn 1920, Fitzpatrick received a fortuitous appointment; the American Commission on Irish Independence asked him to serve as president of its newly constructed labor bureau. CFL activists Ed Nockels and Robert Buck were selected for the executive committee. The purpose of the bureau was officially "to make effective" the diluted AFL resolution in support of the Irish Republic that had been passed in 1919. Specifically, officials on the commission hoped to gain AFL support for a boycott of British goods and to win U.S. recognition of the Irish Republic. But after the defeat of militant Irish independence resolutions on the floor of the AFL convention, Fitzpatrick instead directed his initiatives at central federated bodies.[38]

In January 1921, the bureau sent letters to hundreds of municipal labor organizations asking them to aid the committee in its fight for Irish freedom and to appoint five members to organize local Irish campaigns. Over two hundred bodies responded. Subsequently, the bureau worked through local agents at these central bodies to institute a partial boycott of British goods independent of major national and international unions. Assisting the bureau in many localities was the Irish Women's Consumers League, which dispensed lists of British goods to consumers. For symbolic reasons, boycott advocates particularly targeted British teas. To publicize the boycott of the British national beverage, the Irish Women's Consumers League staged a reenactment of the Boston Tea Party and subsequently established a mail-order service to sell other types of tea to desperate working-class families. Central feder-

37. NM, 11/13/20, 1–2; 11/6/20, 1.
38. See Chapter 3. See also Walsh to Flaherty, 4/9/21, B29; Fitzpatrick to Walsh, 7/13/21, B26; T. J. Vind to Walsh, B29; Labor Bureau on Irish Independence Statement, 1/10/21, B29: WP.

ated bodies distributed and publicized lists of boycotted teas and other products to workers and dispensed literature on the mail-order service. The financial effectiveness of the boycott is difficult to determine. Existing evidence suggests a very loosely organized campaign that varied tremendously in effectiveness from one locale to another. Its impact was dramatic enough in certain heavily Irish-American neighborhoods to inspire lawsuits against the Irish Women's Consumers League for falsely placing some American products on its lists of goods to be boycotted. But it seems dubious that the boycott caused any significant national decline in profits on British imports. More important were the psychological and political ramifications of the boycott campaigns. By even occasionally interjecting international politics into the daily shopping trips of Irish-American workers and their families, the boycott likely nurtured grudges against Wilson for his failure to deliver on wartime promises of self-determination for oppressed nationalities. In so doing, it helped further to discredit Wilsonian internationalist principles and to breed renewed suspicion of international organizations and centralized forms of power sharing promoted by Wilsonians.[39]

The campaign clearly had ramifications for Labor party politics as well, enabling Fitzpatrick to show Irish-Americans the unique kinds of power that labor might wield on their behalf. Immigrant leaders could never independently institute a boycott. Neither could they unite workers of all nationalities in a lobbying campaign. Fitzpatrick's work for the Labor Bureau also gave him access to five workers in numerous communities throughout the country who could work the year round to promote Irish issues. Just as Fitzpatrick had used the CFL to weld Irish loyalties in Chicago to the Labor party, so might these workers help to demonstrate the utility of class-based political action to ethnic workers in their cities. Finally, the Labor Bureau gave Fitzpatrick a chance to cultivate political alliances among other central federated body leaders—always his strongest supporters.

39. Letter from the Labor Bureau, American Commission on Irish Independence to Fitzpatrick, n.d., B9–F67; Report of the Labor Bureau of the American Commission on Irish Independence, B11–F78; Letter from Fitzpatrick to the American Commission on Irish Independence, 8/13/20, B9–F64; Letter from Labor Bureau, American Commission on Irish Independence, to Fitzpatrick, 11/1/20, B9–F67; Report, "Extracts from Replies of Central Bodies," B9–F68; Telegram, Frank Walsh to Fitzpatrick, 6/21/21, B10–F73; Coupon from Irish Women's Purchasing League, B10–F72; Unsigned letter to Victor Olander, 4/15/21, B10–F71: FP. Labor Bureau, American Commission on Irish Independence Memo, B26; Walsh to Leonora O'Reilly, 1/27/21, 5/23/21, B29; Leonora O'Reilly to Walsh 5/28/21, B29; Walsh to Fitzpatrick, 10/25/20, B28: WP. See also NM, 11/20/20, 3; 1/15/21, 1–2; 1/8/21, 2–3; 6/25/23, 4; 2/2/21, 2.

Although initiated to mobilize workers on behalf of Irish independence, Fitzpatrick's plans also seemed to provide an effective blueprint for building a Labor party movement in the absence of support from the AFL. Central federated bodies could become centers for promoting a vast array of nationalist causes, breaking down previous resistance among immigrant workers to Labor party politics and promoting worker solidarity in the midst of ethnic diversity. Central federateds might also provide a perfect network for organizing future Labor party campaigns without extensive funding. These networks would enable the CFL to circumvent hostile mainstream union channels while still building on the strength of the union movement.[40]

Municipal labor leaders also needed to solicit the support of some mainstream ethnic organizations if they were to realign permanently the political loyalties of immigrant workers. The leaders of such groups could help convince workers of the viability of independent labor political action and also neutralize the competing political agendas of middle-class elements within their communities. A number of Irish-American newspaper editors had pledged their support for third parties in 1920, but leading Irish-American organizations proved to be infertile ground for Labor party recruitment.[41] In late 1920, however, Eamon De Valera formed his own organization, the American Association for the Recognition of the Irish Republic (AARIR). Upset with the leaders of major Irish-American groups, De Valera deliberately excluded them. Instead, he asked prominent labor and business leaders who had only played peripheral roles in past Irish-American affairs to help launch the organization in cities throughout the country. Among these was John Fitzpatrick, who created a vigorous Chicago branch from a remnant of the old FOIF council to which he had belonged.

40. That CFL leaders viewed central labor unions as effective centers for foreign policy agitation and for promoting labor political solidarity is illustrated in the documents on Irish campaigns listed in n. 39 and in the documentation on their Indian and Russian campaigns. See Tarknath Das to Walsh, 1/19/21, B10: WP. Agnes Smedley to Fizpatrick, 5/25/19, B8–F60: FP. NM, 4/19/19, 8–9. Speech of Basanta Koomar Roy, Fraternal Delegate from Friends of Freedom for India, *Proceedings of the First National Convention of the Labor Party*, 1919, 32–37. Joseph Manley of Trade Union National Committee for Russian Relief to Walsh, n.d., circa March 1922; Manley to Walsh, 3/8/22: B11, WP. Nockels to Walsh, 9/30/22, B11; Treasurer, Friends of Soviet Russia to Walsh 5/31/22, B9; Walsh to Mr. A. B. Martin of Friends of Soviet Russia, 5/31/22, B9: WP. Foner, *History of the Labor Movement*, 8: 60–62.

41. CC, 7/8/21, 4; 10/22/20, 1; 10/29/20, 3. GA, 10/16/20, 4; 11/13/20, 4. IW, 10/18/19, 4. Walsh to Alexander Scott, 6/2/22, B26: WP.

The Chicago organization worked closely with the Labor party and Labor Bureau in order to make the boycott of British goods effective. It also conducted fund-raising campaigns and collected lists of those Chicago businessmen who supported these campaigns. The *New Majority* then ran advertisements for these businesses. One typical ad for Patterson Mineral Co. claimed that the royalties on every bottle of orange soda went to the cause of Irish freedom and urged its readers to "Drink to the Success of Sinn Fein."[42] The Chicago branch was soon attracting over one thousand people to its weekly meetings. Nationwide, the organization claimed seven hundred thousand members by late 1921—at least four hundred thousand more than its competitor the FOIF.[43]

Unlike other Irish-American organizations, the AARIR did not develop domestic political agendas that competed with those of the Labor party; instead, it limited itself primarily to the issues of winning diplomatic recognition for the Irish Republic and to promoting the boycott. The AARIR proved an ideal partner for the Labor Bureau, lending credibility to its campaigns without simultaneously diverting the political energies of workers away from labor issues. The organization never officially supported the Labor party but, by undercutting the political campaigns of more traditional groups, it opened a window of opportunity within the Irish-American community for Labor party advocates.[44]

Unfortunately, both the AARIR and the Labor Bureau were torn asunder by the signing of the Anglo-Irish treaty in December 1921. The treaty divided Ireland in two; under its provisions, Northern Ireland remained a British province. The South, meanwhile, was denied the independence it sought but was accorded the status of a protectorate. When Dail Eireann voted to accept the treaty by a slim margin of sixty-four to fifty-seven, Eamon De Valera and other opponents walked out and formed a new government. The AARIR split over whom to support. A majority of the executive council voted to endorse the treaty. The

42. *NM*, 4/23/20, 8.
43. *CC*, 1/21/21, 6. *NM*, 4/30/21. Funchion, *Irish-American Voluntary Organizations*, 10. Walsh to Fitzpatrick, 8/13/20, and n.s. letter to Rev. Wm. Cahill, 11/2/20, B28; Fitzpatrick to Walsh, 7/13/21, B26; Thomas Prendergast to Walsh, 7/14/21, B26: FP. Frank Walsh claimed a membership of 965,000 for the AARIR as of October 15, 1921, but I have not found other documentation of this figure. See Walsh to *New York Times*, 10/21/21, B26: WP.
44. See, especially, Walsh to James O'Mara, 4/16/29, B29; Fitzpatrick to Walsh 7/13/21, B26; Thomas Prendergast to Walsh, 7/14/21, B26: WP. Funchion, *Irish-American Voluntary Organizations*, 9–12.

minority who opposed the agreement, however, claimed to represent the true sentiments of rank-and-file AARIR members and conducted separate activities. Both factions subsequently launched smear campaigns against each other that proved disastrous for the organization; by March 1922, membership had declined to about seventy-five thousand. The Labor Bureau also languished, eventually disbanding in the face of bitter divisions within the Irish community.[45]

Fitzpatrick's close association with De Valera earned him the epithet "splitter," or a provocateur of division, and damaged his reputation among important segments of the Irish-American community. When hostilities increased in Ireland during 1922, De Valera's forces became synonymous in the minds of many Irish-Americans with the Bolshevists; like Lenin, De Valera was trying to destroy the duly elected revolutionary government in Ireland. Fitzpatrick's failure to disavow De Valera conveyed to some Irish-Americans that the Labor party was a tool of communists and therefore ought to be shunned.[46]

The CFL's campaigns to win support for the Labor party within the Irish-American community would be further hindered by renewed political activity among older ethnic organizations. Beset by the same divisions over the treaty as the AARIR, mainstream groups increasingly focused on eliminating British influence in America. Reiterating an old theme, they argued that Britain was trying to destroy freedom in the United States as well as in Ireland. British-American big businessmen had seized control of public utility corporations and were using them to subvert municipal governments. Members of this same elite owned most of the presses and papers in the United States and were trying to de-Americanize U.S. history and to Anglicize the American people.[47]

To fight the insidious influence of the British in America, the FOIF launched a new bond drive modeled on the Irish Victory Fund and campaigned for public ownership of utilities. The Ancient Order of Hibernians and other mainstream fraternals worked to get local, state, and national governmental support for the initiative and referendum; officials argued that by adopting these practices the government would be giving more direct control to the people and thereby diminishing the power of England. Other ethnic leaders tried to convince Irish-Americans to withdraw all money from banks handling British securities

45. Funchion, *Irish-American Voluntary Organizations*, 9–12. Basil Manley to Thomas Lyons, 12/14/21, 1–4; Ed Nockels to Frank Walsh, 7/21/21: B26, WP.
46. CC, 7/1/21, 4; 7/22/21, 4. GA, 5/14/21, 14.
47. CC, 2/11/21, 4.

and to work for federal control of insurance companies in order to diminish Britain's economic power in the United States.[48]

The renewed Anglophobia of Irish-American leaders was spurred in part by the bitterness felt toward Britain, and British-Americans, over atrocities committed during the Irish war for independence. But it was also inspired by political ambitions and by collective anxiety over a political system that had seemed to run amok during the years of the Wilson presidency. Like Labor party officials, many Irish-American leaders remained suspicious of the collaborationist arrangements that had developed between big business, trade union leaders, and government officials during 1914 and 1915. This pro-British cabal, they believed, had been decisive in forcing the nation into war against popular wishes. It was also responsible for the catastrophic peace treaty that Wilson had constructed. Irish-Americans continued to be fearful of Wilsonian elites even after helping to defeat the Democrats during the election, arguing that they were using their influence at lesser levels to destroy American democratic institutions and to undermine the political power of oppressed nationality groups.

Similar political concerns helped spur renewed interest on the part of Irish-American leaders in the foreign policy of the Harding administration. Many Irish-Americans had voted for Harding partly because they believed he would reverse Wilson's pro-British policies. But they began to doubt Harding's intentions when he failed to demand that Britain repay war debts due to the United States in 1921. According to Irish-American leaders, these outstanding debts prevented the American government from making loans to home-buyers and also enabled Britain to continue the war in Ireland. Subsequently, Irish-Americans tried to create a bloc in Congress to compel Britain to pay its bills. In response to the lobbying activities of those concerned with the debt question, congressional representatives created a committee to investigate the issue. Much to the chagrin of Irish-Americans, the committee recommended forgiving one-half of the debt and establishing very lenient terms for repayment. The committee's conclusions convinced ethnic leaders that British influence was more pervasive in Washington than they had imagined.[49]

Their views appeared confirmed when the Harding administration called a naval conference in Washington to negotiate arms control

48. *GA*, 5/14/21, 2; 2/18/22, 1; 4/21/21, 1.
49. *CC*, 12/31/20, 8; 2/11/21, 4; 7/4/21, 1; 11/26/20, 4. *GA*, 1/27/23, 1; 2/24/23, 1.

treaties with Britain and several other nations. Participants eventually concluded several important agreements. One, the Five-Power Treaty, established a ten-year moratorium on the construction of capital naval vessels and also placed ceilings on the aircraft carrier tonnage a nation could possess. The Four-Power Treaty abolished the Anglo-Japanese alliance and stated that signatories would respect each other's Pacific territories. Irish-American leaders objected to these agreements on the grounds that they institutionalized British naval superiority. After the conference, they tried to rally isolationists in the Senate against the treaties, but they discovered that many of their most faithful allies had defected to the ranks of the enemy. The treaties subsequently passed by substantial margins.[50]

Like the domestic campaigns of Irish-American leaders, these new foreign policy crusades were clearly designed to increase the unity of the Irish-American voting bloc. The editors at the *Gaelic American*, in justifying continued Irish lobbying, told their readers, "The American people are utterly uninformed on old world politics, and England, being in complete control of foreign news services, takes good care that they are misinformed on all important happenings." They noted that "the work of getting the facts to the American people has been the chief function of citizens of Irish blood for the past twenty-five years." If America was to fulfill its historic world role, then Irish-Americans must continue to fight British influence in America.[51] Anglophobia meshed neatly with political ambition.

In the end, both misfortune and the campaigns of conventional ethnic leaders hindered Fitzpatrick's attempts to build support for independent labor political action and a class-based diplomacy among Irish-Americans. The untimely demise of the Labor Bureau and AARIR deprived Fitzpatrick of forums for demonstrating the continued affinity of labor and Irish nationalist diplomatic goals. Meanwhile, older Irish-American groups launched campaigns that helped to revitalize Anglophobia and to undercut class consciousness. But if the Irish campaigns of municipal labor bodies failed to benefit Labor party politics, they nonetheless suggest that such groups remained important diplomatic actors within older immigrant communities following the election. Local labor activists expanded the scope of Irish-American critiques of

50. GA, 12/3/21, 4; 7/22/21, 4; 12/17/21, 1; 10/28/22, 4. CC, 7/22/21, 4. *Chicago Herald Examiner*, 12/13/21. See also Hoff-Wilson, *American Business and Foreign Policy*, 31–64; Rosenberg, *Spreading the American Dream*, 108–60.
51. GA, 1/21/22, 4.

Wilsonian internationalism and politicized workers in ways that raised class as well as ethnic foreign policy concerns.

The CFL's Indian campaign, though closely linked to its Irish nationalist crusade, failed to have the same political fallout. CFL leaders worked closely with the Friends of Freedom for India to garner trade union support for Indian independence. But the movement did not appear to have the scope of the Irish campaign or seem to effect in any significant way the CFL's relations with other labor or ethnic organizations.[52] The Russian campaigns of the CFL, by contrast, had profound implications. To promote famine relief, the CFL sponsored a Trade Union National Committee for Russian Relief which, like the Labor Bureau on Irish Independence, solicited the help of other municipal labor councils. It also worked closely with the Friends of Soviet Russia and the American Labor Alliance for Trade Relations with Russia, both of which won widespread support among central labor councils. Since Russia and Poland engaged in a bitter conflict over territory after the war, the CFL's Soviet campaigns triggered an angry backlash within Chicago's large and politically important Polish community.[53]

Like the Irish, Poles had been inspired by Wilson's rhetoric about self-determination during the war. After Wilson pronounced his intention to win freedom for oppressed nationalities, both socialist and nonsocialist Polish organizations worked tirelessly to raise money for the war effort. In return for their loyalty, Poles demanded American support for Polish independence.[54] Wilson subsequently aided Poland in attaining its freedom at the peace conference, but he soon discovered that his talk of self-determination had fostered grander dreams among Poles.

When Wilson used the term "self-determination," he referred to the right of different ethnic groups to decide their own political fate. Accordingly, he continued to argue that Polish borders ought to be deter-

52. Tarknath Das to Walsh, 1/19/21, B10: WP. Agnes Smedley to Fizpatrick, 5/25/19, B8–F60, FP. NM, 4/19/19, 8–9. Speech of Basanta Koomar Roy, Fraternal Delegate from Friends of Freedom for India, *Proceedings of the First National Convention of the Labor Party*, 1919, 32–37. Unfortunately, there is less documentation on the CFL's Indian campaigns, so their exact scope is unclear.
53. Joseph Manley of Trade Union National Committee for Russian Relief to Walsh, n.d. circa March 1922, B11; Manley to Walsh, 3/8/22, B11: WP. Nockels to Walsh, 9/30/22, B11; Treasurer, Friends of Soviet Russia, to Walsh, 5/31/22, B9; Walsh to Mr. A. B. Martin of Friends of Soviet Russia, 5/31/22, B9: WP. Foner, *History of the Labor Movement*, 8: 60–62. Foner estimates that central labor unions in seventy-two cities supported the Alliance for Trade Union Relations with Russia.
54. See Chapters 1 and 2; and Gerson, *Woodrow Wilson*, 52–80; Cygan, "Political and Cultural Leadership."

mined on the basis of nationality; those areas in which Poles formed a majority should go to Poland while other land ought to be placed under the control of neighboring states. Many Polish and Polish-American leaders, on the other hand, remained committed to a medieval vision of their homeland's perimeters. They argued that boundaries ought to be determined not by nationality but by Poland's historical claims to territories in Europe. One group suggested that Poland was entitled to vast stretches of land in the east which included parts of White Russia, all of Lithuania, and part of the Ukraine. Poland's claim to this land dated from 1386 when Polish kings from the Jagiellonian dynasty ruled over these areas. Other politicians, known as Piasts, claimed title to western territories on the basis of ancient feudal rights that included land beyond the Oder and additional areas along the Baltic coast. The imperialist ambitions of Polish leaders were reinforced by the power vacuum left in eastern Europe following the signing of the armistice. Upon viewing the chaos surrounding them, some Poles argued that Poland ought to reestablish both the Jagiellonian and Piast empires. Among these were Ignace Paderewski and socialist leader Joseph Pilsudski, who were key figures in establishing a coalition government in Poland after the armistice.[55]

The first hint that Paderewski and Pilsudski planned to act on their ambitions came when they asked Wilson to send munitions in order to ward off the Bolsheviks and requested the services of an interallied battalion that had fought in France during the war. Alarmed by the potential spread of communism, Wilson granted both these requests. The Poles used the equipment and army to launch an offensive against the Ukrainians. When Wilson demanded that the Poles withdraw, the newly formed government refused. Over the course of the next several months, Poland expanded eastward without obstruction. Poles then tried to solidify these gains and win some territories in the west by diplomatic means at the peace conference. A special commission on Poland appointed by the Allies initially recommended giving Poland many of the areas it demanded, including Lithuania, the German city of Danzig, large parts of Silesia, and a corridor along the Baltic. France supported these claims because it desired a powerful ally to check German offensives. Wilson and Lloyd George, however, argued that the commission's proposals grossly violated the principles of self-determination. If the advice of the commission were followed, over two million Germans

55. Gerson, *Woodrow Wilson*, 111–12.

would be expatriated; Lithuania would be placed in a state of vassalage to an alien power with which it shared no common cultural heritage. The objections of British and American diplomats finally forced the Poles to compromise. Danzig was made an international city, while Lithuania was given its independence. Plebiscites were held in other disputed areas. Western Silesia was subsequently given to Germany, but a wealthier industrial section in the east was awarded to Poland.[56]

Polish-Americans remained grateful to Wilson for winning freedom for their homeland in the wake of the peace conference, but his refusal to grant their demands for more territory confirmed their wartime suspicions about his diplomatic abilities. The president, suggested some, was ignorant about European politics. Like Chicago Irish leaders, they argued that Wilson placed too much faith in the League of Nations and that only an equitable distribution of power would ensure world peace.[57]

Antagonism toward Wilson intensified when he sent a League-mandated commission to Poland to investigate allegations of pogroms against Jews and black migrant workers. Wilson subsequently insisted on safeguards for Jews in the treaty guaranteeing Polish freedom. Many Poles believed that Wilson and the commission had violated Poland's sovereignty and questioned whether the League would be used against small nations in the future.[58] The incident also reconfirmed the Polish-American image of Wilson as an innocent well-wisher easily manipulated by other powers. The pogrom stories, some Polish-Americans suggested, were exaggerated. Moreover, there were deeper reasons for the killings of Africans and Jews than appeared on the surface; members of these groups, some immigrant editors argued, had "earned their fate." They claimed that Jews were frequent practitioners of usury while blacks attacked white women.[59] Following the commission's report, one Polish editor counseled his readers to avoid Chicago Jewish businesses so that "we will not have any leaches sucking our life blood."[60]

Despite their increasing disillusionment with Wilsonian diplomacy, Poles supported passage of the treaty. Political activity on its behalf, however, was sporadic because the issue lacked urgency. A Polish government was already functioning; Senate passage of the treaty would

56. Ibid. See also Kantowicz, *Polish-American Politics in Chicago*, 117–18.
57. Gerson, *Woodrow Wilson*, 95. *Narod Polski*, 4/23/19, 1–2; 4/30/19, 3–4: WPA. *Dziennik Zwiazkowy*, 1/26/17, 1: WPA.
58. *Narod Polski*, 8/16/19, 12: WPA. Kantowicz, *Polish-American Politics in Chicago*, 117–18.
59. *Narod Polski*, 5/28/19, 6/18/19, 1–2: WPA.
60. Ibid., 5/28/19, 1.

only give official status to this government. As the elections approached in 1920, Polish-American leaders remained lackadaisical in their support of the president and the Democratic party. Some officials argued that Poles ought to vote Democratic in November out of gratitude for Wilson. Others, while noting their indebtedness to the Democrats, nonetheless remained silent on the issue of whom to support in the presidential election. Still others openly endorsed Harding. A number of leading Polish socialists backed Eugene Debs. Over 61 percent of all Polish voters in Chicago ultimately gave their vote to Warren G. Harding.[61]

The vote signaled to many Labor party activists that the wartime marriage of Poles to the Democratic party had ended. Subsequently, they tried to rekindle support for the Labor party in Chicago's heavily Polish districts. Yet relations between the CFL and Poles had deteriorated since the 1919 mayoral election. CFL officials disapproved of Poland's expansionist foreign policy because they believed it endangered the fledgling revolutionary regime in Russia. During summer 1920, the CFL passed a resolution condemning Poland for its acts of aggression in eastern Europe and calling on the AFL to send aid to Russia.[62] The resolution provoked an angry counterreaction within Chicago's Polish community. "Some American or English Jew at the head of a labor union," wrote the editors of *Narod Polski*, "desires to control the destiny of Poland: Out with such leaders."[63] Continued work by the CFL on behalf of Russia convinced some Polish-American officials that politics was an inappropriate endeavor for the labor movement. "There is something wrong in the ranks of organized labor," argued *Narod Polski*. "The workman is entering a slippery path of international politics for purely economic reasons. Organized Labor desires to dictate laws, first to its own government and later on to other governments and countries." The editors concluded that "Politics should be removed from the Labor unions as soon as possible. If the union leaders desire to play politics, we Poles cannot cooperate with them lest we betray Poland our nation."[64]

Although Fitzpatrick and other party leaders blundered in their attempts at cultivating political alliances with Poles during 1920 and

61. Allswang, *House for All Peoples*, 117–19. See also Kantowicz, *Polish-American Politics in Chicago*, 117; and Gerson, *Hyphenate*, 99.

62. *NM*, 10/23/20, 12.

63. *Narod Polski*, 9/1/20, 1–3: WPA.

64. Ibid. Letter from *Dziennik Ludowy* to Fitzpatrick, 2/1/22, B11–F94; Fitzpatrick article, n.d., B12–F84; Letter from Zygmunt Piotrowski to Fitzpatrick, 5/10/21, B10–F72: FP. Pacyga, *Polish Immigrants*, 246.

1921, they had long possessed an intuitive understanding of the relationship between unionization and political support in new immigrant communities. In late 1921, Fitzpatrick and CFL officials once again initiated campaigns in the stockyards and followed through with a nationwide strike. Polish workers demonstrated particular enthusiasm for the strike, and many immigrant leaders assisted in relief efforts. But the strike was undercut by feuds between union leaders; by divisions among workers along ethnic, racial, and skill lines; and by high unemployment levels. The strike collapsed in February, further eroding support for the local labor movement among area Poles.[65]

CFL organizing and political campaigns in Polonia were also undercut by a case involving the popular Polish labor organizer John Kikulski. A CFL trial committee censured Kikulski for embezzling funds, and he responded by hurling countercharges against local activists. In spring 1920, Kikulski was shot to death near his home. In the wake of the shooting, Polish hostility toward the dominant ethnic groups who controlled the local labor movement increased. The editors at *Dziennik Chicagoski* argued that Kikulski had been like "salt in the eye of the Irish." The staff at *Dziennik Zjednoczenia*, after lambasting area union leaders, advised their Polish readers to avoid becoming a "Goat of Sacrifice" once again. They claimed that "the Poles in the United States constitute a working class" and insisted that "the sympathies of the entire Polish society, and in no less a measure of the press, are on the side of the worker." Polish-Americans should form "purely Polish" unions rather than rely on existing labor organizations. Through their own unions, Poles could independently influence the employer class.[66] Ethnic officials further suggested that Polish-American workers organize publicity crusades to fight the slanderous propaganda of trade union leaders. To aid in this battle, they formed a Polish Information Bureau that disseminated fliers throughout the country.[67]

Nonsocialist Polish-American activists urged their countrymen to seek greater political power for Polonia within the two-party system. "Politics," argued the editor of *Chicago Society News*, "is a selfish

65. Barrett, *Work and Community in the Jungle*, 255–63. For examples of support from Polish organizations during the strike, see *Dziennik Chicagoski*, 1/30/21, 1: WPA. For unfavorable reactions, see *Dziennik Zjednoczenia*, 7/4/22, 1 and 2/3/22, 2: WPA.
66. *Dziennik Chicagoski* quoted in Pacyga, *Polish Immigrants*, 245. *Dziennik Zjednoczenia*, 7/24/22, 1; 12/7/21, 1: WPA. Barrett, *Work and Community in the Jungle*, 229.
67. *Dziennik Chicagoski*, 12/12/21, 3: WPA.

game. Let us be as selfish as others are."[68] Others gave similar advice. "We should, regardless of party affiliations, regardless of our personal views, regardless of our will," claimed one contributor to *Dziennik Zjednoczenia*, "stand united at the polling booth and unanimously elect those candidates who are fellow countrymen." He argued that once Poles were elected to office they would command more respect "and matters of international importance will be investigated more justly in the future."[69]

To further assure that Poles would vote as a bloc, ethnic leaders launched a campaign against radical parties that were making inroads into the Polish community in Chicago. Ethnic leaders claimed that the Communist and Communist Labor parties ought to be opposed because they were controlled by Jews and Irishmen; these two nationalities had always sought to exploit Poles. Moreover, the Communists would give Poles a bad name among native Americans. Socialists were denounced for fanning the flames of class prejudice, while Labor party leaders were labeled disloyal. None of these three groups, according to Polish leaders, would work for Poles. Since these groups were unlikely to win the elections anyway, Poles would only be wasting their votes and diminishing Polish-American political power if they cast ballots for candidates from these parties. A spirit of retrenchment and xenophobia among leading Polish groups combined with the CFL's ill-considered policies toward Polish nationalism to help further erode support for independent labor politics within Polonia.[70]

The history of the CFL's diplomatic initiatives and interaction with Irish- and Polish-American activists illustrates both the possibilities and limits of grass-roots labor foreign policy movements in the wake of the 1920 election. Municipal labor leaders did sometimes succeed temporarily in launching diplomatic campaigns that channeled nationalist and ethnic energies toward city labor councils and helped to promote class-based interpretations of international affairs. But just as often, the international campaigns of city labor groups backfired, provoking increased antagonism toward the labor movement and labor party politics within immigrant communities. Despite their failures, the foreign policy pro-

---

68. *Chicago Society News*, 9/12/23, 4: WPA.
    69. *Dziennik Zjednoczenia*, 11/6/22; 10/23/22, 1: WPA. *Dziennik Zwiazkowy*, 8/15/18, 18, 1–4: WPA.
    70. *Polonia*, 5/19/21, 1; 5/6/20, 1: WPA. *Narod Polski*, 1/12/21, 1; 8/17/21, 1: WPA. *Dziennik Zjednoczenia*, 8/28/22, 1: WPA. On Polish communists, see Cygan, "Political and Cultural Leadership," 117–19.

grams of local labor groups played important roles in increasing the spectrum of debate on foreign policy issues, in politicizing key groups of workers, and in further discrediting Wilsonian and AFL internationalist principles. When Gompers finally succeeded in suppressing municipal insurgencies, it would significantly alter patterns of accommodation and resistance to U.S. foreign policy initiatives within the working class.

CHAPTER SIX

The Final Battle, 1922–1924

As the CFL weathered the storms created by its ethnic activities during 1922, the AFL experienced an equally disastrous year. At the annual convention, AFL leaders lamented the return of reaction and claimed that 99 percent of their time had been spent defeating pernicious legislation. Membership, they noted, had declined by about seven hundred thousand during the preceding twelve months.[1] To some, the labor movement's dire state signaled the need for retrenchment. The AFL, they believed, must focus on shoring up the defenses of existing unions rather than on new organizing campaigns. It must also shun revolutionary politics and instead try to increase the AFL's status and influence as a rational bargaining agent within the capitalist system. The postelection aspirations of conservative labor activists were best captured in a front-page cartoon in the *Unionist* that depicted a large convertible occupied by five passengers. Capital drove the car, while management sat at its side. Labor, invention, and science were all in the back seat enjoying the sun of cooperation that smiled down on them.[2]

If many conservative unionists focused on the need to rekindle collaboration between business and labor in the postelection era, CFL leaders emphasized that the trade union movement must structurally reform itself in ways that would foster more effective strike and political activity. In particular, they encouraged the AFL to hold a conference to establish plans for amalgamating trade unions until there remained "only one

1. *Proceedings of the AFL*, 1922, 115. NM, 6/17/22, 1. NR, 7/5/22, 150.
2. *Unionist*, 9/1/21, cover; 3/24/24, 1; 7/20/21, 1. NR, 7/5/22, 150; 11/2/21, 275–76.

union for each industry." CFL officials also called on the national leadership to develop plans for a union-based labor party. Such drastic actions were necessary because the employers had "solidly united" and, with the help of the government, the courts, and the press, were carrying on a "vicious attack upon the Labor Movement." The unions, by contrast, were "divided against themselves along trade lines" and "thus unable to make united resistance."[3]

The CFL's lobbying on behalf of amalgamation and labor party politics spurred immediate opposition from Gompers. Adding fuel to the fire were the CFL's foreign policy activities, which reaffirmed the AFL president's belief that the Chicago movement was falling under the influence of communists. The AFL's new attacks on the CFL failed to dampen the determination of Chicago labor leaders, but they did trigger disputes within the local movement that weakened the alliance between progressives and communists. A directive from Moscow finally shattered the already fragile partnership between the two moving forces within the CFL: Ordered by Lenin to penetrate the U.S. labor party movement, American communists sabotaged the Farmer-Labor party convention of 1923 and gained control of the party's executive committee. Much disillusioned, Fitzpatrick disavowed his own progeny and pledged the CFL's loyalty to the AFL, bringing an end to the decade-long local insurgency. In an ironic twist, the CFL and AFL subsequently united behind the third-party candidacy of Robert LaFollette. Neither group was truly comfortable with the aging senator, and they only half-heartedly lobbied on his behalf. In the wake of the 1924 presidential election, the AFL reaffirmed its support for nonpartisan politics, bringing a symbolic end to trade union experimentation with third-party politics.

The communists' role in destroying the Chicago insurgency was an ironic one, for they had helped to revitalize the local labor movement in 1921 and 1922. Particularly critical in transforming the federation during these years was William Z. Foster, one of the most important leaders of the wartime packing-house and steel organizing campaigns. Son of an Irish immigrant and one of twenty-three children, Foster grew up in a Philadelphia slum and began working at age ten to help support his family. In contrast to Fitzpatrick, who stayed in Chicago throughout his life, Foster traveled the country during his youth. He also changed politics and allegiances much more frequently than Fitz-

3. *NM*, 3/25/22, 1.

patrick, experimenting with socialism and joining the IWW in his early adulthood. In 1910, Foster traveled to Germany and France, where he was deeply influenced by French syndicalism and became convinced that the best strategy for American radicals lay in "boring from within" the AFL rather than in promoting the dual unionism of the IWW.[4]

Once he returned from Europe, Foster took a job on the railways and joined the Railway Carmen of America—an AFL union—in 1915. He soon became business agent of its Chicago District Council, and he was appointed a delegate to the CFL. Like other municipal labor activists, Foster officially pledged his loyalty to the government during the war, but he initiated and participated in a host of militant organizing and strike campaigns. American communists, who officially organized two political parties in 1919, at first ridiculed Foster for his work with the CFL and for his wartime loyalty. They argued that "trades union-ism" was "the arch enemy of the militant proletariat" and claimed as one of their duties the "destruction of the existing trades union organizations."[5]

The slow growth of communism in Europe and America led Lenin and Comintern to criticize U.S. communists for their alienation from the trade union movement. In summer 1920, the Second Congress of Comintern officially instructed the American communist movement "to work in the A. F. of L. instead of seeking to destroy it."[6] Once hostile to Foster, the communists now eagerly courted him and, in 1921, convinced him to travel to Moscow where he observed the Soviet revolution firsthand and became a convert. Comintern in turn agreed to make the Trade Union Educational League (TUEL), an organization created by Foster to further his syndicalist goals, its official trade union organization.

On March 19, 1922, shortly after his return from the Soviet Union, Foster introduced a resolution at a CFL meeting, without consulting federation leaders, that called on the AFL to stage a conference for the purpose of amalgamating existing AFL unions into several large industrial unions. Theodore Draper suggests that at this time the communists had about twenty-eight delegates in the CFL, or about one-fifth of the total,

4. Draper, *American Communism and Soviet Russia: The Formative Period* (New York: Viking Press, 1960), 61–66, *Roots of American Communism*, 198–200, 311–14; Fine, *Labor and Farmer Parties*, 382.

5. Draper, *Roots of American Communism*, 199–200.

6. Draper, *American Communism and Soviet Russia*, 25.

as well as many allies and sympathizers. The resolution carried by a three-to-one vote.[7]

Gompers's reaction to the resolution was swift. Appearing unexpectedly in Chicago in April, he immediately demanded a meeting of "representative unionists" from the area to discuss the amalgamation resolution. CFL leaders instead asked for a mass meeting on the issue. The ensuing debate laid bare their very different attitudes toward union democracy. Gompers defended his request for a meeting of selected trade union leaders on the grounds that the AFL had found such meetings useful for fostering unity in the past. "If you are chosen the representatives of the great body of workers in your organization," Gompers argued, "then you must certainly have influence with them . . . and can carry some message of clarity of thought and action to the great rank and file."[8] Clearly, Gompers sought a meeting at which he could disseminate information about the AFL's position on amalgamation rather than one at which the issue could be openly discussed.

Fitzpatrick, on the other hand, opposed Gompers's proposed format on the grounds that within the CFL they still had "some measure of democracy." Fitzpatrick also lambasted local conservatives, and indirectly Gompers, for slandering those who were promoting the national meeting on amalgamation. "If it has got so . . . the men and women of the movement are going to vilify the reputations and question the motives of men who dare to ask for a conference," he argued, "then we are in a pitiable situation." Fitzpatrick concluded that "Grown men should be willing to settle their differences by vote."[9]

But ultimately Gompers had his way, holding a meeting of handpicked Chicago trade union representatives on April 12. Despite its carefully orchestrated nature, the meeting was not without fireworks. Gompers opened the session by denouncing Foster, who had apparently not been invited to the gathering and was across town at another rally when a friend caught up with him and informed him that Gompers was destroying his good name. Foster rushed to the meeting and startled Gompers with counteraccusations. A volatile exchange followed in which Gompers insisted that the CFL had "in essence and in fact" called for "one big union." Behind Foster's resolution, he argued, was "noth-

7. NM, 3/25/22, 1; Draper, *American Communism and Soviet Russia*, 67–71, *Roots of American Communism*, 314–20.
8. Conference Minutes: Representative Men of Chicago with President Gompers Presiding and Addressing, 4/12/22, 2: Speeches and Writings Collection (SWC)-GMC.
9. Ibid., 12.

ing more or less than the propaganda of radical revolution designed to overthrow the Government of the United States . . . [and assure the] destruction of the American Federation of Labor." Foster, on the other hand, claimed that the resolution was essentially conservative in nature and called only for fusion within industries to prevent tragedies like the stockyards strike. Not surprisingly, the debate produced no significant shift in the position of either side. Gompers closed the meeting by noting his disappointment with the Chicago Federation of Labor and expressing his hope that those who had quit attending weekly meetings would return and restore the "old spirit."[10] Despite his exhortations, the amalgamation movement spread, and by 1923 "sixteen state federations, fourteen national unions, scores of central labor unions and thousands of local unions" had endorsed proposals for a conference on the issue. Using the CFL as a base, the communists threatened to polarize the trade union movement over the issue of amalgamation.[11]

The communists also sparred with the AFL leadership over foreign policy issues. Once again caught in the cross fire were the leaders of the CFL. Even more than their progressive counterparts in the CFL, Chicago communists saw an organic link between domestic and international issues. Thus, they drew connections between the most critical domestic question of their day—the open shop campaign—and the "economic war" that was raging between different countries. "The nations scramble for trade," proclaimed the Chicago communist paper, the *Voice of Labor*, "and they all are imbued with the one idea of reducing labor to a position where it cannot fight for higher wages. So that by having labor in such a position they can produce their commodities at a lower cost than their competitors." Thus the communists noted that the fight for an open shop was being fought simultaneously in the United States, Germany, France, Italy, Norway, Sweden, England, and other European countries.[12]

The best way to fight against the international business drive for the open shop, suggested Chicago communists, was through international labor organizations. But the communists bitterly attacked both the "Yellow" International Federation of Trade Unions (IFTU) centered in Amsterdam and the International Labor Bureau of the International Labor Organization, or the "Black International," created by Sam Gompers. To Chicago's communists, the IFTU was cowardly in its

10. Ibid., 8, 25, 1–28. Foster, *Pages from a Worker's Life*, 172–77, 275–80.
11. Draper, *American Communism and Soviet Russia*, 71.
12. *Voice of Labor* (VL), 7/8/21, 10.

attempts to defend the world's workers, while the ILO was laughable—not a true labor organization at all. Only the "Red" International, they insisted, could truly protect the rights of workers.[13] Such attacks stung not only Gompers and the AFL hierarchy but also the CFL, which continued to work for closer AFL affiliation with the IFTU. The CFL even warmed to the ILO during 1921 and 1922, as European labor leaders instituted reforms that guaranteed more effective labor representation. By contrast, Gompers's relations with the organization continued to sour in the wake of the election. Thus, the progressive leaders of the CFL found themselves in the position of defending the ILO and the IFTU from attacks by both the AFL leadership and the communists.[14]

CFL leaders were also caught in the middle of debates over AFL policy toward disarmament and Soviet Russia. In April 1921, Gompers was asked by the Harding administration to create an advisory committee, consisting of business and labor representatives, that would advise the Washington Naval Conference on the economic ramifications of disarmament. Gompers quickly seized the opportunity, no doubt in part because he had long been interested in the disarmament issue, and because he believed weapons limitations to be particularly crucial after the failure of the Senate to ratify the peace treaty. Equally important, Gompers may have thought that the appointment would give him a chance to rebuild old corporatist networks. Just as Gompers had struggled during the war to convince Wilson that labor could play a useful auxiliary role on the Council of National Defense, so now he tried to use the disarmament conference to show the Harding administration that the AFL could help to promote its foreign policies. In return for his appointment, Gompers conducted rallies throughout the country to win labor support for disarmament. In addition, Gompers tried to rally trade union movements in Europe behind the agreements.[15]

Progressives within the CFL also favored disarmament, but they argued that the Washington Conference was a fraud. Major powers, they suggested, were using the meetings as a facade behind which to

13. VL, 7/8/21, 10; 10/28/21, 7.
14. On the AFL's postelection relations with the IFTU, see *Proceedings of the AFL*, 1922, 420. Walling to Gompers, 6/5/23, CC-GMC. *Unionist*, 8/4/23. For information on Gompers's attitudes toward the ILO, see Gompers's Public Letter, 2/8/22; Gompers to Albert Thomas, 4/4/22; Gompers to Thomas, 5/30/22; Woll to Gompers, 7/14/22; Gompers to Thomas, 7/18/22: CC-GMC. On disputes between Gompers and Chicago Labor party leaders over the IFTU, see John Walker to Gompers, 1/3/23, enclosed in a letter to Fitzpatrick, 1/5/23, B12–F85: FP.
15. Woll to Gompers, 11/2/21; Greenwood to Gompers, 11/21/21; Gompers to George Sutherland, 11/10/21; Gompers cable to Oudegeest, 12/5/21; Chester Wright, Press Release, 9/30/21: CC-GMC. VL, 10/7/21, 7.

prepare for another war of unprecedented scale. Negotiators had agreed only to limit arms that were obsolete; none had seriously suggested prohibiting the employment of submarines and aircraft, disbanding land forces, or banning conscription. But Fitzpatrick and the CFL leadership avoided directly criticizing Gompers, instead merely asserting that "not the capitalists but the workers of the world will destroy war."[16] By contrast, Chicago communists ferociously attacked Gompers's initiatives. Following the lead of the Red International, the *Voice of Labor* denounced the advisory committee as a farce and suggested that "we do not mind the capitalists having their little joke, but we have a strong objection to the labor movement being made the sucker." They therefore urged American workers to "ignore the Gompers Committee," to strive for solidarity within the labor movement, and to seek affiliation with the Red Labor International.[17]

A similar breakdown occurred over the issue of U.S. policy toward Soviet Russia. Gompers and his closest colleagues remained opposed to recognizing the Soviet Union and to renewing trade with it: Both progressives and communists within the CFL continued to favor these measures, but they disagreed over strategies to promote a change in AFL and U.S. policy. Progressives within the CFL considered launching a new campaign on Russia's behalf in the AFL convention during 1922 but decided against it, because "discretion is the better part of valor." They instead offset Gompers's crusade against Sovietism by continuing to sponsor the Trade Union Committee for Russian Relief and by participating extensively in the campaigns of the Friends of Soviet Russia.[18]

The local communist press, by contrast, waged a personal offensive against Gompers. "It seems, judging by Gompers's attitude toward Soviet Russia," proclaimed the *Voice of Labor,* "that he is not content to starve the millions of Russian workers and peasants, he is also prepared to starve the millions who are out of work in this country." The paper asserted that U.S. workers needed jobs, while Russia needed the goods that American plants could manufacture. Thus, "both races of people could be rescued from starvation" by opening trade between the two countries. But "Gompers—president of the American Federation of

16. *NM,* 1/14/22; 3/31/23, 3.
17. *VL,* 10/7/21, 7; 11/28/21, 1.
18. Joseph Manley to Walsh, 5/15/22, B11; Friends of Soviet Russia Handout, 5/31/22, B9; Walsh to Mr. A. B. Martin, 5/31/22, B9; Manley to Walsh, n.d. circa, March, B11; Nockels to Walsh, 9/30/22, B11; Walsh to Nockels, 6/13/22, B11: WP. Friends of Soviet Russia to Max Hayes, 1/15/24: HP. Gompers and Walling, *Out of Their Own Mouths.*

L-A-B-O-R—says NO." Unfortunately, suggested the editors, Gompers would never retire voluntarily from the AFL presidency but would wait to die in office. It was therefore necessary for militant unionists to wage an aggressive campaign to "smash" the "well-greased" patronage machine on which he relied and then to force the "ouster" of the aging labor czar.[19]

Attempts by CFL progressives to defuse tensions between the central labor union and the AFL hierarchy in 1921 and 1922 were undercut by the vituperative attacks of Chicago communists. Meanwhile, local communists became increasingly critical of what they viewed as the waffling policies of progressive leaders of the CFL. The *Voice of Labor* attacked its counterpart, the *New Majority*, asserting that it was inconsistent on major issues and created "confusion within the minds of the rank and file" that undermined labor solidarity. It also criticized "so called Progressive elements" for not offering a program substantially different than the AFL "machine."[20]

Attacked by both the right and far left wings of the labor movement, prospects for revitalizing the Chicago Farmer-Labor party in 1922 seemed dim. But support for independent labor political action came unexpectedly from a new quarter: the Railroad Brotherhoods. Troubled by government and court actions during rail strikes, the Brotherhoods called for a Conference for Progressive Political Action (CPPA) in February. Delegates from sixteen railroad unions, the Socialist party, the Chicago Farmer-Labor party, and the Minnesota Farmer-Labor party attended. The Brotherhoods made clear that they did not yet want to form a third party; they were interested in greater political coordination among progressive political forces. By contrast, Chicago labor party leaders sought immediately to form a new national labor party. Although the conference failed to produce an agreement, Chicago labor leaders hailed the new spirit of cooperation among progressives and argued that the conference was a step in the right direction.[21]

The second meeting of the CPPA held in December 1922 proved even more important. Once again, delegates from the Railroad Brotherhoods, Socialist party, and Farmer-Labor parties of Minnesota and Chicago attended. But representatives from the Workers' party, the legal political organ of the communist movement, also sought an invitation. Their

19. VL, 7/8/21, 7.
20. VL, 8/8/21; 7/22/21, 10.
21. Weinstein, *Decline*, 277; Fine, *Labor and Farmer Parties*, 402.

interest in the conference was in some respects a surprise, for in 1919 the communists had asserted that there could be "no compromise either with Laborism or a reactionary Socialism." They had also discussed the American Labor party movement as a "minor phase of proletarian unrest" promoted by trade unionists "to conserve what they may have secured as a privileged caste."[22] But Comintern, shortly after changing its policies on communist participation in trade union movements in Europe and the United States, also reversed its position on cooperating with labor party movements in these areas. In December 1921, the international Communist organization officially introduced its policy of a "United Front" among political groups sympathetic to labor causes and especially called on communists in Britain and the United States to support the labor parties in their countries. American communists at first resisted such an alliance but, at Moscow's behest, finally sought admittance to the CPPA.[23]

Among the most adamant supporters of the communists within the CPPA were Chicago Farmer-Labor party representatives, who thought that the conference should include the broadest possible range of candidates. But a majority of delegates at the meeting disagreed, and they voted down the proposal to allow Workers' party delegates. Subsequently, the Railroad Brotherhoods were able to dominate the conference and to defeat Farmer-Labor party proposals calling for the immediate formation of a third party. The communist allies of the Chicago Farmer-Laborites advised them to continue to cooperate with the CPPA anyway, but in March 1923, the Chicago group broke with the conference and issued a call for a new meeting to create a third party in July. Theodore Draper has ably explained the profound repercussions of the split with the CPPA for the Chicago Labor party movement. "As long as the railway unions constituted the Right Wing of the amorphous third-party movement," he writes, "the Farmer-Laborites represented the Left Wing, with the Communists hanging onto their coat-tails, a relatively minor factor at the extreme left. By breaking away from the railway unions, the Farmer-Laborites . . . . placed themselves in the position of the Right Wing in relation to their new allies, the Communists, who promptly pre-empted the position of the only real and true Left Wing."[24]

22. Draper, *American Communism and Soviet Russia*, 31.
23. Ibid., 31–35.
24. Ibid., 37. See also Weinstein, *Decline*, 277–80; Green, "Labor Party," 98–99; *NM*, 2/24/23, 2.

As CFL leaders made preparations for the July convention, they discovered the difficulties of working with their new allies. Shortly after the Chicago Farmer-Labor party dissociated itself from the CPPA, the Workers' party established a committee of three—Charles Krumbein, Arne Swabeck, and Earl Browder—to work with the Chicago group in preparing for the new convention. All three had been active in the Chicago labor movement for years and worked well with the three delegates appointed by the Farmer-Labor party to plan the July meeting: John Fitzpatrick, Ed Nockels, and Jay Brown (secretary of the Farmer-Labor party). From the beginning, Fitzpatrick warned the committee that the Farmer-Labor party must maintain control of the movement. "Let's get the record straight," Fitzpatrick reportedly told Swabeck, "we are willing to go along, but we think you Communists should occupy a backseat in this affair."[25]

Local communists might have been willing to agree to such a relationship. But the New York leadership of the Workers' party, hearing of Fitzpatrick's demand, ordered the Chicago committee to cease discussions with the CFL group. Meanwhile, they made plans to "pack" the July convention with communist delegates in order to ensure Workers' party domination. Fitzpatrick, apparently sensing a communist plot, tried to change the agenda immediately before the convention. He argued that the upcoming meeting should limit itself to creating a committee to gain broader support for the third-party movement: It should avoid immediately forming a new party. But the communists refused to agree to alter the format and goals of the convention, and the plan died.[26]

The July convention attracted several hundred delegates representing a variety of farmer's organizations, local trade unions, political parties, fraternal societies, and four national trade unions. Officially the Workers' party was entitled to only ten delegates at the 1923 convention. But by sending representatives from fraternal groups like the Lithuanian Workers' Literature Society and the United Working Singers, they managed to control about two hundred votes at the convention as compared to fifty for the Farmer-Labor party. Fitzpatrick tried a variety of procedural machinations to unseat the Workers' party delegates, but he failed. Subsequently, the communists dominated the convention, pushing through a proposal for the immediate formation of a new party, the Federated Farmer-Labor party, and electing a left-wing leadership

25. Draper, *American Communism and Soviet Russia*, 41.
26. Ibid., 42–43. Fine, *Labor and Farmer Parties*, 430–32.

against Fitzpatrick's wishes.[27] Not surprisingly, Fitzpatrick bitterly disavowed the new party:

> I know Brother Foster and the others who are identified and connected with him, and if they think they can attract the attention of the rank and file of the working men and women of America to their organization, I say to them and to this organization, that is a hopeless course, and they cannot do it.
>   Then what have they done? They have killed the Farmer-Labor party, and they have killed the possibility of uniting the forces of independent political action in America, and they have broken the spirit of this whole thing so that we will not be able to rally the forces for the next twenty years![28]

After failing to convince the communists to abandon their plans for a new party, Fitzpatrick and his colleagues walked out of the convention that they had organized.[29]

In the wake of the disaster, the leaders of the old Farmer-Labor party tried to regroup while at the same time dissociating themselves from the new party. The Federated Farmer-Labor organization, they declared, was merely the Workers' party reconstituted. It would fail within a few years because "confidence cannot be established with a sledge hammer, a battery ram or a pile driver." The communist leaders of the new party, they argued, were self-righteous dictators who had demonstrated at the convention that they were unable to cooperate even with a sympathetic group. Such individuals would not "permit any federation they were in to make the human-kind rather than the bigot-zealot kind of an approach to unions and farmers groups." As a result, American workers would quickly reject their overtures. By contrast, the real Farmer-Labor party still had a future because it had "no theories for the conduct of the labor movement nor any criticism to make of the conduct of unions." Instead, it sought to give workers what they truly desired: control over their own affairs.[30]

27. Draper, *American Communism and Soviet Russia*, 42–43; Fine, *Farmer and Labor Parties*, 430–32. VL, 7/4/23, 1; 7/5/23, 1. NM, 7/14/23, 5; 7/21/23, 4; 10/13/23, 11.
    28. Draper, *American Communism and Soviet Russia*, 45.
    29. Ibid. VL, 7/4/23, 1; 7/5/23, 1. NM, 7/14/23, 5; 7/21/23, 4; 10/13/23, 11. Foster to Gompers, 7/31/24: CC-GMC. National Committee of the Farmer-Labor Party to Max Hayes, 12/27/22: HP. Foster, *Pages from a Worker's Life*, 275–80, *The Bankruptcy of the American Labor Movement* (Chicago: Trade Union Educational League, 1922); Fine, *Labor and Farmer Parties*, 360, 430; Foner, *History of the American Labor Movement*, 9: 104–69.
    30. NM, 7/21/23, 4–5; 9/15/23, 1.

Postconvention disavowals of the radicals, however, did little to reaffirm the faith of many Labor party members in the old leadership. Gompers had long argued that Fitzpatrick and other CFL officials were the dupes of Foster. Events at the convention seemed to some to confirm Gompers's interpretation. During summer 1923, many local unions withdrew from the old party even while expressing their continued loyalty to Fitzpatrick. The Illinois State Federation of Labor, fearing that association with Foster had damaged its reputation, also rejected a motion to support the Labor party for the first time. To distance itself further from the Communist movement, the state federation overwhelmingly voted down resolutions on amalgamation and diplomatic recognition of Russia that it had endorsed only the year before.[31] With support for the party greatly diminished, Gompers felt free to launch an attack on the instigators of the Labor party and censured both Fitzpatrick and the Federated Press Service. The AFL also cut organizing expenses for the CFL in half.[32]

Not yet ready to surrender, party officials made a last-ditch attempt to win national and international union support at the AFL convention, where a CFL representative pleaded with his colleagues for levelheadedness. "The pity of the situation in our movement today," he proclaimed, "is this. The man who believes in constructive trade unionism is being crushed to death between the two contending factions, the extreme conservatives on the one side, who want at all hazards to keep things as they are, and the extreme radical, who wants to turn the entire system topsy turvy." The CFL, he argued, was for evolutionary change. The representative then joined other progressive unionists in calling for the formation of a Labor party, amalgamation, and recognition of the Russian Republic. These measures, he argued, were moderate ones that would strengthen rather than destroy the AFL. But national and international officials who had been unwilling to support the Labor party at the height of its power were even less inclined to do so in 1923. After extensive debate, the proposed measures were all overwhelmingly defeated.[33]

Farmer-Labor party leaders continued operations for several more months, but in May 1924, Fitzpatrick finally advised the CFL to reem-

31. Ibid., 9/15/23, 5; 10/13/23, 1. *Illinois State Federation of Labor Proceedings*, 1923, 362–64; Green, "Labor Party," 109–12.
32. *NM*, 10/13/23, 4; 10/20/23, 2. Keiser, "John Fitzpatrick," 29, 101.
33. *Proceedings of the AFL*, 1923, 297, 265–68, 286–90, 296–302. *NM*, 8/25/23, 11; 9/5/23.

brace the nonpartisan political policy of the AFL. That action, Fitz-patrick argued, had become necessary in part because "irresponsible elements" had destroyed the good name of the party. But Fitzpatrick also admitted that rank-and-file workers seemed to have lost interest in the party; without their support, he argued, there was "no hope." The CFL followed Fitzpatrick's advice and overwhelmingly endorsed the political programs of the AFL. Robert Buck resigned from the *New Majority* and was replaced by James Bruck, a less-controversial editor who adhered strictly to the AFL's policy guidelines.[34]

Thus died the bold, decade-long insurgency that had inspired the CFL to challenge fundamentally the AFL's industrial, political, and international strategies. But funeral services for the failed rebellion were delayed because of a surprise shift in AFL political policy: Shortly after the CFL reaffirmed its loyalty to the AFL, the AFL hierarchy declared its official support for Robert LaFollette's third-party presidential candidacy. LaFollette was sponsored by the CPPA, the group that the Farmer-Labor party had abandoned in 1922. In announcing the AFL's decision to endorse LaFollette, Gompers argued that the Republicans had shown they were "beyond hope so far as any constructive progressive action was concerned." The Democratic party had also recently come under the control of conservatives; John B. Davis, a prominent corporation lawyer, had been chosen over Alfred Smith and William McAdoo to head the presidential ticket. Gompers believed that Davis was Wall Street's candidate and argued that he was insufficiently progressive to be endorsed by the AFL.[35] LaFollette, on the other hand, supported many of the major reform programs for which the AFL had worked during the past decade, including increased taxes on the wealthy and limiting the authority of the Supreme Court, especially in the use of injunctions. Given the choices, implied Gompers, the AFL seemed almost obligated to support LaFollette.[36] To some, a more moderate version of the union-based third party movement promoted by the CFL seemed on the verge of being born. Although still suspi-

---

34. *NM*, 5/24/24, 12–13; 7/5/24, 4; 8/16/24, 1. Letter from F. J. Smith to Nockels, 6/1/24, B13–F91: FP. *Illinois State Federation of Labor Proceedings*, 1924, 211. Buck to Walsh, 3/21/22, B11; 5/19/24, B13: WP. Keiser, "John Fitzpatrick," 140, 183–84.

35. Gompers to Morrison, 8/19/24: CC-GMC. Walsh to Nockels, 4/12/24; Nockels to Walsh, 4/16/24, B13: WP.

36. See, especially, Gompers to W. B. Wilson, 8/6/24: CC-GMC. *Proceedings of the AFL*, 1924, 65; *Illinois State Federation of Labor Proceedings*, 1924, 211–13; David Thelen, *Robert M. LaFollette and the Insurgent Spirit* (Boston: Little, Brown, 1976), 173–77.

cious of LaFollette and the CPPA, Chicago labor leaders warily rallied behind his campaign.[37]

AFL support for the new progressive political coalition headed by LaFollette proved more cosmetic than real. As a condition for supporting LaFollette, AFL officials made a deal with his staff ensuring that they would be able to continue their nonpartisan policies for local, state, and congressional elections. When questioned about whether they would support the formation of a permanent third party, officials commented that they would wait until the results from the election to make their decision. Privately, however, AFL leaders confided that they doubted LaFollette had any chance of winning and hoped only that he would garner enough votes to convince the Democrats that they needed to restructure the party.[38]

AFL officials were uninterested in creating a new third party in part because they continued to believe that such a party would lack political viability. They were also ill at ease with LaFollette and the progressives who clustered around the aging senator—but for reasons quite different than Farmer-Labor party activists during the 1920 presidential election. During their long careers, both LaFollette and Gompers had sought to curb the abuses of monopolies and had supported some of the same kinds of regulatory legislation. Yet LaFollette was at heart more of a populist than Gompers, and he favored restoring as much power as possible to the average citizen. As governor of Wisconsin, LaFollette had championed both the initiative and the referendum. He had also been among the first governors to establish state commissions designed to oversee large industries and to assure that they served the public interest. At first, LaFollette, like Gompers, welcomed national imitations of the institutions he had developed and prophesied that federal agencies would help prevent exploitation of the common man by capitalists. Yet, over time, LaFollette became wary of big business influence within national agencies like the Interstate Commerce Commission and sought to restore some power to local bodies more easily monitored by the average citizen.[39]

By contrast, Gompers's corporatist blueprints for ensuring industrial stability and class harmony following the armistice overwhelmingly

37. *Federation News* (previously the *New Majority*), 10/11/24, 4; 11/1/24. *Illinois State Federation of Labor Proceedings,* 1924, 211–13; Keiser, "John Fitzpatrick," 147; Fine, *Labor and Farmer Parties,* 365.

38. Gompers to Morrison, 8/19/24; Committee of Morrison, Woll, Wright, Johnston, and Holder to Gompers, 7/12/24; Woll and Wright to Gompers, 7/25/24; Woll to LaFollette, 7/24: CC-GMC.

39. See Thelen, *LaFollette,* 131, 173–77.

emphasized the need for a greater centralization of economic powers within federal agencies. Although such agencies would be designed to encourage voluntary mediation of economic problems by business, state, and labor representatives, they would nonetheless tend to diminish direct popular involvement in industrial regulation.[40] Gompers and LaFollette diverged in their attitudes about the fundamental issue of how power should be distributed within the American political system.

Gompers may also have been suspicious of LaFollette because of his policies toward World War I and his views on diplomatic reform. From the outset of the European conflict, LaFollette accused Wilson of pro-British tendencies and counseled a more neutral policy. When Wilson initiated his preparedness campaign, LaFollette argued that the administration had been unduly influenced by big businessmen seeking to make money of human slaughter. Subsequently, LaFollette joined others in trying to force a referendum vote on the issue of American involvement in the war. After the United States entered the European conflict, LaFollette continued to criticize the government for suppressing the civil rights of dissenters and attacked agencies like the Council of National Defense for allowing big business to profit from the war. During the 1924 election, LaFollette and the CPPA promoted legislation that would make a national referendum mandatory on issues of peace and war. Such policies surely rankled the patriotic Gompers.[41]

Not surprisingly, then, Gompers remained suspicious of plans for a permanent third party led by LaFollette and his allies. During the campaign, he counseled locals and nationals to support the presidential candidate but also to avoid aiding the movement for an independent party.[42] Former Labor party leaders in Chicago abided by this judgment, for they were also lukewarm about a third-party movement headed by LaFollette.[43] Gompers and his cohorts cared little for LaFollette because he sought to give too much power to the average citizen; former Labor party members, on the other hand, faulted LaFollette for not trying to restore more power to American workers. During the Farmer-Labor party campaign of 1920, local activists had applauded LaFollette's populist sentiments but argued that political democracy was useless without

40. See Chapter 3.
41. Thelen, *LaFollette*, 131; Fine, *Labor and Farmer Parties*, 410; Chapter 2.
42. Woll to Gompers, 7/25/24: CC-GMC.
43. *Federation News*, 10/11/24, 4; 11/1/24. *Illinois State Federation of Labor Proceedings*, 1924, 211–13; Keiser, "John Fitzpatrick," 147; Fine, *Labor and Farmer Parties*, 365.

industrial democracy. When LaFollette refused to embrace their platforms on democratic control of industry, they rejected him as their candidate. Leading Labor party advocates were no more enthusiastic about
LaFollette in 1924 than they had been in 1920. But, like Gompers, they
viewed him as the best of a particularly bad assortment of presidential
candidates, and they followed the AFL's lead in offering him a tentative
and noncommittal endorsement.[44]

Also halfheartedly joining the LaFollette coalition were many ethnic
organizations from old immigrant communities, among them leading
Irish-American groups. Irish-American activists supported LaFollette for
the same reasons as the AFL: They sought to restructure the old parties.
Although the leaders of most major Irish-American organizations had
traditionally warned members against wasting votes on independent
candidates, by 1924 they were thoroughly alienated from both the
Republican and the Democratic parties. The Harding and Coolidge
presidencies had demonstrated that the Republicans were as pro-British
as the Democrats. Particularly troubling, according to Irish leaders, was
the drive by the Coolidge administration to enmesh the United States in
the League of Nations through participation in the World Court at the
Hague. Irish groups were also upset by Harding's and Coolidge's
attempts to reduce the size of the American navy, allegedly at Britain's
request. The Republican convention during the summer of 1924 convinced Irish-American leaders that the party would continue to be dominated by Anglophiles in the future.[45]

Likewise, Irish-American officials argued that the Democratic convention signaled that its leaders would remain unreceptive to input from
Irish-Americans. They denounced William McAdoo, a potential Democratic nominee and a former aide to Wilson, as a candidate for the Ku
Klux Klan who deplored not only blacks but Catholics as well. Not surprisingly, Irish-American officials praised Al Smith, but they predicted
that his nomination would be blocked by Wilsonians. When both
McAdoo and Smith were bypassed in favor of Davis, Irish leaders proclaimed that the Democrats had disgraced themselves once again and
would lose the Irish vote as a result. Tammany politicians, they declared, were filled "with the false notion that the Irish in America are
hopelessly divided and therefore a negligible quantity." Such thinking

44. See Keiser, "John Fitzpatrick," 147; Fine, *Labor and Farmer Parties*, 363; Thelen,
LaFollette, 177.
45. *GA*, 3/3/21, 1; 6/2/23, 1; 5/5/23, 3; 10/11/24, 1; Fine, *Labor and Farmer Parties*,
414.

seemed particularly foolish in light of the role Irish-Americans had played in defeating Cox during 1920. Citizens of Gaelic ancestry, they argued, must once and for all disabuse Democrats of their anti-Irish sentiments by shunning Davis and voting for LaFollette.[46]

Irish leaders felt comfortable supporting LaFollette because they advocated many of the same causes as the senator. Groups like the FOIF, the Clan na Gael, and the Ancient Order of Hibernians shared LaFollette's enthusiasm for the initiative and the referendum, public ownership of utilities, and higher taxes for the wealthy. They also agreed with his noninterventionist policies toward Europe and applauded his opposition to American involvement in any League of Nations functions. Had Irish-American leaders been genuinely interested in forming a permanent third party, they might have used these similarities to develop a solid Irish-American base for the CPPA in 1924. Instead, they seemed to devote a majority of their efforts to attacking the Democrats. Davis was accused of being a "dyed in the wool advocate of Wilson's League of Nations" and a pawn of international bankers.[47] The Democratic party was charged with harboring religious prejudice. "Catholics," argued Irish-American editors, "had been insulted by bigots and ignored by the party for which they have been voting for generations." Irish-Americans should therefore "break away from their political affiliation [with the Democrats] and rebuke prejudice and insolence by voting against John W. Davis, President of the English Speaking Union."[48] While Irish campaigns vividly portrayed Davis and other leading Democrats as evil incarnated, LaFollette's virtues received only scant attention.[49]

The failure of Irish groups to take a greater interest in the CPPA is in some respects puzzling. Conventional Irish-American groups had opposed the Labor party because it threatened their power, conflicted with their vision of a pluralist society, and, by its class analysis of America's problems, undermined the credibility of Irish leaders who blamed most of the country's ills on the English. More generally, the Labor party had challenged the ethnic dream of a society in which multifarious special interest groups struggled for power and contributed in their own unique ways to a more just and humane society. The CPPA,

46. GA, 7/19/24, 4; 8/30/24, 4.
47. Ibid., 7/19/24, 1–4; 8/19/24, 4; 8/30/24, 4.
48. Ibid., 8/30/24, 4.
49. See, especially, ibid., 10/11/24, 1; 8/2/24, 4; 10/18/24, 4; 9/16/24, 2; 9/13/24, 4; 11/6/24, 1.

on the other hand, did not seem to threaten the position of ethnic leaders in American society; LaFollette foresaw a loose coalition of groups in which all would be allowed to retain their traditional powers and function as they had previously. Class consciousness seemed clearly as alien to leaders of the progressive coalition as to FOIF officials.

But many Irish-American leaders steeped in the tradition of pluralist politics believed that LaFollette's vision, though not threatening, was unrealistic. Just as light splinters when seen through a prism, so, too, when viewed through the pluralist lenses of some ethnic leaders, the LaFollette coalition seemed a motley assortment of disparate groups destined to fall apart. Unlike LaFollette himself, Irish-American ethnic leaders expressed doubt that heterogeneous groups could be bound together by a common desire to help the underprivileged; invariably, different organizations had very different views about who comprised America's underprivileged and how they could be helped.[50] The Democrats and Republicans, on the other hand, would continue to be sustained by the numerically small but extremely powerful groups of businessmen who controlled these parties. Irish-Americans could gain short-term advantage by voting for LaFollette and expressing their discontent with America's political elites. Ultimately, however, they believed they must seek their political fortunes by forming blocs within the major parties. Like other members of the LaFollette coalition, the support of Irish groups was therefore less than enthusiastic.

The forces arrayed against the coalition, on the other hand, were formidable. A booming economy and Coolidge's reputation for personal honesty won him the endorsement and financial support of large numbers of prominent businessmen, professionals, and prosperous farmers. Sophisticated corporate advertising also fueled the incumbent's campaign, successfully promoting the catchy slogan "Keep Cool with Coolidge."[51] To the surprise of no one, Coolidge won the election decisively, tallying 15,000,000 votes to Davis's 8,500,000 and LaFollette's 4,800,000.[52] Among those lured into the Coolidge net were many voters from new immigrant groups. Chicago's Polish community is illustrative:

50. See articles cited in notes 45–49 above for examples of these attitudes.
51. John Blum et al., *The National Experience: A History of the United States,* 4th ed. (New York: Harcourt Brace, 1977), 600.
52. Blum et al., *National Experience,* 600; *NR,* 1/4/25, 88. On preelection expectations among LaFollette supporters of a massive Coolidge victory, see Walsh to Jacob Billikopf, 8/20/24; Clarence Darrow to Walsh, 9/8/24: B13, WP.

Respective vote tallies were 49 percent Republican, 35 percent Democratic, and 14 percent for LaFollette.[53]

Although Coolidge scored a resounding victory, many were nonetheless taken aback by the large vote for LaFollette. Some noted that LaFollette's tally was comparable to the vote for labor parties on the continent that had been involved in political activities for several years. The statistics, according to these observers, signaled that there was indeed a strong popular base for a third party in the United States.[54] A number of politicians agreed, arguing that LaFollette had "laid a foundation upon which to build an American party of progress and liberalism" that would work for the "broader welfare instead of in the interests of powerful and highly organized classes and cliques." The *New Republic*, though disappointed that the vote for LaFollette was not even larger, also saw potential in the new political coalition and argued that "an opportunity to exert moral pressure would be thrown away if an unreal and unequivocal bargain were made [by LaFollette supporters] with the Democrats" in the wake of the election.[55]

When the CPPA met to consider the future of LaFollette's alliance, however, most major organizations in the coalition decided against forming a third party. The AFL and the railroad unions officially withdrew from the coalition, arguing that the vote signaled what they had known all along: Independent labor political action was not viable in the United States. Socialists, progressives, ethnic leaders, and former Labor party members were less certain about the significance of the election and paid lip service to the idea of forming a third party. They failed to agree, however, on a platform or political agenda. Representatives from these groups finally voted to adjourn the conference with the condition that interested participants meet later to discuss forming a new party. Subsequent meetings failed to yield an agreement, and plans for developing a new coalition were finally abandoned.[56]

Following the dissolution of the LaFollette coalition, the AFL voted to return to its nonpartisan policies and once again campaigned primarily for Democratic candidates.[57] Gompers, for his part, became increasingly enmeshed in the work of the Pan-American Federation of Labor.

53. Allswang, *House for All Peoples*, 42, 47; John Higham, *Strangers in the Land: Patterns of American Nativism, 1860–1925* (New York: Atheneum, [1963] 1981), 306–24.
54. Fine, *Labor and Farmer Parties*, 414–15.
55. *GA*, 11/8/24, 1. *NR*, 11/4/25, 88. See also *NR*, 9/10/24, 36; 10/8/24, 137; 10/22/24, 199, 201; 10/29/24, 221–23.
56. Fine, *Labor and Farmer Parties*, 414–16, 426–27.
57. Ibid. See also *Proceedings of the AFL*, 1925, 61.

During a decade of diplomatic defeats, PAFL had been Gompers's one clear-cut triumph. Created as a regional alternative to the ILO, it seemed to offer proof that labor could play a constructive subsidiary role in the making of diplomacy. At the request of State Department officials, Gompers had on several occasions used the organization to establish contacts with Mexican leader Álvaro Obregón. Gompers had also used PAFL to strengthen conservative trade union movements in Latin America.

In November 1923, Gompers impressed the Coolidge administration by using his PAFL contacts to help arrange a meeting between presidential candidate Plutarco Calles of Mexico and administration advisers. The next year, Gompers personally attended the annual convention of PAFL in Mexico City. Gompers used the occasion to expound on the virtues of constructive unionism and to denounce those Latin American delegates whom he felt had been unduly influenced by European radicals. Partly as a result of his efforts, the Mexican Federation of Labor voted to expel one of its communist delegates. Several other conservative trade union delegations negotiated dual membership agreements with the AFL. But although the conference ended on a successful note, it proved too much for Gompers, who was recuperating from a long illness. As the train carrying the AFL delegation back to the United States wound slowly through the northern hills of Mexico, the Federation's seventy-four-year-old president died quietly in his sleep.[58]

In the wake of Gompers's death, Robert Buck wrote Fitzpatrick from his new home in Virginia and expressed hope that the long-awaited revolution would now occur in the ranks of the AFL. Yet Buck told his old colleague that he feared "the reactionaries have another like Sam who has sufficient political genius to hold the unions together without exercising leadership except toward the stroghold [sic] of the boss."[59] Buck probably meant Matthew Woll, Gompers's long-time confidante and handpicked successor. Much to the surprise of many political observers, Woll was rejected by the badly divided Executive Council. Buck's prophecy nonetheless came true. In place of Woll, AFL officials chose William Green of the United Mine Workers to head the federation. Green was a stout defender of Gompers's domestic and international policies, and he

58. *American Federationist* 32 (January 1925): 61–62. Gompers, *Seventy Years of Life and Labor*, appendix. For a detailed account of the AFL's activities in Mexico during 1923 and 1924, see Andrews, *Shoulder to Shoulder*, 124–39.
59. Robert Buck to John Fitzpatrick, 12/28/24, B13–F95: FP.

firmly aligned the AFL behind these policies during the first year of his presidency.[60]

After Green took over, Chicago labor leaders abandoned any immediate plans for renewing independent political activity. But many were still not ready to offer a final requiem for the Labor party, anticipating that it would one day come back to life. Buck wrote to Fitzpatrick that when questioned by Parley Christensen about his political activities, he replied that he "was not interested in any politics except a labor party and that being on ice, was content to lie by and rest politically until the time seems to have come to take it out and thaw it to life again."[61]

60. See, especially, Irving Bernstein, *The Lean Years: A History of the American Worker* (Boston: Houghton Mifflin, 1960), 96–97.
61. Robert Buck to John Fitzpatrick, 12/28/24, B13–F95: FP.

✿

Conclusion

To many Americans in 1918 the world seemed on the verge of a great democratic revolution that would bring the revolution of 1776 to its logical fruition. Stunned by the horrors of modern warfare, they made sense of the carnage by confidently prophesying that a new social order would rise from the ashes of the old. President Wilson, with his rhetoric about promoting democracy at home and abroad, helped inspire such visions. As the *New Majority* proclaimed, the president had made a "Bargain" with "each soldier sent to Europe." The soldier "agreed to risk life and limb in battle, the United States in turn agreed to make the world safe for democracy. By democracy, we meant, above all, a fair and square deal for the common man in America as well as in Europe."[1] Millions of Americans anticipated that the armistice would not only eliminate autocracy abroad but would also destroy autocratic trusts at home, transform a corrupt American political system, and bring far-reaching changes in the conduct and substance of diplomacy.

If expectations about fundamental changes in industry, politics, and international relations were widespread at war's end, Americans had profoundly different visions of the kinds of democratic reforms that should take place in these spheres. For AFL president Samuel Gompers, corporatist forms of power sharing offered a panacea for democratizing both domestic and international institutions. Much impressed by his participation on the Council of National Defense, Gompers pledged labor's loyalty to the government during the war in part to gain greater

1. *NM*, 4/26/19, 15.

AFL representation on war councils. Following the armistice, Gompers sought to establish a permanent system of arbitration commissions and executive branch agencies modeled on the war boards. The arbitration commissions would encourage business and labor leaders to resolve industrial disputes peaceably under the guidance of government officials. The executive branch agencies would guarantee systematic input by representative experts from important economic sectors on a variety of domestic and international issues. Gompers also tried to increase labor's input on international affairs by creating the ILO, an organization that was modeled on the Council of National Defense. As originally conceived by Gompers, it was to consist of equal numbers of business, labor, and government representatives. Although later altered by European representatives, the original blueprints of the ILO illustrated the strong imprint of Gompers's corporatist thinking. Far from viewing the international interests of business and labor as mutually antagonistic, Gompers believed they shared essentially similar goals. At home, both business and labor benefited from increased industrial productivity. Workers and businessmen from across the globe could likewise benefit from cooperating to increase world economic productivity.

Gompers continued to promote corporatist international principles even after the defeat of the peace treaty in the Senate, repudiating the international labor movement and instead focusing on aligning the AFL behind foreign policies that would serve the "community of interest" shared by American business, labor, and the state. Because Gompers sought a partnership role for labor in shaping international affairs, he opposed independent diplomatic initiatives by labor at home or by international labor organizations abroad that would obstruct state policies. Like Wilson, he also tried to undermine nationalist movements that promoted socialism or communism; such movements were not premised on corporatist principles of collaboration between business, labor, and the state and would therefore impede international productivity. The AFL president became especially active in trying to encourage "constructive," nonsocialist trade unionism and politics in Latin America after 1920, deeming the markets in this area to be critical to U.S. trade expansion.

Many European trade union leaders, like Gompers, also participated in corporatist power-sharing arrangements during the war. Most did not fully reject corporatism after the war, but they did seek to increase labor's bargaining power within corporatist networks. In Britain, labor leaders tried to bring more muscle to the business-state-labor partnership that had developed during the war by strengthening the Labour party at home and by revitalizing the international trade union movement. Labour party leaders like Arthur Henderson shared Gompers's productionist orientation, agreeing with the AFL president that business and labor shared an important community of interest in promoting economic growth. This held true even for many socialists within the party, who argued that the economic chaos fostered by Bolshevism served no one. Instead, they sought an orderly and prosperous transition to public ownership of the means of production.

But most British Labour party leaders, whether socialist or non-socialist, lacked Gompers's faith in voluntary cooperation between business and labor. They argued that business would make concessions to labor at home only if it were compelled to do so by strong state intervention and by the threat of damaging strike activity. Similarly, they suggested that labor could prevent businessmen from practicing the kind of reckless international profiteering that caused wars only if it developed an international trade union organization that could mount economic and political campaigns of its own. During the war and the Paris Peace Conference, Gompers seemed to be winning the diplomatic battle with European trade union officials. By cultivating alliances with important state leaders, he helped to thwart plans for an interbelligerent trade union conference in 1918. He also routed European trade union leaders during the peace conference by convening the Commission on International Labour Legislation while they were still meeting in Berne. But when the Senate rejected the treaty, European labor officials assumed control of the ILO and directed it along lines that Gompers opposed. Gompers subsequently isolated himself from European trade union affairs, and his international influence diminished. Only in Latin America did the AFL continue to wield significant power.

Gompers's diplomatic influence during the critical decade from 1914 to 1924 was also undermined by the persistent opposition of key municipal labor councils like the CFL. Tensions between central labor unions and the AFL hierarchy had been building since the late nineteenth century when the AFL severely curtailed their strike and organizing powers and limited them to only one vote each at the AFL convention. But it took an international crisis—World War I—to catalyze the rebellion among central labor unions. Organically linked to local immigrant communities, large central labor unions like those in Chicago, Seattle, Cleveland, and New York played an important role in antipreparedness activities during 1915 and 1916 and sought to use the labor movement to prevent U.S. intervention in the European conflict. When Gompers pledged labor's loyalty to the government without consulting them or holding a referendum on the issue, many local labor leaders complained bitterly.

After U.S. intervention in the European conflict, most previously dissenting municipal labor councils officially supported the war effort. But while Gompers successfully integrated prominent national union leaders into wartime bureaucracies, he only belatedly turned his attentions to central labor union officials—seeking to use them primarily as patriotic cheerleaders to rally workers' support for war campaigns. Largely excluded from a meaningful role in wartime arbitration agreements, central labor officials quickly became suspicious of the wartime collaboration that developed between business, state, and labor leaders. Mirroring the arguments of the British shop stewards' movement, CFL officials criticized the composition of government arbitration commissions and implied that the independence of the trade union movement was being undermined by an excessive reliance on such commissions.

Determined not to sit by and preserve the industrial status quo during the war, the CFL launched major organizing campaigns in Chicago's stockyards and steel mills during 1917 and 1918. At first pleased by federal intervention during disputes in these industries, the CFL had concluded by war's end that the National War Labor Board was composed of "labor baiters and labor crushers."[2] For Chicago's local labor activists, the AFL's collaborationist foreign policies had negative domestic as well as international consequences.

The extent of disillusionment among municipal labor leaders became apparent when scores of central labor unions defied the AFL's nonpartisan political policies and formed labor parties in the postwar era. Of these, at least twenty rallied behind the national Labor and Farmer-Labor parties created by the CFL. Some fifty other central labor unions sent delegates to Farmer-Labor party functions.[3] Often viewed primarily as an heir to the American socialist and populist traditions, the Farmer-Labor party also reflected the unique concerns and perspectives of a distinct layer of labor leadership: central labor union officials and local union leaders active in their municipal labor movements. Only by understanding this layer of labor leadership can one comprehend the peculiar evolution of the movement and explain why the party ultimately failed to form successful alliances with the Socialist party, leading progressives, national trade union leaders, or communist groups.

2. *CFL Minutes*, 11/3/18, 22; 12/15/18, 6–9.
3. See Chapter 4 for the breakdown on these labor party movements.

Much influenced by their wartime experiences, the Chicago leaders of the Farmer-Labor party movement were preoccupied with preventing the trade union movement from traveling further down the corporatist path paved by Gompers. In their first statement of labor party principles, the CFL implicitly repudiated corporatist forms of power sharing by demanding representation for workers on government councils and in international institutions in proportion to their numbers "in the armies, navies and workshops of the world."[4] As a majority class in American society, suggested CFL leaders, workers did not need to share power with their oppressors. Instead, they should take the reins of government in their own hands through labor party politics. Upon assuming control of government, the foremost goal of the Labor party should be to implement democratic control of industry. This did not mean simply arbitrating favorable wage agreements with "selfish private interests" or "bureaucratic agents of government." Rather, it required that forms of cooperative management be created that would give U.S. workers substantive control over the nation's factories and productive processes.[5]

Like AFL leaders, Farmer-Labor party activists were vitally interested in foreign affairs and diplomatic reform—but for very different reasons. Farmer-Laborites did not believe that foreign trade or investment expansion was critical to the health of the American economy, for they had faith that most of the nation's economic woes would disappear once democratic management of industry was implemented. But they argued that it was critical to watch the international machinations of financial magnates until industry was democratically transformed; otherwise, businessmen would use imperialist ventures to increase their control over workers at home. The platform of the 1920 Farmer-Labor party argued that "Having robbed the people first of their power and then of their wealth, the wielders of financial power seek to extend these enterprises to such lengths that our nation today stands in danger of becoming an empire instead of a republic." It called on the U.S. to withdraw from imperialistic enterprises on which it had already embarked in the Philippines, Hawaii, Cuba, Samoa, and Guam.[6]

In contrast to Gompers, Farmer-Labor party leaders denounced the League of Nations, declaring that it would be dominated by "imperialist governments," who were in turn controlled by "money bosses" seeking

4. *Independent Labor Party Platform*, B7–F51: FP.
5. Ibid.
6. *NM*, 7/4/20, 5.

"to cement an international control of industry by a small group of men who manipulate the bulk of the world's wealth."[7] Until industrial and political reform occurred, a truly democratic league of free peoples would be unrealizable and the role of U.S. workers in shaping international relations must remain a predominantly negative one: They needed to work through the trade union movement, labor politics, and international labor organizations to prevent business and state leaders from destroying democratic workers' movements abroad. But Farmer-Labor party leaders diverged from some radicals in that they also opposed direct U.S. governmental intervention on behalf of revolutionaries. Drawing on traditions of U.S. isolationism, they suggested that the U.S. State Department should avoid economic, political, or military aid to the new governments in the Soviet Union, Ireland, and Mexico and instead focus on quick diplomatic recognition and resumption of trade. Private organizations—including labor unions—would then be free to aid, trade, or invest in these countries as they saw fit. The CFL staged massive relief campaigns and economic boycotts to try to aid numerous revolutionary governments throughout the period from 1919 to 1924.

Taken collectively, the CFL's and Farmer-Labor party's foreign policy programs suggest that significant numbers of municipal labor leaders and activists had by 1919 developed a foreign policy ideology that was fundamentally at odds with that of the AFL. Rejecting the AFL's productionist conceptualization of the relationship between the domestic and international spheres, they suggested that the welfare of American workers ultimately hinged on the democratization of industry rather than on industrial efficiency and foreign economic expansion. They denied that labor shared a community of interest with business and state leaders in undermining socialist, communist, or revolutionary regimes that inhibited the flow of free trade. In contrast to AFL officials, local labor party activists also opposed international organizations, like the League, that fostered greater economic and political cooperation between capitalist powers. Such cooperation, they asserted, enabled financial interests to consolidate their power at the expense of workers in both industrialized and industrializing countries. Rejecting the AFL's corporatist definition of a democratic diplomacy, many local labor militants instead associated the term with independent labor political action, economic campaigns by the trade union movement to thwart imperialist manipulation by business leaders, and international labor solidarity.

7. Ibid., 12/19/19, 8.

The divergent foreign policy ideology of municipal labor activists was probably most clearly articulated in the 1920 Farmer-Labor party platform. It would be a mistake, however, to gauge the diplomatic influence of municipal labor activists by the disappointingly low vote tallies for Parley Christensen in the presidential election. As the *New Republic* made clear, the Farmer-Labor party of 1920 represented "a series of sporadic but widespread local movements rather than a coherent national one."[8] Its attempts to launch a unified national presidential campaign were impeded by the AFL's opposition, by the lack of a "coordinating center," by the Red Scare, by racial and ethnic antagonisms, and by the stubborn opposition of the Farmer-Labor party leadership to an alliance with other left political forces that would compromise the class base of the party.[9] The significance of municipal labor activists in shaping patterns of accommodation and resistance to U.S. foreign policy within the working class can be understood only by examining their role in transforming local subcultures and in altering the process by which workers were politicized on foreign policy issues.

"New" labor historians have ably documented the role of local labor activists in stimulating and leading the militant strike and organizing campaigns of the World War I era. They have also shown how these activities altered working-class communities. But recent studies in labor history have largely failed to explore the Labor party crusades and campaigns against Wilsonian internationalism that often accompanied local organizing activities. The Chicago example suggests that when local labor leaders successfully encroached on the "insular" communities created by immigrant workers through their strike activities, they also often shifted the center of political gravity within those communities.[10] In such instances, the central labor union, and the progressive ethnic organizations with which it was allied, temporarily displaced more traditional nationalist and fraternal organizations as local centers for political agitation. The political activities of central labor unions in turn helped to vitalize continuing strike and organizing campaigns.

Chicago's large Irish and Polish communities provide interesting case studies that illustrate how local labor leaders temporarily disrupted tra-

8. *NR*, 1/5/21, 152.

9. On the term "coordinating center," see Montgomery, "New Tendencies," 110; and Chapter 4.

10. On the concept of insular communities, see Cohen, *Making a New Deal*, 30, 1–52. For a discussion of local labor movements and their role in shifting the centers of gravity within ethnic communities, see Brundage, "Denver's New Departure," 15–18.

ditional ethnic allegiances and shaped alignments on political and foreign policy issues among immigrant workers during the World War I
era. These case studies also help to explain why local labor activists ultimately failed to build a sustainable base for an American labor party in
the ethnic neighborhoods of the nation's large urban centers. Racked by
class and political divisions on the eve of war, all fragments of Chicago's
Irish community temporarily united behind the campaigns of the Friends
of Irish Freedom between 1916 and 1919. But even while participating
in FOIF activities, CFL leaders stressed the class nature of the Irish
nationalist struggle and used the CFL as a center for promoting socialist
forms of Irish republicanism not championed by FOIF leaders. So popular did the cause of Irish republicanism become among immigrant workers of a variety of nationalities that CFL leaders regularly used it as a
rallying cry in strike, organizing, and Labor party activities. American
workers had a responsibility to support the Irish struggle for independence, argued CFL leaders, because "The same imperialistic British capitalists who are grinding down the Irish workers into subjection, through
alliance with the pro-British New York House of Morgan Company and
other supposed American money concerns are exploiting the workers of
the United States."[11] During the peace conference, CFL and Labor party
leaders charged Wilson with bolstering the forces of British imperialism
in ways that hurt both Irish and American workers. They advertised
their perspectives not just at labor activities but also during Irish nationalist parades and at local FOIF meetings. By making it possible to oppose Wilsonian diplomacy in the name of both class solidarity and
nationalist brotherhood, CFL and Labor party leaders added important
momentum to the swelling tide of revulsion against the Democrats
within Chicago's Irish neighborhoods in 1919 and 1920.

When a feud between Irish president Eamon De Valera and the leaders
of the FOIF split Irish America apart in 1920, CFL leaders sided with De
Valera and played a critical role in helping him to create rival Irish organizations. Through groups like the Labor Bureau on Irish Independence
and the American Association for the Recognition of the Irish Republic,
Fitzpatrick more firmly wed the cause of Irish republicanism to an emer-
gent working-class internationalism and undermined support for traditional Irish fraternals. Some two hundred city labor councils eventually
joined the Labor Bureau on Irish Independence.[12] The activities of groups

11. Fitzpatrick, Speech to the First Convention of the American Association for the
Recognition of the Irish Republic, n.d., B11–F78: FP.
12. See Chapter 5, n. 39.

like the Labor Bureau contributed to a political atmosphere that made resuscitation of the Versailles Peace Treaty impossible. But the same kind of schisms that opened a window of political opportunity for labor activists within Irish America also destroyed their initiatives. Civil war in Ireland tore asunder the Labor Bureau and AARIR as members divided over which side to support. The CFL's power to channel the forces of Irish nationalism in ways that encouraged independent labor political action thus proved short-lived.

Meanwhile, the CFL's activities on behalf of Soviet Russia provoked a backlash within Chicago's Polish community. In the 1919 mayoral elections, heavily Polish neighborhoods abutting the stockyards had demonstrated strong support for the Labor party. Such support seemed to be a logical outgrowth of the CFL's successful organizing campaigns in the stockyards. Swept up by the currents of labor internationalism that swirled through the stockyards in 1919, Polish workers even participated in mass demonstrations expressing support for Irish independence. But strike defeats and a feud between CFL leaders and Polish organizer John Kikulski significantly dampened Polish enthusiasm for the local labor movement and Labor party politics by the end of 1920. Adding fuel to the fire was the CFL's insistence on supporting Russia in the Polish-Russian war and its continued sponsorship of the Trade Union Committee for Russian Relief and the American Labor Alliance for Trade Relations with Russia. These policies ultimately led Polish-American activists to conclude that "If the union leaders desire to play politics, we Poles cannot cooperate with them lest we betray Poland our nation."[13]

The organic working-class internationalism promoted by CFL leaders thus ultimately shattered on the shoals of ethnic divisity. If the time was not yet ripe for Labor party politics and diplomacy, the CFL's foreign policy activities nonetheless illustrate that municipal labor leaders were important diplomatic actors within their communities during the World War I era. Utilizing their considerable local contacts and influence, they acted in ways that often undercut the AFL's corporatist brand of internationalism. By rallying workers against the Versailles treaty, local labor activists helped to prevent AFL participation in the ILO. They also indirectly undermined the AFL's foreign policy agenda by providing critical financial aid, through their relief activities, to revolutionary regimes opposed by or ignored by the AFL. Among the most important recipi-

---

13. Letter from *Dziennik Ludowy* to Fitzpatrick, 2/1/22, B11–F94; Fitzpatrick article, n.d., B12–F84; Letter from Zygmunt Piotrowski to Fitzpatrick, 5/10/21, B10–F72: FP. Pacyga, *Polish Immigrants*, 246.

ents of aid from city labor councils were Soviet, Irish, and Indian revolutionaries. Equally significant, municipal labor activists may have forced the AFL to pursue more cautious strategies in such U.S. colonies and protectorates as the Philippines, Guam, and Cuba by helping to stimulate the public debate over U.S. imperialism in the early 1920s. Finally, one must consider the cumulative effect of the militant strike and political activities of local labor activists. Through their campaigns, municipal union officials helped to undermine the AFL's moderate image and to destroy the spirit of business-labor-state cooperation that Gompers deemed essential to creating a corporatist state and to pursuing a collaborationist foreign policy. It was this final consideration that likely spurred Gompers's campaign to crush the Chicago insurgency.

Following the demise of local insurgencies like the one in Chicago, the AFL was able to pursue a more consistently corporatist approach to foreign policy and to commit the U.S. trade union movement to global strategies fundamentally at odds with the internationalist ideology of CFL officials.[14] Even though the AFL emerged the ultimate victor in its battle with the Chicago Federation of Labor, the role of local labor activists in shaping patterns of accommodation and resistance to U.S. foreign policy between 1914 and 1924 deserves to be reclaimed and their alternative vision of a democratic and anti-imperialist diplomacy resurrected.

14. An extensive and rich literature on labor diplomacy since the 1930s has developed over the past twenty years. For general studies, see Radosh, *American Labor and United States Foreign Policy*; and Gary K. Bush, *The Political Role of International Trade Unions* (New York: St. Martin's Press, 1983). For case studies demonstrating the role of U.S. labor in suppressing or undermining radical trade unionism and revolutionary governments abroad, see Nathan Godfried, "Spreading American Corporatism: Trade Union Education for Third World Labour," *Review of African Political Economy* 39 (September 1987): 51–63; Howard Schonberger, "Labor's Cold War in Occupied Japan," *Diplomatic History* 3 (summer 1979): 249–72; Carolyn Eisenberg, "Working-Class Politics and the Cold War: American Intervention in the German Labor Movement, 1945–1949," *Diplomatic History* 7 (fall 1983): 283–306; Al Weinrub and William Bollinger, *The AFL-CIO in Central America: A Look at the American Institute for Free Labor Development (AIFLD)* (Oakland, Calif.: Labor Network on Central America, 1987); Peter Weiler, "The United States, International Labor, and the Cold War: The Break Up of the World Federation of Trade Unions," *Diplomatic History* 5 (winter 1981): 1–22. For studies that illustrate rank-and-file resistance to American labor imperialism, see George Lipsitz, *Class and Culture in Cold War America* (South Hadley, Mass.: Praeger, J. F. Bergin Publishers, 1982); and Jerry Gordon, *Cleveland Labor and the Vietnam War* (Cleveland: Greater Cleveland Labor History Society and Orange Blossom Press, 1990).

Bibliography

Personal Papers and Manuscript Collections
Brennan, James P., and Brentano Family Collection. Chicago Historical Society.
Faherty, Roger. Chicago Historical Society.
Fitzpatrick, John. Chicago Historical Society.
Gompers, Samuel. Wisconsin State Historical Society, Madison.
Hayes, Max. Ohio State Historical Society, Columbus.
Herstein, Lillian. Chicago Historical Society.
Insull, Samuel. Loyola University Library, Chicago.
McDowell, Mary. Chicago Historical Society.
Olander, Victor. Chicago Historical Society.
Saposs, David. Wisconsin State Historical Society, Madison.
Walker, John. Illinois Historical Survey Library, University of Illinois, Urbana-
    Champaign.
Walsh, Frank. New York Public Library.

Unpublished Memoirs
Frey, John. "The Reminiscences of John P. Frey." 1957. Columbia University
    Oral History Collection, Butler Library, Columbia University, New York.
Walsh, Frank. "Diary of Frank P. Walsh at the Peace Conference, 1919, 2
    April–12 June, 1919." Box 29, Walsh Papers, New York Public Library.

Proceedings, Minutes, and Reports
American Federation of Labor. *Labor and the War: The American Federation
    of Labor and the Labor Movements of Europe and Latin America.* Wash-
    ington, D.C.: American Federation of Labor, 1918.
——. *Proceedings of the AFL.* Washington, D.C.: 1914–1924.
Chicago Federation of Labor. *Chicago Federation of Labor Minutes.* Chicago,
    1914–1924.

Illinois State Council of Defense. Minute Books; Record Books; Final Reports. Springfield, Ill., 1917–1919 (Insull Papers).

Illinois State Federation of Labor. *Illinois State Federation of Labor Proceedings.* Springfield, Ill., 1914–1924.

International Labor Organization. Minutes and Documents of the Commission on International Labour Legislation, February 1 to March 24, 1919; Documents of the First International Labor Conference. In *The Origins of the International Labor Organization*, vol. 2, edited by James T. Shotwell. New York: Columbia University Press, 1934.

National Labor Party of the United States. *Proceedings of the First National Convention of the Labor Party of the U.S..* November 22–25, 1919. Chicago, Ill., 1919.

U.S. Military Intelligence. U.S. Military Intelligence Reports: Surveillance of Radicals in the United States, 1917–1941. Microfilm Collection. Frederick, Md.: University Publications of America.

Pamphlet and Rare Book Collections

Communist Pamphlet Collection. Chicago Historical Society.

Gompers, Samuel. Pamphlet Collection. Wisconsin State Historical Society, Madison.

Illinois Labor Party Pamphlet Collection. Chicago Historical Society.

Irish-American Societies Pamphlet Collection. Chicago Historical Society.

Rare Book and Pamphlet Collection. Cambridge University Library, Cambridge, England.

Newspapers and Periodicals

American Federationist

Chicago American

Chicago Citizen

Chicago Herald Examiner

Chicago Tribune

Gaelic American

Illinois State Federation of Labor Bulletin

Irish World and American Industrial Liberator

Labor Herald

Nation

New Majority (changes to *Federation News* in 1924)

New Republic

Polish-American Newspapers: Chicago Foreign Language Press Survey, Works Progress Administration. Chicago Historical Society.

Chicago Society News

Dziennik Chicagoski

Dziennik Ludowy

Dziennik Zjednoczenia

Dziennik Zwiazkowy

Narod Polski
Polonia
The Unionist
Voice of Labor

Secondary Sources

Adler, Selig. *The Isolationist Impulse: Its Twentieth-Century Reaction.* New York: Abelard-Schuman, 1957.

Allswang, John M. *A House for All Peoples: Ethnic Politics in Chicago, 1890–1936.* Lexington: University Press of Kentucky, 1971.

Ambrosius, Lloyd. *Woodrow Wilson and the American Diplomatic Tradition: The Treaty Fight in Perspective.* New York: Cambridge University Press, 1987.

Anderson, Benedict R. *Imagined Communities: Reflections on the Origin and Spread of Nationalism.* London: Verso, 1983.

Andrews, Gregg. *Shoulder to Shoulder? The American Federation of Labor, the United States, and the Mexican Revolution, 1910–1924.* Berkeley: University of California Press, 1991.

Asher, Robert. "Union Nativism and Immigrant Response." *Labor History* 23 (summer 1982): 325–82.

Babcock, Robert H. *Gompers in Canada: A Study in American Continentalism before the First World War.* Toronto: University of Toronto Press, 1974.

Bailey, Thomas A., and Paul B. Ryan. *The Lusitania Disaster: An Episode in Modern Warfare and Diplomacy.* New York: Free Press, 1975.

Barrett, James R. "Unity and Fragmentation: Class, Race, and Ethnicity on Chicago's South Side, 1900–1922." In *"Struggle a Hard Battle": Essays on Working-Class Immigrants,* ed. Dirk Hoerder, 229–53. Dekalb: Northern Illinois University Press, 1986.

———. *Work and Community in the Jungle: Chicago's Packinghouse Workers, 1894–1922.* Urbana: University of Illinois Press, 1987.

Beckner, Earl R. "The Trade Union Educational League and the American Labor Movement." Master's thesis, University of Chicago, 1924.

Bernstein, Irving. *The Lean Years: A History of the American Worker, 1920–1933.* Boston: Houghton Mifflin, 1960.

Bigham, Truman Cicero. "The Chicago Federation of Labor." Master's thesis, University of Chicago, 1925.

Bing, Alexander M. *War-time Strikes and Their Adjustment.* Ed. Leon Stein and Philip Taft. New York: Arno Press and the *New York Times,* 1971 [1921].

Biskupski, M. B. "Paderewski as Leader of American Polonia, 1914–1918." *Polish-American Studies* 43 (spring 1986): 37–56.

Bodnar, John E. *The Transplanted: A History of Immigrants in Urban America.* Bloomington: Indiana University Press, 1985.

Brody, David. *The Butcher Workmen: A Study of Unionization.* Cambridge: Harvard University Press, 1964.

——. *Steelworkers in America: The Nonunion Era*. Cambridge: Harvard University Press, 1960.

Brundage, David. "Denver's New Departure: Irish Nationalism and the Labor Movement in the Gilded Age." *Southwest Economy and Society* 5 (winter 1981): 10–23.

Buckley, John Patrick. *The New York Irish: Their View of American Foreign Policy, 1914–1921*. New York: Arno Press, 1976.

Chern, Kenneth S. "The Politics of Patriotism: War, Ethnicity, and the New York Mayoral Campaign, 1917." *New York Historical Quarterly* 63 (October 1979): 291–313.

Chicago Department of Development and Planning. *Chicago's Irish Population*. Chicago, 1976.

Cohen, Lizabeth. *Making a New Deal: Industrial Workers in Chicago, 1919–1939*. Cambridge: Cambridge University Press, 1990.

Conner, Valerie Jean. *The National War Labor Board: Stability, Social Justice, and the Voluntary State in World War I*. Chapel Hill: University of North Carolina Press, 1983.

Coogan, John W. *The End of Neutrality: The United States, Britain, and Maritime Rights, 1899–1915*. Ithaca, N.Y.: Cornell University Press, 1981.

Cooper, John Milton. *The Vanity of Power: American Isolationism and the First World War, 1914–1917*. Westport, Conn.: Greenwood, 1969.

Costigliola, Frank. *Awkward Dominion: American Political, Economic, and Cultural Relations with Europe, 1919–1933*. Ithaca, N.Y.: Cornell University Press, 1984.

Cronin, James E., and Carmen Sirianni, eds. *Work, Community, and Power: The Experience of Labor in Europe and America, 1900–1925*. Philadelphia: Temple University Press, 1983.

Cuddy, Joseph Edward. *Irish America and National Isolationism*. New York: Arno Press, 1976.

Cumbler, John T. *Working-Class Community in Industrial America: Work, Leisure, and Struggle in Two Industrial Cities, 1880–1930*. Westport, Conn.: Greenwood Press, 1979.

Cygan, Mary. "Political and Cultural Leadership in an Immigrant Community: Polish-American Socialism, 1880–1950." Ph.D. diss., Northwestern University, 1989.

Dawse, Robert E. "The Independent Labour Party and Foreign Politics, 1918–1923." *International Review of Social History* 7 (1962): 33–46.

Dawson, Andrew. "The Paradox of Dynamic Technological Change and the Labor Aristocracy in the United States." *Labor History* 20 (summer 1979): 325–51.

DeConde, Alexander. *Ethnicity, Race, and American Foreign Policy: A History*. Boston: Northeastern University Press, 1992.

Draper, Theodore. *American Communism and Soviet Russia: The Formative Period*. New York: Viking Press, 1960.

——. *The Roots of American Communism*. New York: Viking Press, 1957.

Fine, Nathan. *Labor and Farmer Parties in the United States 1828–1928.* New York: Rand School of Social Science, 1928. Reprint. New York: Russell and Russell, 1961.

Fite, Gilbert C., and H. C. Peterson. *Opponents of War: 1917–1918.* Seattle: University of Washington Press, 1957.

Foner, Eric. "Class, Ethnicity, and Radicalism in the Gilded Age: The Land League and Irish-America." *Marxist Perspectives* 1 (summer 1978): 6–55.

Foner, Philip S. *History of the Labor Movement in the United States,* vols. 1–9. New York: International Publishers, 1947–1991.

Foster, William Z. *American Trade Unionism: Principles and Organization, Strategy and Tactics.* New York: International Publishers, 1947.

———. *The Bankruptcy of the American Labor Movement.* Chicago: Trade Union Educational League, 1922.

———. *The Great Steel Strike and Its Lessons.* New York: B. W. Huebsch, 1920.

———. *History of the Communist Party of the United States.* New York: International Publishers, 1952.

———. *Pages from a Worker's Life.* New York: International Publishers, 1939.

———. *Trade Unions in America.* Chicago: Daily Workers Publishing Co., 1925.

Frank, Dana Lynn. "At the Point of Consumption: Seattle Labor and the Politics of Consumption, 1919–1927." Ph.D. diss., Yale University, 1988.

———. *Purchasing Power: Consumer Organizing, Gender, and the Seattle Labor Movement, 1919–1929.* Cambridge: Cambridge University Press, 1994.

Friedheim, Robert L. *The Seattle General Strike.* Seattle: University of Washington Press, 1964.

Friedheim, Robert L., and Robin Friedheim. "The Seattle Labor Movement, 1919–1920." *Pacific Northwest Quarterly* 55 (October 1964): 146–56.

Funchion, Michael. *Chicago's Irish Nationalists.* New York: Arno Press, 1976.

———. *Irish-American Voluntary Organizations.* Westport, Conn.: Greenwood Press, 1983.

Gaddis, John Lewis. "The Corporatist Synthesis: A Skeptical View." *Diplomatic History* 10 (fall 1986): 357–62.

Gerson, Louis L. *The Hyphenate in Recent American Politics and Diplomacy.* Lawrence: University of Kansas Press, 1964.

———. *Woodrow Wilson and the Rebirth of Poland, 1914–1920: A Study in the Influence on American Policy of Minority Groups of Foreign Origin.* New Haven, Conn.: Yale University Press, 1952.

Gifford, Ernest. *William Z. Foster: Fool or Faker?* Chicago: Ernest Gifford, 1923.

Godfried, Nathan. *Bridging the Gap between Rich and Poor: American Economic Development Policy toward the Arab East, 1942–1949.* New York: Greenwood Press, 1987.

———. "Spreading American Corporatism: Trade Union Education for Third World Labour." *Review of African Political Economy* 39 (September 1987): 51–63.

Gompers, Samuel. *American Labor and the War.* New York: George H. Doran Company, 1919.

——. *Seventy Years of Life and Labor: An Autobiography.* New York: E. P. Dutton, 1925.

Gompers, Samuel, with the collaboration of William English Walling. *Out of Their Own Mouths: A Revelation and an Indictment of Sovietism.* New York: E. P. Dutton, 1921.

Gordon, Michael R. *Conflict and Consensus in Labour's Foreign Policy, 1914–1965.* Stanford, Calif.: Stanford University Press, 1969.

Gosnell, Harold. "Machine Politics: Chicago Model." Master's thesis, University of Chicago, 1937.

Gould, J. D. "European Inter-Continental Emigration, The Road Home: Return Migration from the U.S.A." *Journal of European Economic History* 9 (spring 1980): 41–112.

Green, Charles. "The Labor Party Movement in Illinois, 1919–1924." Master's thesis, University of Illinois, 1959.

Green, James R. *The World of the Worker: Labor in Twentieth-Century America.* New York: Hill and Wang, 1980.

Green, Marguerite. *The National Civic Federation and the American Labor Movement, 1900–1925.* Washington: Catholic University of America Press, 1956. Reprint, Westport, Conn.: Greenwood Press, 1973.

Greene, Julia Marie. "The Strike at the Ballot Box: Politics and Partisanship in the American Federation of Labor, 1881–1916." Ph.D. diss., Yale University, 1990.

Grubbs, Frank. *The Struggle for Labor Loyalty: Gompers, the A.F. of L., and the Pacifists, 1917–1920.* Durham, N.C.: Duke University Press, 1968.

Haessler, Stephen J. "Carl J. Haessler and the Federated Press: Essays on the History of American Labor Journalism." Master's thesis, University of Wisconsin, 1979.

Hawley, Ellis. *The Great War and the Search for a Modern Order: A History of the American People and Their Institutions, 1917–1933.* New York: St. Martin's Press, 1979.

Henderson, Arthur. *The League of Nations and Labour.* Oxford: Oxford University Press, 1918.

Hendrickson, Kenneth E. "The Prowar Socialists, the Social Democratic League, and the Ill-Fated Drive for Industrial Democracy in America, 1917–1920." *Labor History* (summer 1970): 304–22.

Higham, John. *Strangers in the Land: Patterns of American Nativism, 1860–1925.* New York: Atheneum, 1963.

Hinton, James. *The First Shop Stewards' Movement.* London: George Allen and Unwin, 1973.

——. *Labour and Socialism: A History of the British Labour Movement, 1867–1974.* Amherst: University of Massachusetts Press, 1983.

Hirsch, Eric L. "Revolution or Reform: An Analytical History of an Urban Labor Movement." Ph.D. diss., University of Chicago, 1981.

Hoerder, Dirk, ed. *"Struggle a Hard Battle"*: *Essays on Working-Class Immigrants*. Dekalb: Northern Illinois University Press, 1986.

Hogan, Michael J. "Corporatism." *Journal of American History* 77 (June 1990): 153–60.

——. *Informal Entente: The Private Structure of Cooperation in Anglo-American Economic Diplomacy, 1918–1928*. Columbia: University of Missouri Press, 1977.

——. "Revival and Reform: America's Twentieth-Century Search for a New Economic Order Abroad." *Diplomatic History* 8 (fall 1984): 287–310.

Horowitz, Roger. "The Failure of Independent Political Action: The Labor Party of Cook County, 1919–20." Bachelor's essay, University of Chicago, 1982.

Hunt, E. H. *British Labor History, 1815–1914*. Atlantic Highlands, N.J.: Humanities Press, 1981.

Hunt, Michael. "Ideology and American Foreign Policy." *Journal of American History* 77 (June 1990): 108–15.

Jeffreys-Jones, Rhodri. "Massachusetts Labour and the League of Nations Controversy, 1919." *Irish Historical Studies* 19 (September 1975): 396–416.

Judd, Richard W. *Socialist Cities: Municipal Politics and the Grass Roots of American Socialism*. Albany: State University of New York Press, 1989.

Jung, Norman Oliver. "Chicago's Foreign Language Press in World War I." Master's thesis, University of Chicago, 1959.

Kantowicz, Edward. *Polish-American Politics in Chicago*. Chicago: University of Chicago Press, 1975.

Kaufman, Burton. *Efficiency and Expansion: Foreign Trade Organization in the Wilson Administration, 1913–1921*. Westport, Conn.: Greenwood Press, 1974.

Kazin, Michael. *Barons of Labor: The San Francisco Building Trades and Union Power in the Progressive Era*. Urbana: University of Illinois Press, 1987.

——. "The Great Exception Revisited: Organized Labor and Politics in San Francisco and Los Angeles, 1870–1940." *Pacific Historical Review* 55 (1986): 371–402.

Keil, Hartmut, and John B. Jentz, eds. *German Workers in Industrial Chicago 1850–1910: A Comparative Perspective*. Dekalb: Northern Illinois University Press, 1983.

Keiser, John. "John Fitzpatrick and Progressive Unionism, 1915–1925." Ph.D. diss., Northwestern University, 1965.

Kennedy, David M. *Over Here: The First World War and American Society*. New York: Oxford University Press, 1980.

Kolko, Gabriel. "The Decline of American Radicalism." *Studies on the Left* 6 (September–October, 1966): 9–26.

Kolko, Gabriel. *The Triumph of Conservatism: A Reinterpretation of American History, 1900–1916*. Chicago: Quadrangle Books, 1967.

Larson, Simeon. *Labor and Foreign Policy: Gompers, the AFL, and the First World War, 1914–1918*. London: Associated University Presses, 1975.

Lasch, Christopher. *The American Liberals and the Russian Revolution.* New York: Columbia University Press, 1962.

Laslett, John H. M. *Labor and the Left: A Study of Socialist and Radical Influences in the American Labor Movement, 1881–1924.* New York: Basic Books, 1970.

Leffler, Melvyn P. *The Elusive Quest: America's Pursuit of European Stability and French Security, 1919–1933.* Chapel Hill: University of North Carolina Press, 1979.

Lens, Sidney. *Left, Right, and Center: Conflicting Forces in American Labor.* Hinsdale, Ill.: H. Regnery, 1949.

Levenstein, Harvey A. *Labor Organizations in the United States and Mexico: A History of their Relations.* Westport, Conn.: Greenwood Press, 1971.

Leventhal, F. M. *Arthur Henderson.* Manchester: Manchester University Press, 1989.

Levin, Norman Gordon. *Woodrow Wilson and World Politics: America's Response to War and Revolution.* Oxford: Oxford University Press, 1968.

Linderman, Gerald F. *The Mirror of War: American Society and the Spanish-American War.* Ann Arbor: University of Michigan Press, 1974.

Link, Arthur S. *Wilson the Diplomatist: A Look at His Major Foreign Policies.* Baltimore, Md.: Johns Hopkins University Press, 1957.

——. *Woodrow Wilson: Revolution, War, and Peace.* Arlington Heights, Ill.: Harlan Davidson, 1979.

Lorwin, Lewis L. *Labor and Internationalism.* New York: Macmillan, 1929.

McCaffrey, Lawrence. *Ireland: From Colony to Nation State.* Englewood Cliffs, N.J.: Prentice-Hall, 1979.

——. *Irish Diaspora in America.* Bloomington: Indiana University Press, 1976.

——, ed. *Irish Nationalism and the American Contribution.* New York: Arno Press, 1976.

——, et al. *The Irish in Chicago.* Urbana: University of Illinois Press, 1987.

McCormick, Thomas. "Drift or Mastery? A Corporatist Synthesis for American Diplomatic History." *Reviews in American History* 10 (December 1982): 318–30.

McDonald, Forrest. *Insull.* Chicago: University of Chicago Press, 1962.

MacDonald, J. Ramsey. *National Defence: A Study in Militarism.* London: George Allen and Unwin, 1921.

McKee, Delber Lee. "The American Federation of Labor and American Foreign Policy, 1886–1912." Ph.D. diss., Stanford University, 1952.

McKillen, Beth. "The Corporatist Model, World War I, and the Public Debate over the League of Nations." *Diplomatic History* 15 (spring 1991): 171–97.

Marwick, Arthur. *The Deluge: British Society and the First World War.* Boston: Little, Brown, 1966. London: Macmillan, 1991.

Maurer, James H. *It Can Be Done: The Autobiography of James Hudson Maurer.* New York: Rand School Press, 1938.

Mayer, Arno J. *Political Origins of the New Diplomacy 1917–1918.* New York: Howard Fertig, 1969.

Merriam, Charles Edward. *Chicago: A More Intimate View of Urban Politics.* New York: Macmillan, 1929.

Mink, Gwendolyn. *Old Labor and New Immigrants in American Political Development: Union, Party, and State, 1875–1920.* Ithaca, N.Y.: Cornell University Press, 1986.

Montgomery, David. *The Fall of the House of Labor: The Workplace, the State, and American Labor Activism, 1865–1925.* New York: Cambridge University Press, 1987.

——. "Immigrants, Industrial Unions, and Social Reconstruction in the United States, 1916–1923." *Labour/LeTravail* 13 (spring 1984): 101–13.

——. "Nationalism, American Patriotism, and Class Consciousness among Immigrant Workers in the United States in the Epoch of World War I." In *"Struggle a Hard Battle": Essays on Working-Class Immigrants,* ed. Dirk Hoerder, 327–50. Dekalb: Northern Illinois University Press, 1986.

——. "New Tendencies in Union Struggles and Strategies in Europe and the United States, 1916–1922." In *Work, Community, and Power: The Experience of Labor in Europe and America, 1900–1925,* edited by James E. Cronin and Carmen Sirianni, 88–116. Philadelphia: Temple University Press, 1983.

——. *Workers' Control in America: Studies in the History of Work, Technology, and Labor Struggles.* New York: Cambridge University Press, 1979.

Morlan, Robert. *Political Prairie Fire: The Nonpartisan League, 1915–1922.* Minneapolis: University of Minnesota Press, 1955.

Murray, Robert K. *Red Scare: A Study in National Hysteria, 1919–1920.* Minneapolis: University of Minnesota Press, 1955.

Noble, David F. *America by Design: Science, Technology, and the Rise of Corporate Capitalism.* New York: Alfred Knopf, 1979.

Nolan, Mary. *Social Democracy and Society: Working-Class Radicalism in Dusseldorf, 1890–1920.* Cambridge: Cambridge University Press, 1981.

O'Connor, Harvey. *Revolution in Seattle: A Memoir.* New York: Monthly Review Press, 1964.

O'Grady, Joseph. *The Immigrants' Influence on Wilson's Peace Policies.* Lexington: University of Kentucky Press, 1967.

Pacyga, Dominic A. *Polish Immigrants and Industrial Chicago: Workers on the South Side, 1880–1922.* Columbus: Ohio State University Press, 1991.

Paterson, Thomas G., J. Garry Clifford, and Kenneth J. Hagan. *American Foreign Policy: A History,* 3d ed. Lexington, Mass.: D. C. Heath, 1988.

Pelling, Henry. *A Short History of the Labour Party,* 3d ed. New York: St. Martin's Press, 1968.

Perkin, Harold. *The Rise of Professional Society: England since 1880.* London: Routledge, 1989.

Pierce, Bessie Louise, ed. *As Others See Chicago: Impressions of Visitors, 1673–1933.* Chicago: University of Chicago Press, 1933.

Radosh, Ronald. *American Labor and United States Foreign Policy.* New York: Random House, 1969.

——. "The Corporate Ideology of American Labor Leaders from Gompers to Hillman." *Studies on the Left* 6 (1966): 66–88.

Rosenberg, Emily S. *Spreading the American Dream: American Economic and Cultural Expansion, 1890–1945.* New York: Hill and Wang, 1982.

Saposs, David. *Left Wing Unionism: A Study of Radical Policies and Tactics.* New York: International Publishers, 1926; rpt. Russell and Russell, 1967.

Schonberger, Howard. "Labor's Cold War in Occupied Japan." *Diplomatic History* 3 (summer 1979): 249–72.

Sell, Harry B. "The A.F. of L. and the Labor Party Movement of 1918–1920." Master's thesis, University of Chicago, 1922.

Shannon, David. *The Socialist Party of America: A History.* New York: Macmillan, 1955.

Shapiro, Stanley. "'Hand and Brain': The Farmer-Labor Party of 1920." *Labor History* 26 (summer 1985): 405–22.

——. "Hand and Brain: The Farmer-Labor Party of 1920." Ph.D. diss., University of California at Berkeley, 1967.

Shotwell, James, ed. *The Origins of the International Labor Organization.* New York: Columbia University Press, 1934.

Simonson, David F. "The Labor Party of Cook County, Ill., 1918–19." Master's thesis, University of Chicago, 1959.

Sklar, Martin J. *The Corporate Reconstruction of American Capitalism, 1890–1916: The Market, the Law, and Politics.* New York: Cambridge University Press, 1988.

Smith, Daniel. *The Great Departure: The United States and World War I, 1914–1920.* New York: John Wiley and Sons, 1965.

Staley, Eugene. *History of the Illinois State Federation of Labor.* Chicago: University of Chicago Press, 1930.

Stansky, Peter. *The Left and the War.* New York: Oxford University Press, 1969.

Tallion, Paul. "The American Federation of Labor and Expansionism: 1890–1910." Senior thesis, Northwestern University, 1985.

Thelen, David. *Robert M. LaFollette and the Insurgent Spirit.* Boston: Little, Brown, 1976.

Thompson, John. *Reformers and War: American Progressive Publicists and the First World War.* New York: Cambridge University Press, 1987.

Tomlins, Christopher L. "AFL Unions in the 1930s: Their Performance in Historical Perspective." *Journal of American History* 65 (March 1979): 1021–42.

Tuttle, William M., Jr. *Race Riot: Chicago in the Red Summer of 1919.* New York: Atheneum, 1970.

Weinstein, James. *The Corporate Ideal and the Liberal State, 1900–1918.* Boston: Beacon Press, 1968.

——. *The Decline of Socialism in America, 1912–1925.* New York: Monthly Review Press, 1967.

——. "The Socialist Party: Its Roots and Strengths, 1912–19." *Studies on the Left* 1 (winter 1960): 5–27.

Welch, Richard E. *Response to Imperialism: The United States and the Philippine-American War, 1899–1902.* Chapel Hill: University of North Carolina Press, 1979.

Wiebe, Robert. *The Search for Order, 1877–1920.* New York: Hill and Wang, 1967.

Zake, Louis J. "The National Department and the Polish-American Community, 1916–1923." *Polish-American Studies* 38 (autumn 1981): 16–25.

Zeman, Douglas E. "E Pluribus Unum: A Study of Four Catholic Ethnic Groups in Chicago." Ph.D. diss., University of Chicago, 1973.

Index